the McLUHAN EXPLOSION

the McLUHAN EXPLOSION

A Casebook on **MARSHALL McLUHAN**
and *Understanding Media*

HARRY H. CROSBY and **GEORGE R. BOND**
BOSTON UNIVERSITY

AMERICAN BOOK COMPANY

HOW TO USE THIS CASEBOOK

For some readers, this anthology will serve only as a source of information about Marshall McLuhan and his ideas. Others, particularly students in college Freshman English courses, may use this collection as a casebook.

The development of the casebook is the result of a need in higher education. Although almost everyone agrees that one of the functions of a Freshman English course is to give students an opportunity to prepare a research paper and have practice using standard manuscript and footnote techniques, no one has devised a completely acceptable method. A large university in particular just cannot flood three or four thousand students onto its library without overtaxing its staff and rendering its facilities useless for any other service. If all the students are working on one subject, there cannot be enough copies of books and magazines to go around. If the faculty permits students to select their own subjects, each teacher has the unprofessional task of judging a paper written on a subject about which he knows little. Too many instructors have had to comment sagaciously about anthropods, the cathedral at Chartres, cybernetics, cryogenics, Notre Dame football, food chemistry, the religion of John Dewey, and the quadratic sum, all in one evening. Ignorant about a theme's subject, the teacher cannot make such comments as "You ignored the valuable contributions of such-and-such an authority," or "You missed one important issue," or "You have taken this comment out of context and garbled it."

The McLuhan Explosion provides, under one cover for all students in a course, a selection of articles about one subject. The instructor and students can thus read all the information and treat it just as though they read it in the original periodicals and books. The instructor will know what the student omitted and how appropriately the student used his inclusions.

This casebook can be used in several ways. Some instructors, wishing to avoid any conditioning of the students' minds, will have their students read

Understanding Media before they touch the casebook. Other instructors will prefer to have their students know what is expected of them before they begin to read McLuhan's book. Such instructors may have their students read the "Introduction" and "Projects," perhaps even making a tentative decision about issues which particularly interest them. Then students can turn to the critics' articles and those by McLuhan contained in the casebook. On the assumption that some classes will stay in step as they read the article in this casebook, discussion and writing projects have been provided for each article. Even the student making his way through the articles at his own rate may be helped by the questions to focus his attention on important issues.

The "Introduction" briefly outlines McLuhan's rise to fame and makes three suggestions about how his work may be approached meaningfully: by analyzing and evaluating McLuhan's message, by analyzing his style and evaluating its relevance to modern communication methods, and by using a synopticon method of note-taking and organization of information.

The "Projects" section provides questions for discussion and topics for writing assignments. They are organized according to whether library facilities are necessary. Since an ideal situation for a freshman English paper is that the first experience be the "controlled-research" type—that is, with the student reading material with which the teacher is familiar—some instructors may assign two research papers for their students, with the second topic growing out of individual student reaction to this casebook's library projects. The topics which require library use are deliberately chosen to encourage the use of standard library reference tools.

As you read the articles you will notice italicized numbers inserted in brackets. For convenience in making footnotes, the numbers indicate the turning of the page; thus [63–64] marks the end of page 63 and the beginning of page 64 in the article as it was printed in the original source.

No college textbook is exclusively the product of its authors and editors, and we wish at this time to acknowledge our debt and appreciation to Professor Marshall McLuhan; to the authors of the critical articles; to Karen Woolis of the Boston University Library; to Dean Horatio M. LaFauci, Marilyn Morgillo, and the faculty of the Rhetoric Division of Boston University's College of Basic Studies; and to our wives, Jean E. Crosby and Ava Bond.

Harry H. Crosby
George R. Bond

Contents

UNDERSTANDING MEDIA (In Part)

McLUHAN AND HIS IDEAS

CONTENTS

the McLUHAN EXPLOSION

INTRODUCTION

Marshall McLuhan existed before 1964, but his light was under a bushel. Prior to 1951 he turned out the usual spate of scholarly articles which are expected of English professors on the way up. In 1951, he published a book, *The Mechanical Bride*, which started him on the road toward his position today as a controversial, irritating, pop philosopher and communication consultant, on the one hand respected and on the other hand rejected—but on neither hand ignored.

In *The Mechanical Bride*, Professor McLuhan widened the definition of communication and art. Anything that made an impression or conveyed a message was an aspect of communication; any part of culture, whether popular or more serious, was art. Society itself became a phase of communication and art. Instead of being shaped by society, communication and art shaped society. Modern advertising was construed to be one of the strongest and most insidious influences on society.

But there was little new in *The Mechanical Bride* and it was not expressed in the provocative style which was to serve McLuhan later—and there was no stir. Today, copies of the book are collectors' items—now that it is important in retrospect—and it has been reissued in paperback by Beacon Press and in hardcover by Vanguard.

In 1962, Professor McLuhan came closer to the style and message which was to make him a modern idol: he wrote *The Gutenberg Galaxy*, in which he attempted to "trace the ways in which the *forms* of experience and of mental outlook have been modified, first by the phonetic alphabet and then by printing." He quoted Peter Drucker, who had written, "There is still one thing we do not know about the Technological Revolution, but it is essential: What happened to bring about the basic changes in attitudes, beliefs, and values which released it?" McLuhan asserted, "*The Gutenberg Galaxy* . . . attempts to 'supply the one thing we do not know.'" Contending that "In our time the sudden shift from the mechanical technology of the wheel to the technology of electrical circuitry represents one of the major shifts of all time," he advanced the thesis that the development of the printing press was the key to recent civilization since it changed man's acquisition of information from a multi-sense but primarily oral method to a sequential, visual experience.

McLuhan was hitting his stride. In his brash book he attempted to bring the whole of western intellectual history into one pattern, and he succeeded in catching the attention of the intellectual and educational community. Ian Snowton wrote that *Gutenberg Galaxy* "offers casual erudition that's appalling in scope and variety . . . It leaves an English professor like myself feeling somewhat of a cross between a dodo and an astronaut with a heart condition."

The real bomb burst late in 1964. Few reviewers had marked the publication of either *The Mechanical Bride* or *The Gutenberg Galaxy*, but few of them missed *Understanding Media* when it was published by McGraw-Hill and later in paperback by Signet. In June, Dwight Macdonald, the distinguished perennial viewer-with-alarm, viewed *Media* with 5800 words, most of them with alarm, the alarm being heightened by Macdonald's contention that the work was "impure nonsense," nonsense diluted with just enough sense to make it attractive.

A survey of two standard library reference books provides a quantitative indication of how McLuhan has hit the public eye. In 1953, *Readers' Guide to Periodical Literature* listed one article by Herbert Marshall McLuhan. It was a statement that advertising is increasingly shaping modern taste. In 1954, *Readers' Guide* listed two articles by Herbert Marshall McLuhan, one in *Poetry* and the other in *Commonweal,* the point to each being loosely that lineal visual poetry, a line at a time, an idea at a time, is being supplanted by a literature of total impact, based on sound and compounded impressions. From 1955 to 1963 there was silence by and about McLuhan; in 1964, an article in the *Nation* (December 28, 1964), "Notes on Burroughs," by McLuhan was listed. In 1965, the *Readers' Guide* listed four articles about McLuhan, one in *Commentary,* two in the *New Yorker,* and one in *Harper's.* The furore was on.

In 1964 and 1965, most of the attention to Marshall McLuhan was in the form of book reviews, and thus most of the attention is demonstrated by a second library reference work, *Book Review Digest.* In 1964, many reviews of *Understanding Media* were listed, one in *Book Week* by Dwight Macdonald, one in the *Canadian Forum* by Paul West, and another in *Christian Science Monitor.* In the 1965 edition of *Book Review Digest* reviews were listed from *Commentary,* (by Neil Compton), *Commonweal* (C. J. Fox), *Library Journal* (E. M. Oboler), *Nation* (D. A. Holmes and George Zabriskie), *New Statesman* (Christopher Ricks), *New York Review of Books* (Frank Kermode), *Time Magazine,* the *London Times Supplement, America* (J. E. Page), and *Commonweal* (Richard Kostelanetz). That Marshall McLuhan was becoming someone to remark is indicated not only by the number of articles and reviews but also by the number of words in each review. An article about McLuhan almost invariably is about three times as long as the average of the given magazine. A second observation is that the editors of *Book Review Digest,* who usually mark a review with a + (plus) to indicate a favorable review and a — (minus) to indicate an unfavorable one, had difficulty deciding whether the review was praise or pan, and left the marks out completely. It was obvious by 1965, that Marshall McLuhan was a celebrity, and a controversial one.

Fame and notoriety are hard to assess and quantitative evaluation of anything so subjective is often almost a joke. Nevertheless, a count of articles by and about Professor McLuhan is impressive.

Between January 20, 1967, and April 20, 1967, there were eight articles about McLuhan. To be sure there were sixteen about Jacqueline Kennedy (mostly about her reactions to the Manchester book), and 32 about Senator Robert Kennedy, but they are in a different class. In the same period there were nine about Defense Secretary Robert McNamara and nine about Cassius Clay. In the same period there was none about Martin Luther King and none about Norman Mailer. There were ten about Pope Paul VI, and three about Episcopal Bishop James Pike, mostly about his alleged heresy. There were few articles about philosophers or college professors. There was just one about Jean Paul Sartre, four about John Kenneth Galbraith, and two about Arthur Schlesinger. That the latter almost made it in the same class as Mc-Luhan was a reference to Professor Schlesinger as the "swinging soothsayer."

In 1966 and 1967 Marshall McLuhan burst out everywhere. Articles about him or reference to him appeared in *Fortune, Newsweek, Life, Esquire, Craft Horizon, National Review, Architectural Record, Partisan Review, Look, New Yorker, New Mexico Quarterly, Publisher's Weekly, America, National Catholic Reporter, Saturday Review, New York Times Magazine, Forbes, Popular Photography, Library Journal, Encounter, Senior Scholastic,* and *The Family Circle.* His face appeared on the covers of *Newsweek* and *Saturday Review* and on New York educational television. For a handsome fee he was hired to talk to executives of Bell Telephone, IBM, Container Corp. of America and General Motors. He was referred to as the "intellectuals' pinup boy," in the *New Yorker.* Benjamin DeMott wrote, "He's swinging, switched on, with it, and NOW. And wrong." George Steiner wrote, "McLuhan's teaching is radical, new, animated by high intelligence, and capable of moving people to social action. It is not possible to give a rational summary of McLuhan's ideas. His writing is deliberately antilogical: circular, repetitious, unqualified, gnomic, outrageous." Arthur M. Schlesinger, Jr., wrote, [McLuhanism] is "a chaotic combination of bland assertion, astute guesswork, fake analogy, dazzling insight, hopeless nonsense, shockmanship, showmanship, wisecracks, and oracular mystification, all mingling cockily and indiscriminately in an endless and random monologue. It also, in my judgment, contains a deeply serious argument. After close study, one comes away with the feeling that here is an intelligent man who, for reasons of his own, prefers to masquerade as a charlatan."

Hugh Kenner commented that "Marshall McLuhan's name flies about these days the way 'Technocracy' did in the Thirties," noting a "picture story in *Life,* a reference to him in the *Time* Essay, random allusions in the columns of every journal one picks up." A group of professors set up a festival to celebrate McLuhan's ideas of the New World. An article in *Nation* (December, 1966), called McLuhan "the medium guru from Toronto" with a "native talent for delivering remarks designed to make readers splutter over their morning coffee." According to *Newsweek,* (March 6, 1967, p. 53) *Understanding Media* became "the fastest selling non-fiction book at Harvard and at Ann Arbor." Students liked its breezy McLuhan style and responded by treating him breezily, for instance, the student who abbreviated *Gutenberg Galaxy* to "Gut Gal." In intellectual, industrial, and academic circles, Marshall McLuhan is very much a conversation piece.

Marshall McLuhan has something in common with John Maynard Keynes and Sigmund Freud. Everyone talks about them but few people read their works. Since we wish to deprive no one of the exposure to McLuhan we hesitate to synopsize *Understanding Media*. However, since so many people read him differently and come to different conclusions about what he has said, we offer this interpretation as a sort of hypothesis. When you read *Understanding Media,* see whether you agree that this is a fair interpretation.

McLUHAN'S MESSAGE

History, according to McLuhan, is made up of three stages: (1) Preliterate or the tribal, in which men lived close together and communicated orally; (2) the Gutenberg or Individual stage in which men communicated by the printed word and thinking was done in lineal-sequential patterns; and (3) the neo-Tribal or Electric, in which computers, television and other electronic communication media have moved men back together ("implosion"). Professor McLuhan fears that man is not able to function properly under the bombardment of instantaneous, mosaic communication.

The first seven chapters ("Part I") of *Understanding Media* contain the general remarks which precede an individual analysis of each medium. According to Professor McLuhan, technology is any development which makes man more efficient; the "media" are any developments which extend man's senses, as the radio makes men able to hear speech uttered miles away. The "media" have a content, that is, the information conveyed by the words literally, and a "message," that is, "the change of scale or pace or pattern" that they introduce into human affairs. This message, which is also characteristic of technology, is more important than the content; in fact, McLuhan argues, "The medium *is* the message." Anything which affects mankind's actions is a medium, even a light bulb or a cigarette. Human development ("history") is the record of gradual fragmentation by technology, with man taking smaller parts of human endeavor as his own responsibility.

Each new medium has a challenging and often numbing effect on man. Prior to the printing press (the "Gutenberg Galaxy"), man received information all at once, in patterns or "configurations"; in contrast, print transmits information lineally and sequentially, and man had to learn to think lineally and sequentially. Each new medium affects the balance between patterned, simultaneous transmissions.

The media are either "hot" (with much detail—or "definition"—being supplied by the transmitter, leaving the receptor little to add from his own experiences or knowledge) or "cool" (with little detail, but requiring much contribution, or "involvement," from the receptor). A "hot" medium extends *one single sense* in high definition. History is often a process in which a cool medium replaces a hot medium, or the opposite. Often the transition causes such "overheat" that society is disrupted. For instance, print changed society from tribal culture to nationalism (since all users of one language could use it) but television has "reversed" man to tribal culture since we can experience distant occurrences with more senses and more involvement. Thus, the population explosion is really an "implosion," *i.e.*, problems occur because of the increased togetherness. This is an example of the "reversal" which comes from the energy caused by a "hybrid media," made up of several extended senses.

Men tend to become "gadget lovers," fascinated by extensions of themselves, (like Narcissus) but often the energy generated by joining media is so great that a numbing sets in, for instance, when man becomes so saturated by television commercials that he is "numb" to them. Media, like art, "translate" experience, *i.e.*, convert it to something we can grasp or comprehend, as a metaphor transmits information. New technologies and media present a challenge to which man must adjust; the artist makes the adjustment first and helps society avoid "numbing" or "collapse." One form of collapse is "auto-amputation" in which man voluntarily or unknowingly cuts off a new sense extension (turns off a medium). Man's greatest problem ("challenge") today is how to avoid the crises brought on by new technology and media.

Some specifics to illustrate McLuhan thought: Print is hotter than oral communication because it must supply much detail via one sense—with sight, smell, and hearing being frustrated. It is "high detail, low involvement." Television is cooler than radio because it extends, not one sense, but several. The viewer can identify more with the action even though less detail may be presented. Television is more instantaneous (or "patterned," or "configurational") than print which must transmit a fragment at a time, lineally or sequentially. James Dean is cool, since he supplied little detail and demanded involvement. The "hard sell" is hot; it is one-sided, requires little involvement, and is filled with detail. A lecture is hot, but a class discussion is cool. The electric light bulb is the essential McLuhan-type medium since it contains no "content" but has much message, *i.e.*, effect on man (change in the pace or form of man's actions"). Progress is always a "fragmentation"; each man becomes more of a specialist.

Obviously as you read McLuhan and his critics, your first task is to understand them and evaluate them. This task is somewhat less than easy, but synopticon reading and note-taking may help you. The task of understanding and evaluating McLuhan is made the more hazardous because of his style—and the second responsibility you probably will assume is to decide just what *you* think of the way *he* thinks, and writes.

McLUHAN'S STYLE: THE MOSAIC VERSUS THE PROSAIC

Marshall McLuhan has a maddening yet provocative writing style. Some of his critics condemn his perverse opaqueness; others predict that his style anticipates the communication of the future. He throws everything at you at once—as you are bombarded with low-detail information in advertising, as spectators were bombarded with a hundred pictures at once at Expo 67. In the fall of 1967, when the Boston Red Sox, the Chicago White Sox, the Detroit Tigers, and the Minnesota Twins were bunched within one game of the top of the league, radio and television followed the McLuhan method and broadcast the games of all four teams at once. Orderly, lineal, idea-at-a-time writing may be a voice of the past; mosaic impressions may be the communication of the future. As you read, you should gather evidence or impressions which will help you decide whether McLuhan's style talks to you.

THE SYNOPTICON: A READING TECHNIQUE

As you pass through life in college and afterwards, you will need to organize information that you accumulate, and you can begin now, during your study of McLuhan, to develop an effective technique, the synopticon. When you read philosophy, for instance, you find that philosophers are concerned with about the same questions: What is the nature of life, man, God, knowledge, society, and what is the relationship among them? You can increase your comprehension of philosophy by preparing summaries and answers to these questions. As you read McLuhan and his critics, you will find that they also are preoccupied with certain questions, and you can understand and evaluate McLuhan by starting a synopticon notebook.

We have listed below ten topics which seem most to preoccupy McLuhan and his critics; you may select others. We suggest that you start your McLuhan synopticon by writing each topic at the top of a blank page in your notebook. Then, as you come across information relevant to the topic, jot down a paraphrase or quotation. Use direct quotes frequently because you may wish to use an author's exact words later in one of your papers. Be sure too to indicate source. (Compton, 79) would be a shorthand way of indicating that your note came from page 79 of the *Commentary* article written by Neil Compton.

1. The McLuhan vocabulary. (Jot down such terms as *media, technology, message, cool, hot, lineal, sequential, fragmentation, definition, involvement, reversal, numbing, tribal culture, Narcissus, translate, implosion,* and *autoamputation,* and then insert his definitions or the definitions you infer.)

2. The nature of history. (How does McLuhan characterize history? How does his interpretation differ from others? What are the stages of history according to McLuhan and other historians?)

3. McLuhan's perception of the effect of media on society. (What are the media? How are they "Extensions of Man"?)

4. Education. (Why does McLuhan find traditional educational methods so unsatisfactory for today's problems and today's children? What reforms do you infer to be necessary?)

5. McLuhan's writing style. (What is the proportion of specific to general? Is his style humorous, cheeky, breezy, serious, or what? How does he use metaphor and analogy? Is his vocabulary technical, esoteric, ordinary, or what?)

6. McLuhan's method of thinking. (Where does he get his ideas? On what basis does he generalize? Does he use primary or secondary sources?)

7. The application of McLuhanism. (How are McLuhan's concepts used to explain various modern occurrences?)

8. Evaluation of McLuhan. (What do you think of McLuhan's ideas? In a sentence or so, what is each critic's evaluation of McLuhan personally and his ideas specifically and generally?)

9. The biography of McLuhan. (To evaluate his ideas, you and the critics will need to know McLuhan's training and experience— and the sources of his ideas.)

10. Evaluation of the critics. (Does the writer catch the essence of McLuhan? Is his information complete and accurate? Is his interpretation influenced by the writer's interests, background, or occupation? Do his comments improve your perception of McLuhan?)

If your instructor will test you on your comprehension of the information you are studying, your synopticon will provide help in preparing for inevitable essay questions. Whatever writing projects you undertake, the synopticon will provide clues and information ready for insertion at the appropriate places.

UNDERSTANDING MEDIA: THE EXTENSIONS OF MAN

Marshall McLuhan

INTRODUCTION TO THE SECOND EDITION

Jack Paar mentioned that he once had said to a young friend, "Why do you kids use 'cool' to mean 'hot'?" The friend replied, "Because you folks used up the word 'hot' before we came along." It is true that "cool" is often used nowadays to mean what used to be conveyed by "hot." Formerly a "hot argument" meant one in which people were deeply involved. On the other hand, a "cool attitude" used to mean one of detached objectivity and disinterestedness. In those days the word "disinterested" meant a noble quality of fairmindedness. Suddenly it got to mean "couldn't care less." The word "hot" has fallen into similar disuse as these deep changes of outlook have developed. But the slang term "cool" conveys a good deal besides the old idea of "hot." It indicates a kind of commitment and participation in situations that involves all of one's faculties. In that sense, one can say that automation is cool, whereas the older mechanical kinds of specialist or fragmented "jobs" are "square." The "square" person and situation are not "cool" because they manifest little of the habit of depth involvement of our faculties. The young now say, "Humor is not cool." Their favorite jokes bear this out. They ask, "What is purple and hums?" Answer, "An electric grape." "Why does it hum?" Answer, "Because it doesn't know the words." Humor is presumably not "cool" because it inclines us to laugh *at* something, instead of getting us emphatically involved in something. The story line is dropped from "cool" jokes and "cool" movies alike. The Bergman and Fellini movies demand far more involvement than do narrative shows. A story line encompasses a set of events much like a melodic line in music. Melody, the *melos modos,* "the road round," is a continuous, connected, and repetitive structure that is not used in the "cool" art of the Orient. The [*vii–viii*] art and poetry of Zen creates involvement by means of the *interval,* not by the *connection* used in the visually organized Western world. Spectator becomes artist in oriental art because he must supply all the connections.

The section on "media hot and cool" confused many reviewers of *Understanding Media* who were unable to recognize the very large structural changes in human outlook that are occurring today. Slang offers an immediate index to changing perception. Slang is based not on theories but on immediate experience. The student of media will not only value slang as a guide to changing perception, but he will also study media as bringing about new perceptual habits.

The section on "the medium is the message" can, perhaps, be clarified by pointing out that any technology gradually creates a totally new human environment. Environments are not passive wrappings but active processes. In his splendid work *Preface to Plato* (Harvard University Press, 1963), Eric Havelock contrasts the oral and written cultures of the Greeks. By Plato's time the written word had created a new environment that had begun to detribalize man. Previously the Greeks had grown up by benefit of the process of the *tribal encyclopedia.* They had memorized the poets. The poets provided specific operational wisdom for all the contingencies of life—Ann Landers in verse. With the advent of individual detribalized man, a new education was needed. Plato devised such a new program for literate men. It was based on the Ideas. With the phonetic alphabet, classified wisdom took over from the operational wisdom of Homer and Hesiod and the tribal encyclopedia. Education by classified data has been the Western program ever since.

Now, however, in the electronic age, data classification yields to pattern recognition, the key phrase at IBM. When data move instantly, classification is too fragmentary. In order to cope with data at electric speed in typical situations of "information overload," men resort to the study of configurations, like the sailor in Edgar Allan Poe's *Maelstrom.* The drop-out situation in our schools at present has only begun to develop. The young student today grows up in an electrically configured world. It is a world not of wheels but of circuits, not of fragments but of integral patterns. The student today *lives* mythically and in depth. At school, however, he encounters a situation organized by means of classified information. The subjects are unrelated. They are visually conceived in terms of a blueprint. The student can find no possible means of involvement for himself, nor can he discover [viii–ix] how the educational scene relates to the "mythic" world of electronically processed data and experience that he takes for granted. As one IBM executive puts it, "My children had lived several lifetimes compared to their grandparents when they began grade one."

"The medium is the message" means, in terms of the electronic age, that a totally new environment has been created. The "content" of this new environment is the old mechanized environment of the industrial age. The new environment reprocesses the old one as radically as TV is reprocessing the film. For the "content" of TV is the movie. TV is environmental and imperceptible, like all environments. We are aware only of the "content" or the old environment. When machine production was new, it gradually created an environment whose content was the old environment of agrarian life and the arts and crafts. This older environment was elevated to an art form by the new mechanical environment. The machine turned Nature into an art form. For the first time men began to regard Nature as a source of aesthetic and spiritual values. They began to marvel that earlier ages had been so unaware of the world of Nature as Art. Each new technology creates an environment that is itself regarded as corrupt and degrading. Yet the new one turns its predecessor into an art form. When writing was new, Plato transformed the old oral dialogue into an art form. When printing was new the Middle Ages became an art form. "The Elizabethan world view" was a view of the Middle Ages. And the industrial age turned the Renaissance into an art form as seen in the work of Jacob Burckhardt. Siegfried Giedion, in turn, has in the electric age taught us how to see the entire process of mechanization as an art process. (*Mechanization Takes Command*)

As our proliferating technologies have created a whole series of new environments, men have become aware of the arts as "anti-environments" or "counter-environments" that provide us with the means of perceiving the environment itself. For, as Edward T. Hall has explained in *The Silent Language*, men are never aware of the ground rules of their environmental systems or cultures. Today technologies and their consequent environments succeed each other so rapidly that one environment makes us aware of the next. Technologies begin to perform the function of art in making us aware of the psychic and social consequences of technology.

Art as anti-environment becomes more than ever a means of training perception and judgment. Art offered as a con-[ix–x]sumer commodity rather than as a means of training perception is as ludicrous and snobbish as always. Media study at once opens the doors of perception. And here it is that the young can do top-level research work. The teacher has only to invite the student to do as complete an inventory as possible. Any child can list the effects of the telephone or the radio or the motor car in shaping the life and work of his friends and his society. An inclusive list of media effects opens many unexpected avenues of awareness and investigation.

Edmund Bacon, of the Philadelphia town-planning commission, discovered that school children could be invaluable researchers and colleagues in the task of remaking the image of the city. We are entering the new age of education that is programmed for discovery rather than instruction. As the means of input increase, so does the need for insight or pattern recognition. The famous Hawthorne experiment, at the General Electric plant near Chicago, revealed a mysterious effect years ago. No matter how the conditions of the workers were altered, the workers did more and better work. Whether the heat and light and leisure were arranged adversely or pleasantly, the quantity and quality of output improved. The testers gloomily concluded that testing distorted the evidence. They missed the all-important fact that when the workers are permitted to join their energies to a process of learning and discovery, the increased efficiency is phenomenal.

Earlier it was mentioned how the school drop-out situation will get very much worse because of the frustration of the student need for participation in the learning process. This situation concerns also the problem of "the culturally disadvantaged child." This child exists not only in the slums but increasingly in the suburbs of the upper-income homes. The culturally disadvantaged child is the TV child. For TV has provided a new environment of low visual orientation and high involvement that makes accommodation to our older educational establishment quite difficult. One strategy of cultural response would be to raise the visual level of the TV image to enable the young student to gain access to the old visual world of the classroom and the curriculum. This would be worth trying as a temporary expedient. But TV is only one component of the electric environment of instant circuitry that has succeeded the old world of the wheel and nuts and bolts. We would be foolish not to ease our transition from the fragmented visual world of the existing educational establishment by every possible means.

The existential philosophy, as well as the Theater of the [x–xi] Absurd, represents anti-environments that point to the critical pressures of the new electric environment. Jean-Paul Sartre, as much as Samuel Beckett and Arthur Miller, has declared the futility of blueprints and classified data and "jobs" as a way out. Even the words "escape" and "vicarious living" have dwindled from the new scene of electronic involvement. TV engineers have begun to explore the braille-like character of the TV image as a means of enabling the blind to see by having this image projected directly onto their skins. We need to use all media in this wise, to enable us to see our situation.

On page 16 there are some lines from *Romeo and Juliet* whimsically modified to make an allusion to TV. Some reviewers have imagined that this was an involuntary misquotation.

The power of the arts to anticipate future social and technological developments, by a generation and more, has long been recognized. In this century Ezra Pound called the artist "the antennae of the race." Art as radar acts as "an early alarm system," as it were, enabling us to discover social and psychic targets in lots of time to prepare to cope with them. This concept of the arts as prophetic, contrasts with the popular idea of them as mere self-expression. If art is an "early warning system," to use the phrase from World War II, when radar was new, art has the utmost relevance not only to media study but to the development of media controls.

When radar was new it was found necessary to eliminate the balloon system for city protection that had preceded radar. The balloons got in the way of the electric feedback of the new radar information. Such may well prove to be the case with much of our existing school curriculum, to say nothing of the generality of the arts. We can afford to use only those portions of them that enhance the perception of our technologies, and their psychic and social consequences. Art as a radar environment takes on the function of indispensable perceptual training rather than the role of a privileged diet for the elite. While the arts as radar feedback provide a dynamic and changing corporate image, their purpose may be not to enable us to change but rather to maintain an even course toward permanent goals, even amidst the most disrupting innovations. We have already discovered the futility of changing our goals as often as we change our technologies.   [xi]

1 · THE MEDIUM IS THE MESSAGE

In a culture like ours, long accustomed to splitting and dividing all things as a means of control, it is sometimes a bit of a shock to be reminded that, in operational and practical fact, the medium is the message. This is merely to say that the personal and social consequences of any medium—that is, of any extension of ourselves—result from the new scale that is introduced into our affairs by each extension of ourselves, or by any new technology. Thus, with automation, for example, the new patterns of human association tend to eliminate jobs, it is true. That is the negative result. Positively, automation creates roles for people, which is to say depth of involvement in their work and human association that our preceding mechanical technology had destroyed. Many people would be disposed to say that it was not the machine, but what one did with the machine, that was its meaning or message. In terms of the ways in which the machine altered our relations to one another and to ourselves, it mattered not in the least whether it turned out cornflakes or Cadillacs. The restructuring of human work and association was shaped by the technique of fragmentation that is the essence of machine technology. The essence of automation technology is the opposite. It is integral and decentralist in depth, just as the machine was fragmentary, centralist, and superficial in its patterning of human relationships.

The instance of the electric light may prove illuminating in this connection. The electric light is pure information. It is a medium without a message, as it were, unless it is used to spell out some verbal ad or name. This fact, characteristic of all media, means that the "content" of any medium is always another medium. The content of writing is speech, just as the [23–24] written word is the content of print, and print is the content of the telegraph. If it is asked, "What is the content of speech?," it is necessary to say, "It is an actual process of thought, which is in itself nonverbal." An abstract painting represents direct manifestation of creative thought processes as they might appear in computer designs. What we are considering here, however, are the psychic and social consequences of the designs or patterns as they amplify or accelerate existing processes. For the "message" of any medium or technology is the change of scale or pace or pattern that it introduces into human affairs. The railway did not introduce movement or transportation or wheel or road into human society, but it accelerated and enlarged the scale of previous human functions, creating totally new kinds of cities and new kinds of work and leisure. This happened whether the railway functioned in a tropical or a northern environment, and is quite independent of the freight or content of the railway medium. The airplane, on the other hand, by accelerating the rate of transportation, tends to dissolve the railway form of city, politics, and association, quite independently of what the airplane is used for.

Let us return to the electric light. Whether the light is being used for brain surgery or night baseball is a matter of indifference. It could be argued that these activities are in some way the "content" of the electric light, since they could not exist without the electric light. This fact merely underlines the point that "the medium is the message" because it is the medium that shapes and controls the scale and form of human association and action. The content or uses of such media are as diverse as they are ineffectual in shaping the form of human association. Indeed, it is only too typical that the "content" of any medium blinds us to the character of the medium. It is only today that industries have become aware of the various kinds of business in which they are engaged. When IBM discovered that it was not in the business of making office equipment or business machines, but that it was in the business of processing information, then it began to navigate with clear vision. The General Electric Company makes a considerable portion of its profits from electric light bulbs and lighting systems. It has not yet discovered that, quite as much as A.T.&T., it is in the business of moving information.

The electric light escapes attention as a communication medium just because it has no "content." And this makes it an invaluable instance of how people fail to study media at all. [24–25] For it is not till the electric light is used to spell out some brand name that it is noticed as a medium. Then it is not the light but the "content" (or what is really another medium) that is noticed. The message of the electric light is like the message of electric power in industry, totally radical, pervasive, and decentralized. For electric light and power are separate from their uses, yet they eliminate time and space factors in human association exactly as do radio, telegraph, telephone, and TV, creating involvement in depth.

A fairly complete handbook for studying the extensions of man could be made up from selections from Shakespeare. Some might quibble about whether or not he was referring to TV in these familiar lines from *Romeo and Juliet:*

> But soft! what light through yonder window breaks?
> It speaks, and yet says nothing.

In *Othello*, which, as much as *King Lear*, is concerned with the torment of people transformed by illusions, there are these lines that bespeak Shakespeare's intuition of the transforming powers of new media:

> Is there not charms
> By which the property of youth and maidhood
> May be abus'd? Have you not read, Roderigo,
> Of some such thing?

In Shakespeare's *Troilus and Cressida,* which is almost completely devoted to both a psychic and social study of communication, Shakespeare states his awareness that true social and political navigation depend upon anticipating the consequences of innovation:

> The providence that's in a watchful state
> Knows almost every grain of Plutus' gold,
> Finds bottom in the uncomprehensive deeps,
> Keeps place with thought, and almost like the gods
> Does thoughts unveil in their dumb cradles.

The increasing awareness of the action of media, quite independently of their "content" or programming, was indicated in the annoyed and anonymous stanza:

> In modern thought, (if not in fact)
> Nothing is that doesn't act,
> So that is reckoned wisdom which
> Describes the scratch but not the itch.   [25–26]

The same kind of total, configurational awareness that reveals why the medium is socially the message has occurred in the most recent and radical medical theories. In his *Stress of Life,* Hans Selye tells of the dismay of a research colleague on hearing of Selye's theory:

> When he saw me thus launched on yet another enraptured description of what I had observed in animals treated with this or that impure, toxic material, he looked at me with desperately sad eyes and said in obvious despair: "But Selye, try to realize what you are doing before it is too late! You have now decided to spend your entire life studying the pharmacology of dirt!"
>
> (Hans Selye, *The Stress of Life*)

As Selye deals with the total environment situation in his "stress" theory of disease, so the latest approach to media study considers not only the "content" but the medium and the cultural matrix within which the particular medium operates. The older unawareness of the psychic and social effects of media can be illustrated from almost any of the conventional pronouncements.

In accepting an honorary degree from the University of Notre Dame a few years ago, General David Sarnoff made this statement: "We are too prone to make technological instruments the scapegoats for the sins of those who wield them. The products of modern science are not in themselves good or bad; it is the way they are used that determines their value." That is the voice of the current somnambulism. Suppose we were to say, "Apple pie is in itself neither good nor bad; it is the way it is used that determines its value." Or, "The smallpox virus is in itself neither good nor bad; it is the way it is used that determines its value." Again, "Firearms are in themselves neither good nor bad; it is the way they are used that determines their value." That is, if the slugs reach the right people firearms are good. If the TV tube fires the right ammunition at the right people it is good. I am not being perverse. There is simply nothing in the Sarnoff statement that will bear scrutiny, for it ignores the nature of the medium, of any and all media, in the true Narcissus style of one hypnotized by the amputation and extension of his own being in a new technical form. General Sarnoff went on to explain his attitude to the technology of print, saying that it was true that print caused much trash to circulate, but it had also disseminated the Bible and the thoughts of seers and philosophers. It has [26–27] never occurred to General Sarnoff that any technology could do anything but *add* itself on to what we already are.

Such economists as Robert Theobald, W. W. Rostow, and John Kenneth Galbraith have been explaining for years how it is that "classical economics" cannot explain change or growth. And the paradox of mechanization is that although it is itself the cause of maximal growth and change, the principle of mechanization excludes the very possibility of growth or the understanding of change. For mechanization is achieved by fragmentation of any process and by putting the fragmented parts in a series. Yet, as David Hume showed in the eighteenth century, there is no principle of causality in a mere sequence. That one thing follows another accounts for nothing. Nothing follows from following, except change. So the greatest of all reversals occurred with electricity, that ended sequence by making things instant. With instant speed the causes of things began to emerge to awareness again, as they had not done with things in sequence and in concatenation accordingly. Instead of asking which came first, the chicken or the egg, it suddenly seemed that a chicken was an egg's idea for getting more eggs.

Just before an airplane breaks the sound barrier, sound waves become visible on the wings of the plane. The sudden visibility of sound just as sound ends is an apt instance of that great pattern of being that reveals new and opposite forms just as the earlier forms reach their peak performance. Mechanization was never so vividly fragmented or sequential as in the birth of the movies, the moment that translated us beyond mechanism into the world of growth and organic interrelation. The movie, by sheer speeding up the mechanical, carried us from the world of sequence and connection into the world of creative configuration and structure. The message of the movie medium is that of transition from lineal connections to configurations. It is the transition that produced the now quite correct observation: "If it works, it's obsolete." When electric speed further takes over from mechanical movie sequences, then the lines of force in structures and in media become loud and clear. We return to the inclusive form of the icon.

To a highly literate and mechanized culture the movie appeared as a world of triumphant illusions and dreams that money could buy. It was at this moment of the movie that cubism occurred, and it has been described by E. H. Gombrich (*Art and Illusion*) as "the most radical attempt to stamp out ambiguity and to enforce one reading of the picture—that of a man-made construction, a colored canvas." For [27–28] cubism substitutes all facets of an object simultaneously for the "point of view" or facet of perspective illusion. Instead of the specialized illusion of the third dimension on canvas, cubism sets up an interplay of planes and contradiction or dramatic conflict of patterns, lights, textures that "drives home the message" by involvement. This is held by many to be an exercise in painting, not in illusion.

In other words, cubism, by giving the inside and outside, the top, bottom, back, and front and the rest, in two dimensions, drops the illusion of perspective in favor of instant sensory awareness of the whole. Cubism, by seizing on instant total awareness, suddenly announced that *the medium is the message*. Is it not evident that the moment that sequence yields to the simultaneous, one is in the world of the structure and of configuration? Is that not what has happened in physics as in painting, poetry, and in communication? Specialized segments of attention have shifted to total field, and we can now say, "The medium is the message" quite naturally. Before the electric speed and total field, it was not obvious that the medium is the message. The message, it seemed, was the "content," as people used to ask what a painting was *about*. Yet they never thought to ask what a melody was about, nor what a house or a dress was about. In such matters, people retained some sense of the whole pattern, of form and function as a unity. But in the electric age this integral idea of structure and configuration has become so prevalent that educational theory has taken up the matter. Instead of working with specialized "problems" in arithmetic, the structural approach now follows the lines of force in the field of number and has small children meditating about number theory and "sets."

Cardinal Newman said of Napoleon, "He understood the grammar of gunpowder." Napoleon had paid some attention to other media as well, especially the semaphore telegraph that gave him a great advantage over his enemies. He is on record for saying that "Three hostile newspapers are more to be feared than a thousand bayonets."

Alexis de Tocqueville was the first to master the grammar of print and typography. He was thus able to read off the message of coming change in France and America as if he were reading aloud from a text that had been handed to him. In fact, the nineteenth century in France and in America was just such an open book to de Tocqueville because he had learned the grammar of print. So he, also, knew when that grammar did not apply. He was asked why he did not write [28–29] a book on England, since he knew and admired England. He replied:

> One would have to have an unusual degree of philosophical folly to believe oneself able to judge England in six months. A year always seemed to me too short a time in which to appreciate the United States properly, and it is much easier to acquire clear and precise notions about the American Union than about Great Britain. In America all laws derive in a sense from the same line of thought. The whole of society, so to speak, is founded upon a single fact; everything springs from a simple principle. One could compare America to a forest pierced by a multitude of straight roads all converging on the same point. One has only to find the center and everything is revealed at a glance. But in England the paths run criss-cross, and it is only by travelling down each one of them that one can build up a picture of the whole.

De Tocqueville, in earlier work on the French Revolution, had explained how it was the printed word that, achieving cultural saturation in the eighteenth century, had homogenized the French nation. Frenchmen were the same kind of people from north to south. The typographic principles of uniformity, continuity, and lineality had overlaid the complexities of ancient feudal and oral society. The Revolution was carried out by the new literati and lawyers.

In England, however, such was the power of the ancient oral traditions of common law, backed by the medieval institution of Parliament, that no uniformity or continuity of the new visual print culture could take complete hold. The result was that the most important event in English history has never taken place; namely, the English Revolution on the lines of the French Revolution. The American Revolution had no medieval legal institutions to discard or to root out, apart from monarchy. And many have held that the American Presidency has become very much more personal and monarchical than any European monarch ever could be.

De Tocqueville's contrast between England and America is clearly based on the fact of typography and of print culture creating uniformity and continuity. England, he says, has rejected this principle and clung to the dynamic or oral common law tradition. Hence the discontinuity and unpredictable quality of English culture. The grammar of print cannot help to construe the message of oral and nonwritten culture and institutions. The English aristocracy was properly classified as barbarian by Matthew Arnold because its power and status [29–30] had nothing to do with literacy or with the cultural forms of typography. Said the Duke of Gloucester to Edward Gibbon upon the publication of his *Decline and Fall:* "Another damned fat book, eh, Mr. Gibbon? Scribble, scribble, scribble, eh, Mr. Gibbon?" De Tocqueville was a highly literate aristocrat who was quite able to be detached from the values and assumptions of typography. That is why he alone understood the grammar of typography. And it is only on those terms, standing aside from any structure or medium, that its principles and lines of force can be discerned. For any medium, that its principles and lines of force can be discerned. For any medium has the power of imposing its own assumption on the unwary. Prediction and control consist in avoiding this subliminal state of Narcissus trance. But the greatest aid to this end is simply in knowing that the spell can occur immediately upon contact, as in the first bars of a melody.

A Passage to India by E. M. Forster is a dramatic study of the inability of oral and intuitive oriental culture to meet with the rational, visual European patterns of experience. "Rational," of course, has for the West long meant "uniform and continuous and sequential." In other words, we have confused reason with literacy, and rationalism with a single technology. Thus in the electric age man seems to the conventional West to become irrational. In Forster's novel the moment of truth and dislocation from the typographic trance of the West comes in the Marabar Caves. Adela Quested's reasoning powers cannot cope with the total inclusive field of resonance that is India. After the Caves: "Life went on as usual, but had no consequences, that is to say, sounds did not echo nor thought develop. Everything seemed cut off at its root and therefore infected with illusion."

A Passage to India (the phrase is from Whitman, who saw America headed Eastward) is a parable of Western man in the electric age, and is only incidentally related to Europe or the Orient. The ultimate conflict between sight and sound, between written and oral kinds of perception and organization of existence is upon us. Since understanding stops action, as Nietzsche observed, we can moderate the fierceness of this conflict by understanding the media that extend us and raise these wars within and without us.

Detribalization by literacy and its traumatic effects on tribal man is the theme of a book by the psychiatrist J. C. Carothers, The African Mind in Health and Disease (World Health Organization, Geneva, 1953). Much of his material appeared in an article in Psychiatry magazine, November, 1959: "The Culture, Psychiatry, and the Written Word." Again, it is [30–31] electric speed that has revealed the lines of force operating from Western technology in the remotest areas of bush, savannah, and desert. One example is the Bedouin with his battery radio on board the camel. Submerging natives with floods of concepts for which nothing has prepared them is the normal action of all of our technology. But with electric media Western man himself experiences exactly the same inundation as the remote native. We are no more prepared to encounter radio and TV in our literate milieu than the native of Ghana is able to cope with the literacy that takes him out of his collective tribal world and breaches him in individual isolation. We are as numb in our new electric world as the native involved in our literate and mechanical culture.

Electric speed mingles the cultures of prehistory with the dregs of industrial marketeers, the nonliterate with semiliterate and the postliterate. Mental breakdown of varying degrees is the very common result of uprooting and inundation with new information and endless new patterns of information. Wyndham Lewis made this a theme of his group of novels called The Human Age. The first of these, The Childermass, is concerned precisely with accelerated media change as a kind of massacre of the innocents. In our own world as we become more aware of the effects of technology on psychic formation and manifestation, we are losing all confidence in our right to assign guilt. Ancient prehistoric societies regard violent crime as pathetic. The killer is regarded as we do a cancer victim. "How terrible it must be to feel like that," they say. J. M. Synge took up this idea very effectively in his *Playboy of the Western World.*

If the criminal appears as a nonconformist who is unable to meet the demand of technology that we behave in uniform and continuous patterns, literate man is quite inclined to see others who cannot conform as somewhat pathetic. Especially the child, the cripple, the woman, and the colored person appear in a world of visual and typographic technology as victims of injustice. On the other hand, in a culture that assigns roles instead of jobs to people— the dwarf, the skew, the child create their own spaces. They are not expected to fit into some uniform and repeatable niche that is not their size anyway. Consider the phrase "It's a man's world." As a quantitative observation endlessly repeated from within a homogenized culture, this phrase refers to the men in such a culture who have to be homogenized Dagwoods in order to belong at all. It is in our I.Q. testing that we have produced the greatest flood of misbegotten standards. Unaware of our [31–32] typographic cultural bias, our testers assume that uniform and continuous habits are a sign of intelligence, thus eliminating the ear man and the tactile man.

C. P. Snow, reviewing a book of A. L. Rowse (*The New York Times Book Review,* December 24, 1961) on *Appeasement* and the road to Munich, describes the top level of British brains and experience in the 1930s. "Their I.Q.'s were much higher than usual among political bosses. Why were they such a disaster?" The view of Rowse, Snow approves: "They would not listen to warnings because they did not wish to hear." Being anti-Red made it impossible for them to read the message of Hitler. But their failure was as nothing compared to our present one. The American stake in literacy as a technology or uniformity applied to every level of education, government, industry, and social life is totally threatened by the electric technology. The threat of Stalin or Hitler was external. The electric technology is within the gates, and we are numb, deaf, blind, and mute about its encounter with the Gutenberg technology, on and through which the American way of life was formed. It is, however, no time to suggest strategies when the threat has not even been acknowledged to exist. I am in the position of Louis Pasteur telling doctors that their greatest enemy was quite invisible, and quite unrecognized by them. Our conventional response to all media, namely that it is how they are used that counts, is the numb stance of the technological idiot. For the "content" of a medium is like the juicy piece of meat carried by the burglar to distract the watchdog of the mind. The effect of the medium is made strong and intense just because it is given another medium as "content." The content of a movie is a novel or a play or an opera. The effect of the movie form is not related to its program content. The "content" of writing or print is speech, but the reader is almost entirely unaware either of print or of speech.

Arnold Toynbee is innocent of any understanding of media as they have shaped history, but he is full of examples that the student of media can use. At one moment he can seriously suggest that adult education, such as the Workers Educational Association in Britain, is a useful counterforce to the popular press. Toynbee considers that although all of the oriental societies have in our time accepted the industrial technology and its political consequences: "On the cultural plane, however, there is no uniform corresponding tendency." (Somervell, I. 267) This is like the voice of the literate man, floundering in a milieu of ads, who boasts, "Personally, I pay no [32–33] attention to ads." The spiritual and cultural reservations that the oriental peoples may have toward our technology will avail them not at all. The effects of technology do not occur at the level of opinions or concepts, but alter sense ratios or patterns of perception steadily and without any resistance. The serious artist is the only person able to encounter technology with impunity, just because he is an expert aware of the changes in sense perception.

The operation of the money medium in seventeenth-century Japan had effects not unlike the operation of typography in the West. The penetration of the money economy, wrote G. B. Sansom (in *Japan*, Cresset Press, London, 1931) "caused a slow but irresistible revolution, culminating in the breakdown of feudal government and the resumption of intercourse with foreign countries after more than two hundred years of seclusion." Money has reorganized the sense life of peoples just because it is an *extension* of our sense lives. This change does not depend upon approval or disapproval of those living in the society.

Arnold Toynbee made one approach to the transforming power of media in his concept of "etherialization," which he holds to be the principle of progressive simplification and efficiency in any organization or technology. Typically, he is ignoring the *effect* of the challenge of these forms upon the response of our senses. He imagines that it is the response of our opinions that is relevant to the effect of media and technology in society, a "point of view" that is plainly the result of the typographic spell. For the man in a literate and homogenized society ceases to be sensitive to the diverse and discontinuous life of forms. He acquires the illusion of the third dimension and the "private point of view" as part of his Narcissus fixation, and is quite shut off from Blake's awareness or that of the Psalmist, that we become what we behold.

Today when we want to get our bearings in our own culture, and have need to stand aside from the bias and pressure exerted by any technical form of human expression, we have only to visit a society where that particular form has not been felt, or a historical period in which it was unknown. Professor Wilbur Schramm made such a tactical move in studying *Television in the Lives of Our Children*. He found areas where TV had not penetrated at all and ran some tests. Since he had made no study of the peculiar nature of the TV image, his tests were of "content" preferences, viewing time, and vocabulary counts. In a word, his approach to the problem was a literary one, albeit unconsciously so. Consequently, he [33–34] had nothing to report. Had his methods been employed in 1500 A.D. to discover the effects of the printed book in the lives of children or adults, he could have found out nothing of the changes in human and social psychology resulting from typography. Print created individualism and nationalism in the sixteenth century. Program and "content" analysis offer no clues to the magic of these media or to their subliminal charge.

Leonard Doob, in his report *Communication in Africa,* tells of one African who took great pains to listen each evening to the BBC news, even though he could understand nothing of it. Just to be in the presence of those sounds at 7 P.M. each day was important for him. His attitude to speech was like ours to melody—the resonant intonation was meaning enough. In the seventeenth century our ancestors still shared this native's attitude to the forms of media, as is plain in the following sentiment of the Frenchman Bernard Lam expressed in *The Art of Speaking* (London, 1696):

> 'Tis an effect of the Wisdom of God, who created Man to be happy, that whatever is useful to his conversation (way of life) is agreeable to him . . . because all victual that conduces to nourishment is relishable, whereas other things that cannot be assimulated and be turned into our substance are insipid. A Discourse cannot be pleasant to the Hearer that is not easie to the Speaker; nor can it be easily pronounced unless it be heard with delight.

Here is an equilibrium theory of human diet and expression such as even now we are only striving to work out again for media after centuries of fragmentation and specialism.

Pope Pius XII was deeply concerned that there be serious study of the media today. On February 17, 1950, he said:

> It is not an exaggeration to say that the future of modern society and the stability of its inner life depend in large part on the maintenance of an equilibrium between the strength of the techniques of communication and the capacity of the individual's own reaction.

Failure in this respect has for centuries been typical and total for mankind. Subliminal and docile acceptance of media impact has made them prisons without walls for their human users. As A. J. Liebling remarked in his book *The Press,* a man is not free if he cannot see where he is going, even if he has a gun to help him get there. For each of the media is [34–35] also a powerful weapon with which to clobber other media and other groups. The result is that the present age has been one of multiple civil wars that are not limited to the world of art and entertainment. In *War and Human Progress,* Professor J. U. Nef declared: "The total wars of our time have been the result of a series of intellectual mistakes. . . ."

If the formative power in the media are the media themselves, that raises a host of large matters that can only be mentioned here, although they deserve volumes. Namely, that technological media are staples or natural resources, exactly as are coal and cotton and oil. Anybody will concede that society whose economy is dependent upon one or two major staples like cotton, or grain, or lumber, or fish, or cattle is going to have some obvious social patterns of organization as a result. Stress on a few major staples creates extreme instability in the economy but great endurance in the population. The pathos and humor of the American South are embedded in such an economy of limited staples. For a society configured by reliance on a few commodities accepts them as a social bond quite as much as the metropolis does the press. Cotton and oil, like radio and TV, become "fixed charges" on the entire psychic life of the community. And this pervasive fact creates the unique cultural flavor of any society. It pays through the nose and all its other senses for each staple that shapes its life.

That our human senses, of which all media are extensions, are also fixed charges on our personal energies, and that they also configure the awareness and experience of each one of us, may be perceived in another connection mentioned by the psychologist C. G. Jung:

> Every Roman was surrounded by slaves. The slave and his psychology flooded ancient Italy, and every Roman became inwardly, and of course unwittingly, a slave. Because living constantly in the atmosphere of slaves, he became infected through the unconscious with their psychology. No one can shield himself from such an influence (*Contributions to Analytical Psychology*, London, 1928).   [35–36]

2 · MEDIA HOT AND COLD

"The rise of the waltz," explained Curt Sachs in the *World History of the Dance*, "was a result of that longing for truth, simplicity, closeness to nature, and primitivism, which the last two-thirds of he eighteenth century fulfilled." In the century of jazz we are likely to overlook the emergence of the waltz as a hot and explosive human expression that broke through the formal feudal barriers of courtly and choral dance styles.

There is a basic principle that distinguishes a hot medium like radio from a cool one like the telephone, or a hot medium like the movie from a cool one like TV. A hot medium is one that extends one single sense in "high definition." High definition is the state of being well filled with data. A photograph is, visually, "high definition." A cartoon is "low definition," simply because very little visual information is provided. Telephone is a cool medium, or one of low definition, because the ear is given a meager amount of information. And speech is a cool medium of low definition, because so little is given and so much has to be filled in by the listener. On the other hand, hot media do not leave so much to be filled in or completed by the audience. Hot media are, therefore, low in participation, and cool media are high in participation or completion by the audience. Naturally, therefore, a hot medium like radio has very different effects on the user from a cool medium like the telephone.

A cool medium like hieroglyphic or ideogrammic written characters has very different effects from the hot and explosive medium of the phonetic alphabet. The alphabet, when pushed to a high degree of abstract visual intensity, became typography. The printed word with its specialist intensity burst the bonds of medieval corporate guilds and monasteries, creating extreme individualist patterns of enterprise and monopoly. But the typical reversal occurred when extremes of monopoly brought back the corporation, with its impersonal [36–37] empire over many lives. The hotting-up of the medium of writing to repeatable print intensely led to nationalism and the religious wars of the sixteenth century. The heavy and unwieldy media, such as stone, are time binders. Used for writing, they are very cool indeed, and serve to unify the ages; whereas paper is a hot medium that serves to unify spaces horizontally, both in political and entertainment empires.

Any hot medium allows of less participation than a cool one, as a lecture makes for less participation than a seminar, and a book for less than dialogue. With print many earlier forms were excluded from life and art, and many were given strange new intensity. But our own time is crowded with examples of the principle that the hot form excludes, and the cool one includes. When ballerinas began to dance on their toes a century ago, it was felt that the art of the ballet had acquired a new "spirituality." With this new intensity, male figures were excluded from ballet. The role of women had also become fragmented with the advent of industrial specialism and the explosion of home functions into laundries, bakeries, and hospitals on the periphery of the community. Intensity or high definition engenders specialism and fragmentation in living as in entertainment, which explains why any intense experience must be "forgotten," "censored," and reduced to a very cool state become it can be "learned" or assimilated. The Freudian "censor" is less of a moral function than an indispensable condition of learning. Were we to accept fully and directly every shock to our various structures of awareness, we would soon be nervous wrecks, doing double-takes and pressing panic buttons every minute. The "censor" protects our central system of values, as it does our physical nervous system by simply cooling off the onset of experience a great deal. For many people, this cooling system brings on a life-long state of psychic *rigor mortis*, or of somnambulism, particularly observable in periods of new technology.

An example of the disruptive impact of a hot technology succeeding a cool one is given by Robert Theobald in *The Rich and the Poor*. When Australian natives were given steel axes by the missionaries, their culture, based on the stone axe, collapsed. The stone axe had not only been scarce but had always been a basic status symbol of male importance. The missionaries provided quantities of sharp steel axes and gave them to women and children.

The men had even to borrow these from the women, causing a collapse of male dignity. A tribal and feudal hierarchy of traditional kind collapses quickly when it meets any hot medium of the mechanical, uniform, [37–38] and repetitive kind. The medium of money or wheel or writing, or any other form of specialist speedup of exchange and information, will serve to fragment a tribal structure. Similarly, a very much greater speedup as occurs with electricity, may serve to restore a tribal pattern of intense involvement such as took place with the introduction of radio in Europe, and is now tending to happen as a result of TV in America. Specialist technologies detribalize. The nonspecialist electric technology retribalizes. The process of upset resulting from a new distribution of skills is accompanied by much culture lag in which people feel compelled to look at new situations as if they were old ones, and come up with ideas of "population explosion" in an age of implosion. Newton, in an age of clocks, managed to present the physical universe in the image of a clock. But poets like Blake were far ahead of Newton in their response to the challenge of the clock. Blake spoke of the need to be delivered "from single vision and Newton's sleep," knowing very well that Newton's response to the challenge of the new mechanism was itself merely a mechanical repetition of the challenge. Blake saw Newton and Locke and others as hypnotized Narcissus types quite unable to meet the challenge of mechanism. W. B. Yeats gave the full Blakean version of Newton and Locke in a famous epigram:

> Locke sank into a swoon;
> The garden died;
> God took the spinning jenny
> Out of his side.

Yeats presents Locke, the philosopher of mechanical and lineal associationism, as hypnotized by his own image. The "garden," or unified consciousness, ended. Eighteenth-century man got an extension of himself in the form of the spinning machine that Yeats endows with its full sexual significance. Woman, herself, is thus seen as a technological extension of man's being.

Blake's counterstrategy for his age was to meet mechanism with organic myth. Today, deep in the electric age, organic myth is itself a simple and automatic response capable of mathematical formulation and expression, without any of the imaginative perception of Blake about it. Had he encountered the electric age, Blake would not have met its challenge with a mere repetition of electric form. For myth *is* the instant vision of a complex process that ordinarily extends over a long period. Myth is contraction or implosion of any process, [38–39] and the instant speed of electricity confers the mythic dimension on ordinary industrial and social action today. We *live* mythically but continue to think fragmentarily and on single planes.

Scholars today are acutely aware of a discrepancy between their ways of treating subjects and the subject itself. Scriptural scholars of both the Old and New Testaments frequently say that while their treatment must be linear, the subject is not. The subject treats of the relations between God and man, and between God and the world, and of the relations between man and his neighbor—all these subsist together, and act and react upon one another at the same time. The Hebrew and Eastern mode of thought tackles problem and resolution, at the outset of a discussion, in a way typical of oral societies in general. The entire message is then traced and retraced, again and again, on the rounds of a concentric spiral with seeming redundancy. One can stop anywhere after the first few sentences and have the full message, if one is prepared to "dig" it. This kind of plan seems to have inspired Frank Lloyd Wright in designing the Guggenheim Art Gallery on a spiral, concentric basis. It is a redundant form inevitable to the electric age, in which the concentric pattern is imposed by the instant quality, and overlay in depth, of electric speed. But the concentric with its endless intersection of planes is necessary for insight. In fact, it is the technique of insight, and as such is necessary for media study, since no medium has its meaning or existence alone, but only in constant interplay with other media.

The new electric structuring and configuring of life more and more encounters the old lineal and fragmentary procedures and tools of analysis from the mechanical age. More and more we turn from the content of messages to study total effect. Kenneth Boulding put this matter in *The Image* by saying, "The meaning of a message is the change which it produces in the image." Concern with *effect* rather than *meaning* is a basic change of our electric time, for effect involves the total situation, and not a single level of information movement. Strangely, there is recognition of this matter of effect rather than information in the British idea of libel: "The greater the truth, the greater the libel."

The effect of electric technology had at first been anxiety. Now it appears to create boredom. We have been through the three stages of alarm, resistance, and exhaustion that occur in every disease or stress of life, whether individual or collective. At least, our exhausted slump after the first encounter with the electric has inclined us to expect new problems. However, [39–40] backward countries that have experienced little permeation with our own mechanical and specialist culture are much better able to confront and to understand electric technology. Not only have backward and nonindustrial cultures no specialist habits to overcome in their encounter with electromagnetism, but they have still much of their traditional oral culture that has the total, unified "field" character of our new electromagnetism. Our old industrialized areas, having eroded their oral traditions automatically, are in the position of having to rediscover them in order to cope with the electric age.

In terms of the theme of media hot and cold, backward countries are cool, and we are hot. The "city slicker" is hot, and the rustic is cool. But in terms of the reversal of procedures and values in the electric age, the past mechanical time was hot, and we of the TV age are cool. The waltz was a hot, fast mechanical dance suited to the industrial time in its moods of pomp and circumstance. In contrast, the Twist is a cool, involved and chatty form of improvised gesture. The jazz of the period of the hot new media of movie and radio was hot jazz. Yet jazz of itself tends to be a casual dialogue form of dance quite lacking in the repetitive and mechanical forms of the waltz. Cool jazz came in quite naturally after the first impact of radio and movie had been absorbed.

In the special Russian issue of *Life* magazine for September 13, 1963, it is mentioned that in Russian restaurants and night clubs, "though the Charleston is tolerated, the Twist is taboo." All this is to say that a country in the process of industrialization is inclined to regard hot jazz as consistent with its developing programs. The cool and involved form of the Twist, on the other hand, would strike such a culture at once as retrograde and incompatible with its new mechanical stress. The Charleston, with its aspect of a mechanical doll agitated by strings, appears in Russia as an avant-garde form. We, on the other hand, find the *avant-garde* in the cool and the primitive, with its promise of depth involvement and integral expression.

The "hard" sell and the "hot" line become mere comedy in the TV age, and the death of all the salesmen at one stroke of the TV axe has turned the hot American culture into a cool one that is quite unacquainted with itself. America, in fact, would seem to be living through the reverse process that Margaret Mead described in *Time* magazine (September 4, 1954): "There are too many complaints about society having to move too fast to keep up with the machine. There is great advantage in moving fast if you move completely, if [40–41] social, educational, and recreational changes keep pace. You must change the whole pattern at once and the whole group together—and the people themselves must decide to move."

Margaret Mead is thinking here of change as uniform speed-up of motion or a uniform hotting-up of temperatures in backward societies. We are certainly coming within conceivable range of a world automatically controlled to the point where we could say, "Six hours less radio in Indonesia next week or there will be a great falling off in literary attention." Or, "We can program twenty more hours of TV in South Africa next week to cool down the tribal temperature raised by radio last week." Whole cultures could now be programmed to keep their emotional climate stable in the same way that we have begun to know something about maintaining equilibrium in the commercial economies of the world.

In the merely personal and private sphere we are often reminded of how changes of tone and attitude are demanded of different times and seasons in order to keep situations in hand. British clubmen, for the sake of companionship and amiability, have long excluded the hot topics of religion and politics from mention inside the highly participational club. In the same vein, W. H. Auden wrote, ". . . this season the man of goodwill will wear his heart up his sleeve, not on it. . . . the honest manly style is today suited only to Iago" (Introduction to John Betjeman's *Slick But Not Streamlined*). In the Renaissance, as print technology hotted up the social *milieu* to a very high point, the gentleman and the courtier (Hamlet-Mercutio style) adopted, in contrast, the casual and cool nonchalance of the playful and superior being. The Iago allusion of Auden reminds us that Iago was the *alter ego* and assistant of the intensely earnest and very non-nonchalant General Othello. In imitation of the earnest and forthright general, Iago hotted up his own image and wore his heart on his sleeve, until General Othello read him loud and clear as "honest Iago," a man after his own grimly earnest heart.

Throughout *The City in History,* Lewis Mumford favors the cool or casually structured towns over the hot and intensely filled-in cities. The great period of Athens, he feels, was one during which most of the democratic habits of village life and participation still obtained. Then burst forth the full variety of human expression and exploration such as was later impossible in highly developed urban centers. For the highly developed situation is, by definition, low in opportunities of participation, and rigorous in its demands of specialist fragmentation from those who would control it. For example, [41–42] what is known as "job enlargement" today in business and in management consists in allowing the employee more freedom to discover and define his function. Likewise, in reading a detective story the reader participates as co-author simply because so much has been left out of the narrative. The open-mesh silk stocking is far more sensuous than the smooth nylon, just because the eye must act as hand in filling in and completing the image, exactly as in the mosaic of the TV image.

Douglas Cater in *The Fourth Branch of Government* tells how the men of the Washington press bureaus delighted to complete or fill in the blank of Calvin Coolidge's personality. Because he was so like a mere cartoon, they felt the urge to complete his image for him and his public. It is instructive that the press applied the word "cool" to Cal. In the very sense of a cool medium, Calvin Coolidge was so lacking in any articulation of data in his public image that there was only one word for him. He was real cool. In the hot 1920s, the hot press medium found Cal very cool and rejoiced in his lack of image, since it compelled the participation of the press in filling in an image of him for the public. By contrast, F.D.R. was a hot press agent, himself a rival of the newspaper medium and one who delighted in scoring off the press on the rival hot medium of radio. Quite in contrast, Jack Paar ran a cool show for the cool TV medium, and became a rival for the patrons of the night spots and their allies in the gossip columns. Jack Paar's war with the gossip columnists was a weird example of clash between a hot and cold medium such as had occurred with the "scandal of the rigged TV quiz shows." The rivalry between the hot press and radio media, on one hand, and TV on the other, for the hot ad buck, served to confuse and to overheat the issues in the affair that pointlessly involved Charles Van Doren.

An Associated Press story from Santa Monica, California, August 9, 1962, reported how

> Nearly 100 traffic violators watched a police traffic accident film today to atone for their violations. Two had to be treated for nausea and shock. . . .

> Viewers were offered a $5.00 reduction in fines if they agreed to see the movie, *Signal 30,* made by Ohio State police.

> It showed twisted wreckage and mangled bodies and recorded the screams of accident victims.

Whether the hot film medium using hot content would cool off the hot drivers is a moot point. But it does concern any [42–43] understanding of media. The effect of hot media treatment cannot include much empathy or participation at any time. In this connection an insurance ad that featured Dad in an iron lung surrounded by a joyful family group did more to strike terror into the reader than all the warning wisdom in the world. It is a question that arises in connection with capital punishment. Is a severe penalty the best deterrent to serious crime? With regard to the bomb and the cold war, is the threat of massive retaliation the most effective means to peace? Is it not evident in every human situation that is pushed to a point of saturation that some precipitation occurs? When all the available resources and energies have been played up in an organism or in any structure there is some kind of reversal of pattern. The spectacle of brutality used as deterrent can brutalize. Brutality used in sports may humanize under some conditions, at least. But with regard to the bomb and retaliation as deterrent, it is obvious that numbness is the result of any prolonged terror, a fact that was discovered when the fallout shelter program was broached. The price of eternal vigilance is indifference.

Nevertheless, it makes all the difference whether a hot medium is used in a hot or a cool culture. The hot radio medium used in cool or nonliterate cultures has a violent effect, quite unlike its effect, say in England or America, where radio is felt as entertainment. A cool or low literacy culture cannot accept hot media like movies or radio as entertainment. They are, at least, as radically upsetting for them as the cool TV medium has proved to be for our high literacy world.

And as for the cool war and the hot bomb scare, the cultural strategy that is desperately needed is humor and play. It is play that cools off the hot situations of actual life by miming them. Competitive sports between Russia and the West will hardly serve that purpose of relaxation. Such sports are inflammatory, it is plain. And what we consider entertainment or fun in our media inevitably appears as violent political agitation to a cool culture.

One way to spot the basic difference between hot and cold media uses is to compare and contrast a broadcast of a symphony performance with a broadcast of a symphony rehearsal. Two of the finest shows ever released by the CBC were of Glenn Gould's procedure in recording piano recitals, and Igor Stravinsky's rehearsing the Toronto symphony in some of his new work. A cool medium like TV, when really used, demands this involvement in process. The neat tight package [43–44] is suited to hot media, like radio and gramophone. Francis Bacon never tired of contrasting hot and cool prose. Writing in "methods" or complete packages, he contrasted with writing in aphorisms, or single observations such as "Revenge is a kind of wild justice." The passive consumer wants packages, but those, he suggested, who are concerned in pursuing knowledge and in seeking causes will resort to aphorisms, just because they are incomplete and require participation in depth.

The principle that distinguishes hot and cold media is perfectly embodied in the folk wisdom: "Men seldom make passes at girls who wear glasses." Glasses intensify the outward-going vision, and fill in the feminine image exceedingly, Marion the Librarian notwithstanding. Dark glasses, on the other hand, create the inscrutable and inaccessible image that invites a great deal of participation and completion.

Again, in a visual and highly literate culture, when we meet a person for the first time his visual appearance dims out the sound of the name, so that in self-defense we add: "How do you spell your name?" Whereas, in an ear culture, the *sound* of a man's name is the overwhelming fact, as Joyce knew when he said in *Finnegans Wake,* "Who gave you that numb?" For the name of a man is a numbing blow from which he never recovers.

Another vantage point from which to test the difference between hot and cold media is the practical joke. The hot literary medium excludes the practical and participant aspect of the joke so completely that Constance Rourke, in her *American Humor,* considers it as no joke at all. To literary people, the practical joke with its total physical involvement is as distasteful as the pun that derails us from the smooth and uniform progress that is typographic order. Indeed, to the literary person who is quite unaware of the intensely abstract nature of the typographic medium, it is the grosser and participant forms of art that seem "hot," and the abstract and intensely literary form that seems "cool." "You may perceive, Madam," said Dr. Johnson, with a pugilistic smile, "that I am well-bred to a degree of needless scrupulosity." And Dr. Johnson was right in supposing that "well-bred" had come to mean a white-shirted stress on attire that rivaled the rigor of the printed page. "Comfort" consists in abandoning a visual arrangement in favor of one that permits casual participation of the senses, a state that is excluded when any one sense, but especially the visual sense, is hotted up to the point of dominant command of a situation.

On the other hand, in experiments in which all outer sensa-[44–45] tion is withdrawn, the subject begins a furious fill-in or completion of senses that is sheer hallucination. So the hotting-up of one sense tends to result in hallucination.

3 · REVERSAL OF THE OVERHEATED MEDIUM

A headline for June 21, 1963, read:

WASHINGTON-MOSCOW HOT LINE
TO OPEN IN 60 DAYS

The *Times* of London Service, Geneva:

The agreement to establish a direct communication link between Washington and Moscow for emergencies was signed here yesterday by Charles Stelle of the United States and Semyon Tsarapkin of the Soviet Union. . . .

The link, known as the hot line, will be opened within sixty days, according to U.S. officials. It will make use of leased commercial circuits, one cable and the other wireless, using teleprinter equipment.

The decision to use the hot printed medium in place of the cool, participational, telephone medium is unfortunate in the extreme. No doubt the decision was prompted by the literary bias of the West for the printed form, on the ground that it is more impersonal than the telephone. The printed form has quite different implications in Moscow from what it has in Washington. So with the telephone. The Russians' love of this instrument, so congenial to their oral traditions, is owing to the rich nonvisual involvement it affords. The Russian uses the telephone for the sort of effects we associate with the eager conversation of the lapel-gripper whose face is twelve inches away.

Both telephone and teleprinter as amplifications of the unconscious cultural bias of Moscow, on one hand, and of Washington, on the other, are invitations to monstrous misunder-[45–46]standings. The Russian bugs rooms and spies by ear, finding this quite natural. He is outraged by our visual spying, however, finding this quite unnatural.

The principle that during the stages of their development all things appear under forms opposite to those that they finally present is an ancient doctrine Interest in the power of things to reverse themselves by evolution is evident in a great diversity of observations, sage and jocular. Alexander Pope wrote

> Vice is a monster of such frightful mien
> As to be hated needs but to be seen;
> But seen too oft, familiar with its face,
> We first endure, then pity, then embrace.

A caterpillar gazing at the butterfly is supposed to have remarked. "Waal, you'll never catch me in one of those durn things."

At another level we have seen in this century the change-over from the debunking of traditional myths and legends to their reverent study. As we begin to react in depth to the social life and problems of our global village, we become reactionaries. Involvement that goes with our instant technologies transforms the most "socially conscious" people into conservatives. When Sputnik had first gone into orbit a schoolteacher asked her second-graders to write some verse on the subject. One child wrote:

> The stars are so big,
> The earth is so small,
> Stay as you are.

With man his knowledge and the process of obtaining knowledge are of equal magnitude. Our ability to apprehend galaxies and subatomic structure, as well, is a movement of faculties that includes and transcends them. The second-grader who wrote the words above *lives* in a world much vaster than any which a scientist today has instruments to measure, or concepts to describe. As W. B. Yeats wrote of this reversal, "The visible world is no longer a reality and the unseen world is no longer a dream."

Associated with this transformation of the real world into science fiction is the reversal now proceeding apace, by which the Western world is going Eastern, even as the East goes Western. Joyce encoded this reciprocal reverse in his cryptic phrase: [46–47]

> The West shall shake the East awake
> While ye have the night for morn.

The title of his *Finnegans Wake* is a set of multi-leveled puns on the reversal by which Western man enters his tribal, or Finn, cycle once more, following the track of the old Finn, but wide awake this time as we re-enter the tribal night. It is like our contemporary consciousness of the Unconscious.

The stepping-up of speed from the mechanical to the instant electric form reverses explosion into implosion. In our present electric age the imploding or contracting energies of our world now clash with the old expansionist and traditional patterns of organization. Until recently our institutions and arrangements, social, political, and economic, had shared a one-way pattern. We still think of it as "explosive," or expansive; and though it no longer obtains, we still talk about the population explosion and the explosion in learning. In fact, it is not the increase of numbers in the world that creates our concern with population. Rather, it is the fact that everybody in the world has to live in the utmost proximity created by our electric involvement in one another's lives. In education, likewise, it is not the increase in numbers of those seeking to learn that creates the crisis. Our new concern with education follows upon the changeover to an interrelation in knowledge, where before the separate subjects of the curriculum had stood apart from each other. Departmental sovereignties have melted away as rapidly as national sovereignties under conditions of electric speed. Obsession with the older patterns of mechanical, one-way expansion from centers to margins is no longer relevant to our electric world. Electricity does not centralize, but decentralizes. It is like the difference between a railway system and an electric grid system: the one requires railheads and big urban centers. Electric power, equally available in the farmhouse and the Executive Suite, permits any place to be a center, and does not require large aggregations. This reverse pattern appeared quite early in electrical "labor-saving" devices, whether a toaster or washing machine or vacuum cleaner. Instead of saving work, these devices permit everybody to do his own work. What the nineteenth century had delegated to servants and housemaids we now do for ourselves. This principle applies *in toto* in the electric age. In politics, it permits Castro to exist as independent nucleus or center. It would permit Quebec to leave the Canadian union in a way quite inconceivable under the regime of the railways. The railways require a uniform political and economic space. [47–48] On the other hand, airplane and radio permit the utmost discontinuity and diversity in spatial organization.

Today the great principle of classical physics and economics and political science, namely that of the divisibility of each process, has reversed itself by sheer extension into the unified field theory; and automation in industry replaces the divisibility of process with the organic interlacing of all functions in the complex. The electric tape succeeds the assembly line.

In the new electric Age of Information and programmed production, commodities themselves assume more and more the character of information, although this trend appears mainly in the increasing advertising budget. Significantly, it is those commodities that are most used in social communication, cigarettes, cosmetics, and soap (cosmetic removers), that bear much of the burden of the upkeep of the media in general. As electric information levels rise, almost any kind of material will serve any kind of need or function, forcing the intellectual more and more into the role of social command and into the service of production.

It was Julien Benda's *Great Betrayal* that helped to clarify the new situation in which the intellectual suddenly holds the whip hand in society. Benda saw that the artists and intellectuals who had long been alienated from power, and who since Voltaire had been in opposition, had now been drafted for service in the highest echelons of decision-making. Their great betrayal was that they had surrendered their autonomy and had become the flunkies of power, as the atomic physicist at the present moment is the flunky of the war lords.

Had Benda known his history, he would have been less angry and less surprised. For it has always been the role of intelligentsia to act as liaison and as mediators between old and new power groups. Most familiar of such groups is the case of the Greek slaves, who were for long the educators and confidential clerks of the Roman power. And it is precisely this servile role of the confidential clerk to the tycoon—commercial, military, or political—that the educator has continued to play in the Western world until the present moment. In England "the Angries" were a group of such clerks who had suddenly emerged from the lower echelons by the educational escape hatch. As they emerged into the upper world of power, they found that the air was not at all fresh or bracing. But they lost their nerve even quicker than Bernard Shaw lost his. Like Shaw, they quickly settled down to whimsy and to the cultivation of entertainment values.

In his *Study of History*, Toynbee notes a great many rever-[48–49]sals of form and dynamic, as when, in the middle of the fourth century A.D., the Germans in the Roman service began abruptly to be proud of their tribal names and to retain them. Such a moment marked new confidence born of saturation with Roman values, and it was a moment marked by the complementary Roman swing toward primitive values. (As Americans saturate with European values, especially since TV, they begin to insist upon American coach lamps, hitching posts, and colonial kitchenware as cultural objects.) Just as the barbarians got to the top of the Roman social ladder, the Romans themselves were disposed to assume the dress and manners of tribesmen out of the same frivolous and snobbish spirit that attached the French court of Louis XVI to the world of shepherds and shepherdesses. It would have seemed a natural moment for the intellectuals to have taken over while the governing class was touring Disneyland, as it were. So it must have appeared to Marx and his followers. But they reckoned without understanding the dynamics of the new media of communication. Marx based his analysis most untimely on the machine, just as the telegraph and other implosive forms began to reverse the mechanical dynamic.

The present chapter is concerned with showing that in any medium or structure there is what Kenneth Boulding calls a "break boundary at which the system suddenly changes into another or passes some point of no return in its dynamic processes." Several such "break boundaries" will be discussed later, including the one from stasis to motion, and from the mechanical to the organic in the pictorial world. One effect of the static photo had been to suppress the conspicuous consumption of the rich, but the effect of the speed-up of the photo had been to provide fantasy riches for the poor of the entire globe.

Today the road beyond its break boundary turns cities into highways, and the highway proper takes on a continuous urban character. Another characteristic reversal after passing a road break boundary is that the country ceases to be the center of all work, and the city ceases to be the center of leisure. In fact, improved roads and transport have reversed the ancient pattern and made cities the centers of work and the country the place of leisure and of recreation.

Earlier, the increase of traffic that came with money and roads had ended the static tribal state (as Toynbee calls the nomadic food-gathering culture). Typical of the reversing that occurs at break boundaries is the paradox that nomadic mobile man, the hunter and food-gatherer, is socially static. [49–50] On the other hand, sedentary, specialist man is dynamic, explosive, progressive. The new magnetic or world city will be static and iconic or inclusive.

In the ancient world the intuitive awareness of break boundaries as points of reversal and of no return was embodied in the Greek idea of *hubris*, which Toynbee presents in his *Study of History,* under the head of "The Nemesis of Creativity" and "The Reversal of Roles." The Greek dramatists presented the idea of creativity as creating, also, its own kind of blindness, as in the case of Oedipus Rex, who solves the riddle of the Sphinx. It was as if the Greeks felt that the penalty for one break-through was a general sealing-off of awareness to the total field. In a Chinese work—*The Way and Its Power* (A. Waley translation)—there is a series of instances of the overheated medium, the overextended man or culture, and the peripety or reversal that inevitably follows:

> He who stands on tiptoe does not stand firm;
> He who takes the longest strides does not walk the fastest . . .
> He who boasts of what he will do succeeds in nothing;
> He who is proud of his work achieves nothing that endures.

One of the most common causes of breaks in any system is the cross-fertilization with another system, such as happened to print with the steam press, or with radio and movies (that yielded the talkies). Today with microfilm and micro-cards, not to mention electric memories, the printed word assumes again much of the handicraft character of a manuscript. But printing from movable type was, itself, the major break boundary in the history of phonetic literacy, just as the phonetic alphabet had been the break boundary between tribal and individualist man.

The endless reversals or break boundaries passed in the interplay of the structures of bureaucracy and enterprise include the point at which individuals began to be held responsible and accountable for their "private actions." That was the moment of the collapse of tribal collective authority. Centuries later, when further explosion and expansion had exhausted the powers of private action, corporate enterprise invented the idea of Public Debt, making the individual privately accountable for group action.

As the nineteenth century heated up the mechanical and dissociative procedures of technical fragmentation, the entire attention of men turned to the associative and the corporate. [50–51] In the first great age of the substitution of machine for human toil Carlyle and the Pre-Raphaelites promulgated the doctrine of *work* as a mystical social communion, and millionaires like Ruskin and Morris toiled like navvies for esthetic reasons. Marx was an impressionable recipient of these doctrines. Most bizarre of all the reversals in the great Victorian age of mechanization and high moral tone is the counter-strategy of Lewis Carroll and Edward Lear, whose nonsense has proved exceedingly durable. While the Lord Cardigans were taking their blood baths in the Valley of Death, Gilbert and Sullivan were announcing that the boundary break had been passed.   [51]

FEEDBACK

FEEDBACK *McLUHAN*

FEEDBACK *and*

HIS IDEAS

THE IMPORTANCE OF
MARSHALL McLUHAN

Arthur W. Foshay

Some of us have become aware of Marshall McLuhan. He is like a thunderclap; you cannot overlook him once you have been nearby. There are those, of course, who do not like thunderclaps. The collies hide under the dining table. The poodles and the terriers variously bark and yap. The Great Danes look pained.

Mr. McLuhan has written another book: *The Gutenberg Galaxy* (University of Toronto Press, 1962), and has thus created another sensation. With enormous erudition, he has brought the whole Western intellectual tradition into a single hypothesis: that the basic experience of western man has been shaped mainly by the invention of type.

The great difference between McLuhan and everyone else is that he sees the basic forms of experience both as critical and as modifiable. What is a "basic form"? It is the form in which you put the raw data you think about and the form, therefore, of your thoughts. It matters—scarcely anyone realizes

ARTHUR W. FOSHAY is a member of the faculty of Teachers College, Columbia University.

This article is from *Educational Leadership,* October 1963, pp. 35–39 and is reprinted with permission of the Association for Supervision and Curriculum Development, and of Arthur W. Foshay. © October 1963 by the Association for Supervision and Curriculum Development.

how much it matters—whether you perceive information (data) all-at-once, or sequentially. Is your basic experience of the world lineal or simultaneous? Do you really believe things when they are written *out,* or written *up,* or *down,* or *in;* or none of these? Do you see the data of experience in a line or as a swarm? It makes all the difference which you do.

It makes you a member of the Renaissance—a Gutenberg man—a typographic man—if you arrange experiences in lineal form. For after Gutenberg, the most significant things that happened were *said* and *written* and *printed,* and every one of these is a sequential form in which the data are arranged all in a row.

Not so the medieval man, who entered the great stimulus of his time—the cathedral—and was assaulted from every direction, simultaneously, with the most significant happenings in his culture. He lived in an oral culture, not a print culture. His ear and eye had to cooperate. To be blind after Gutenberg was to be helpless, but a deaf man could even compose music. Not so during the pre-Gutenberg period.

McLuhan presents his hypothesis as a

> . . . mosaic or field approach to its problems. Such a mosaic image of numerous data and quotations in evidence offers the only practical means of revealing causal operations in history.
>
> The alternative procedure would be to offer a series of views of fixed relationships in pictorial space. Thus the galaxy or con-[35–37]stellation of events upon which the present study concentrates is itself a mosaic of perpetually interacting forms that have undergone kaleidoscopic transformation—particularly in our own time.

THIS EXPLOSIVE MAN

McLuhan's description of his method, above, does not describe the effect his book has. The book presents an array of explosive statements, each supported by argument. There is a minimum of bridging. Here are some of his explosions (he calls them "chapter glosses"—an arcane double pun that no doubt arises from his extensive, scholarly interest in James Joyce):

> Civilization gives the barbarian or tribal man an eye for an ear and is now at odds with the electronic world.

> Cervantes confronted typographic man in the figure of Don Quixote.

> Nobody ever made a grammatical error in a non-literate society.

> Typography cracked the voices of silence.

Why should we pay attention to such a book? For one thing—and perhaps this is enough to say—it exists. It has happened, and it is not possible to act as if it has not.

In our various educational roles, however, the book has a special importance. At the root of our thinking about education is our conception of the nature of knowledge, the nature of knowing, the nature of experience. Here is a man who says that the development of the electronic forms for experience wholly transforms it: that the culture-shift we are a half-century or more into is as fundamental as the shift from medieval to Renaissance experience.

Now, *that* is something to think about. For it is inevitable that the straining between the generations, between tea-[37–39]chers and taught, will reflect this strain. It already does. We, the older generation, think of the difference between the generations as action-reaction, as the swinging pendulum. The young sense it, not as anything on one plane, but as an explosion. It is appropriate that the one to tell us of it is this explosive man, Marshall McLuhan, who is called by a professor of English now at Harvard, "the most seminal mind on the continent."   [39]

1. Note that Prof. Foshay calls McLuhan's reference to his *Gutenberg Galaxy* "chapter glosses" an "arcane double pun." What does the *punning* consist of in the expression "chapter glosses"?

2. One of Foshay's quotations from *Gutenberg Galaxy* is "Nobody ever made a grammatical error in a non-literate society." Is this statement quite literally true? What significance does it have for grammar teachers?

REVIEW OF UNDERSTANDING MEDIA

Eli M. Oboler

This unusual book gives a fresh, original view of the influence of the mass media, very broadly considered, on modern society. To the author—director of the Center for the Extension of Man at the University of Toronto—the electric light, jet travel, the book, radio, TV, music, art, the movies, clocks, comics, all these and many more, are examples of the mass media. Indeed, he says, "to the student of media structures every detail of the total mosaic of the contemporary world is vivid with meaningful life." So he cites authorities as disparate as Spengler and *Mad* magazine, as Lewis Carroll and Arnold Toynbee. Stimulating and penetrating, a *sui generis* volume, probably for a limited audience, but worth considering for all academic and larger libraries. [*2359*]

The last sentence of this 1964 review projects the future career of *Understanding Media* as Mr. Oboler foresaw it at that time. How accurate was the prediction? What would have prompted the reviewer to make that judgment?

ELI OBOLER is a research librarian who has edited a number of professional journals in the field of library science and has contributed regularly to periodicals.

BLOWING HOT AND COLD

Unsigned
Review of *Understanding Media*

Every so often, the semi-intellectual communities at the fringes of the arts, the universities, and the communications industries are hit by a new book, which becomes a fad or a parlor game. This summer's possible candidate, with what may be just the right combination of intelligence, arrogance and pseudo science, is Marshall McLuhan's *Understanding Media*.

Seamless Web. Author McLuhan is a University of Toronto professor and literary critic, who writes books (first was *The Gutenberg Galaxy*) to prove that books are responsible for most of the ills of modern man. Nationalism, war, industrialization, population explosion, the breakdown of human relations in urbanized chaos—McLuhan blames them all on Gutenberg's invention of movable type, and the resulting growth of both the audience and the technology for communication-by-print.

The trouble is that print is what McLuhan calls a "hot" medium of communication: sharp in definition, filled with data, exclusively visual and verbal, but (a key and debatable point) psychologically damaging and low in audience participation. Other hot media by McLuhan's rules are photography, movies, competitive spectator sports and radio. Hot media make men think logically and independently, instead of naturally, "mythically" and communally. This is bad. What McLuhan likes are cool media. These are fuzzy, low in information, but richly demanding on the audience to fill in what is

Time Magazine, July 3, 1964, p. 88. Courtesy *Time;* Copyright Time Inc., 1964.

missing. The telephone, modern painting, but pre-eminently television are cool and good. Television and other "electric media" are oral-auditory, tactile, visceral, and involve the individual almost without volition. As a result McLuhan believes that the world is rapidly becoming a "global village," in which mankind communicates in a supermodern version of the way tribal societies were once related. In the coming overthrow of typographic and literate communications McLuhan expresses his grotesque hope that modern man can be put "back into the tribal or oral pattern with its seamless web of kinship and interdependence."

Pseudo Science. As an intellectual game called "cool and hot," the system has great possibilities for a chatty weekend at Big Sur or Martha's Vineyard. Clocks (hot), money (hot), clothes (getting cooler in the U.S.), nudity (very cool), and almost anything else can be interpreted as media by McLuhan's rules. "Backward countries are cool, and we are hot." Autos are hot. The "blurry, shaggy texture of Kennedy" was a natural for cool TV, which is why "sharp, intense" Nixon lost the debates. Private enterprise is hot; public debt is cool. Iago is cool, but Othello hot. Girls who wear glasses don't get passes— because they are hot.

Yet McLuhan is not playing games. He is in humorless earnest. And if the book is taken seriously, it must be judged as fuzzy-minded, lacking in perspective, low in definition and data, redundant, and contemptuous of logical sequence—which is to say that McLuhan has perfectly illustrated the cool qualities he most values in communications. McLuhan's solemn pseudo science at work: "What do we know about the social or psychic energies that develop by electric fusion or implosion when literate individuals are suddenly gripped by an electromagnetic field, such as occurs in the new Common Market pressure in Europe?" Or: "Had TV occurred on a large scale during Hitler's reign, he would have vanished quickly." [88]

Observe the review's tone in this *Time* article on *Understanding Media*. How much of its evaluation of the book is implied by the style of expression? Point out where the reviewer's choice of words and phrases conveys critical judgments. Is the title consistent with the general tone of the review?

NEVER LOSE YOUR COOL

Paul West
Review of *Understanding Media*

"Revolutionary," says the blurb, is Mr. McLuhan's word; and, for a naughty moment, before proper academic gravity reasserts itself, one envisions an academic big wheel playing Canadian roulette and always, in the thirty-three chapter-throws he permits himself, coming to the rest at the same number. What number? The number of the age; Mr. McLuhan has it, and in this book he keeps telling us so—not, I hasten to add, arrogantly or tediously, but with an anecdotal facility and a passion for vivid detail that are enchanting and rare. Most of the prose is trenchant and the tone compact of Alastair Cooke and André Malraux. Now he studs in the details with a dry amenity ("Walt Kelly's *Pogo* looks very much indeed like a gothic page"; "The open-mesh silk stocking is far more sensuous than the smooth nylon"), now he slides into the costive rhetoric we associate with *The Voices of Silence* ("After three thousand years of specialist explosion and of increasing specialism and alienation in the technological extensions of our bodies, our world has become compressional by dramatic reversal"). Thank goodness there is more of the studding than of the jargon. Mr. McLuhan does communicate the exhilaration of his quest;

PAUL WEST is a novelist and critic whose books include *Byron and the Spoiler's Art* and *The Modern Novel*.

This review of *Understanding Media* appeared in the October, 1964, edition of *The Canadian Forum*, pp. 165–166, and is reprinted by permission.

he is a man in love with what William James called life's "big blooming buzzing confusion," and it is quite possible (even a joy) to read *Understanding Media* as field-work toward the novel of electronic manners. No doubt of it, Mr. McLuhan has compiled something amazing.

I have been looking at this book for a month; I have picked up a fortifying mass of information, and I shall pillage Mr. McLuhan's pages for years to come. But I must confess that, when I come to his argument, I am lost: some parts of it I cannot fathom at all, and the parts I think I follow I disagree with on what seems very ordinary grounds. According to Mr. McLuhan, "the medium is the message": the form of the medium, rather than its content, determines what is being said. And he cites "electric light" as a medium: "The electric light escapes attention as a communication medium just because it has no 'content' . . . it is not till the electric light is used to spell out some brand name that it is noticed as a medium." Well now. Would we call human breath a *medium?* Surely Mr. McLuhan has the wrong word; he means form of energy. He thinks that brand names (like brain surgery and night baseball) are somehow part of the content of electric light as they could not exist without such light. True, perhaps; but because, without light, something cannot exist or go on as we now know it, does it follow that the something is part of light's alleged content and not, rather, one of the realized possible uses to which raw energy can be put? I am baffled when I find that both language and electric light are *media;* man invented language; electricity was there from the first, functioning in accordance with laws man did not invent. I am not arguing that media do not distort—impede in a characteristic way—what is put into them: you cannot paint your refutation of Croce's aesthetics; you cannot translate Beethoven's music into words; you cannot make music out of paint or sentences out of the twelve-tone scale. It seems to me that what Mr. McLuhan thinks is a [165–166] medium—TV, telephone, radio, movie, photograph, ad—is not a medium but a medium-aid. Just because you milk a cow by machine instead of by hand doesn't mean that the machine is a new kind of milk. The media, as I understand the term, are words, non-verbal pictures, notes in music, and so on. And when what I call medium-aids bring us spoken or printed words or non-verbal pictures or permutations of musical notes, they are not changing the essence of those things although they may be distorting it. I think Mr. McLuhan's book is not about media at all but truly about "extensions" which, let him say what he likes, are mere valves, vessels, conduits, and so on. If he had made this clear, he would not have involved himself in what seem wilful casuistries about the "message" of "any medium or technology" (revealing alternatives, aren't they) as being "the change of scale or pace or pattern that it introduces into human affairs." When he says message he means impact. In other words, when I hail a ship through a megaphone, I resort to the verbal medium which communicates a message and do so by employing a tool which gives me a better chance of being successful. The megaphone's amplification is its impact, and the fact that the megaphone makes my voice louder does not mean the megaphone itself is a message.

Consider now what Mr. McLuhan says about the telephone and the TV. (He has already assumed that thought is non-verbal; I wonder how he knows.) Anyway, I see no difference between the messages when I hear, from the TV while I am watching, than from the phone because a friend has called up, that it is raining. Each time, it rains. Same message, each way. Now Mr. McLuhan says this:

> There is a basic principle that distinguishes a hot medium like radio from a cool one like the telephone, or a hot medium like the movie from a cool one like TV. A hot medium is one that extends one single sense in "high definition." High definition is the state of being well filled with data.

Radio is hot; phone is cool. Yet, if we grant a ready talker, the ear will get "well filled with data" from either. I cannot for the life of me see why listening to Bertrand Russell on the radio is "hotter" than having him call me up for fifteen minutes. And while he is talking I can imagine as richly as I want. It depends who has your ear, and not how. Again, why does Mr. McLuhan say "Telephone is cool . . . because the ear is given a meager amount of information?" Has he never had a faculty wife call him up about the Red Cross Bingo, etc.? Let that pass; perhaps he means not *amount* of information, but various appeals to different senses. But we read: "speech is a cool medium . . . because so little is given and so much has to be filled in by the listener." On the phone I cannot see my interlocutor's face and gestures. Face to face with him, I can, and surely the same is roughly true when I watch TV. TV, speech, phone, are cool; radio is hot, like movie. Hot media, we are told, permit little participation: but what then of the radio play, something in which we participate intensely and imaginatively, filling in whenever we need to? Cool media invite participation: but are we participating that much when we watch TV? Isn't it a fact that we often cannot get into the act at all, so flooded are our visual and aural senses, so little being left to the imagination? These categories are erratic; indeed, Mr. McLuhan even mixes himself up: cool isn't antithetical to hot. Why not cold and hot? Or cool and warm? Behold: Chapter 2 is titled "Media Hot and Cold", but the text doesn't use "Cold". Give me, if I must at all, mild and bitter, chilled.

Two more quotations must come in now. "A lecture", says Mr. McLuhan, "makes for less participation than a seminar." I wonder; students are supposed to be *thinking* while listening. So participation must be vocal then, or gesticulatory, which seems a very miserly view of it. Is it true that students are failed for not shouting up during lectures and for pondering during seminars? All I can console myself with is the fact that electronic professors stay within the medium of electronic English. Mr. McLuhan is much too civilized, too literate, too much in touch with the swarming world to join them; but occasionally he does offer this kind of thing, perhaps to prove he is not the gracious polymath this book contains: "Is it not evident in every human situation that is pushed to a point of saturation that some precipitation occurs?" Do you, sir, sweat when *you* are drunk?

Mr. McLuhan must have the penultimate word here, however. "Those who panic now about the threat of the newer media and about the revolution we are forging, vaster in scope than that of Gutenberg, are obviously lacking in cool visual detachment and gratitude for that most potent gift bestowed on Western man by literacy and typography: his power to act without reaction or involvement." Maybe: Mr. Barzun is the only one I know of who is getting worked up, and he certainly isn't panicking. I agree with Mr. McLuhan: scorn not the telly. What worries me is his assumption, in the words just quoted, that the supposed panickers lack "cool" visual detachment; which means, I think, they are hot or warm, and therefore are like radio and the movie. Are these people media? Anyway, the moral seems to be: never lose your cool. I just wish Mr. McLuhan had not gone so Aristotelian in reporting brilliantly and punchily what is going on around us. His book is one that I shall treasure, although I confess unhappily, for the wrong reasons. But we cannot read *Understanding Media* without multiplying our awareness one thousand fold of the way things are with us; and that surely is what Mr. McLuhan wants, categories or no.   [*166*]

1. Mr. West's first paragraph comments on McLuhan's prose style. Does this view coincide with the general opinion you have observed among various critics of McLuhan as a writer? In what specific ways does it agree with or diverge from the consensus?

2. West submits a concept he calls "medium-aids" by which he counters McLuhan's definition of "media." Can you distinguish clearly, and with examples, just what objection he has to McLuhan's use of the term "media," and why he insists on a substitute?

THE
CYBERNETIC
CAVEMAN

Deborah A. Holmes
and George Zabriskie

Marshall McLuhan's previous book, *The Gutenberg Galaxy,* presented the thesis that the invention of the alphabet, and later the printing press, progressively transformed an oral, tactile, tribal culture into a specialized, fragmented society characterized by visual perception, the use of logical, sequential organization and a fixed point of view. Earlier, McLuhan, who is director of the Center for Culture and Technology at the University of Toronto, had written *The Mechanical Bride,* an elaborate spoof on the stereotyped excesses of a society dominated by mechanical technology. In *Understanding Media,* which carries history up to President Kennedy's assassination, he returns to the final theme in *The Gutenberg Galaxy:* electronic technology will take us back to oral, tactile tribalism.

The Gutenberg Galaxy, published in 1962, contained the promise of *Understanding Media* in its final section. With only two years between books,

DEBORAH A. HOLMES is an editor with the National Academy of Sciences.

GEORGE ZABRISKIE is a free-lance writer.

Reprinted from *The Nation,* October 5, 1964, pp. 194–196, by permission.

it seems that McLuhan was pressed to finish this new one and many of its disappointments (including an astonishing number of typos and the lack of a bibliography) must be charged to haste—both on his part and that of his publisher. Insights on the nature of cultural processes will keep at least another season. These flaws are some of the most obvious ones; deeper problems appear more slowly. Yet the book represents fresh and constructive thinking—insights, to use the author's own vocabulary—on the nature of media and their psychic and social consequences. In the wake of considerable controversy over his ideas, it is time to take a close look at what McLuhan is up to in *Understanding Media*.

McLuhan's concept of media includes not only the technology of communications but *any* socially affective technology. He treats media as extensions of the human personality, an approach adapted from the psychology of William MacDougall, who considered personality extension to begin with such simple things as the use of hand tools. McLuhan carries this MacDougallian theory into all things, with an inclusive view of media and the broadest possible interpretation of their effects. Clothing, housing, clocks, transportation, weapons, automation are treated along with TV, radio, comic books and other means of verbal or visual projection more commonly considered as media. Furthermore, to McLuhan, media as extensions of personality have particular analogies to parts of the human body: electric technology is an extension of the central nervous system.

From his view of media as extensions of personality, McLuhan proceeds to his second thesis: the medium is the message. He explains: ". . . the 'message' of any medium or technology is the change of scale or pace or pattern that it introduces into human affairs." In other words, the social effects resulting from the action of any medium of communication, and from its interaction with other media, transcend the cognitive content of the medium. Media of pure technology, such as artificial illumination, of course have a content *only* in terms of the message, i.e., the social implications.

The content of one medium is always another. The content of writing is speech; the content of speech is thought. Speech "is an actual process of thought, which is in itself nonverbal." He continues:

> An abstract painting represents direct manifestations of creative thought processes as they might appear in computer designs. What we are considering here, however, are the psychic and social consequences of the designs or patterns as they amplify or accelerate existing processes.

This paragraph defines McLuhan's fundamental interests and the basis of his dynamics. One need add only his particular definition of hot and cold media:

> A hot media is one that extends one single sense in "high definition." High definition is the state of being well filled with data. A photograph is, visually, "high definition." A cartoon is "low definition" simply because very little visual information is provided. . . . Hot media are, therefore, low in participation, and cool media are high in participation or completion by the audience.

This polarity of "hot" and "cold," which pervades the book, is Mc-Luhan's chief methodological error. It has the superficial appearance of crispness, but lends itself to fuzziness and meaningless categorizations which have little to do with McLuhan's central ideas. Polarities can be useful intellectual tools, but they tend to inhibit the description of dynamic processes, which seems to be the function of *Understanding Media*.

Radio and television are McLuhan's main interests. Radio is a hot medium (little audience participation) while TV is cool (great audience participation). He tends to disregard the highly auditory construction of much American programing, in which the visual image actually play a subsidiary role. His theoretical TV audience gives constant and undivided attention to the shadow land of the screen, watching programs in which the visual constructs are all-meaningful. Actually, it is possible to experience many TV programs without looking at the picture. Here again, McLuhan's hodge-podge methodology betrays him.

Television, he affirms, is "tactile" and "tribal." Tactile, because it lacks definition; tribal, because it is "preliterate." The TV image ". . . is not photo in any sense, but a ceaselessly forming contour of things limned by the scanning finger. The resulting plastic contour appears by light *through,* not light *on,* and the image so formed has the quality of sculpture and icon, rather than of picture." Hence, "tactility," in effect, is a metaphor. The ill-defined TV image, to some an eye-straining blur, charms the nonliterate because he is forced to participate in fulfilling its creation. In McLuhan's view, the intellectual tends to reject the specific experience and its quality, while the young and non-intellectual, and those of subliminal literacy, identify with the experience without understanding it. He lists the social and psychological [194–195] changes: the dead-pan expressions of the young, the virtual abolishment of adolescence in the traditional sense, a move toward involvement and participation in *depth*—or "getting with it."

His terminology of "tactile" and "tribal," when applied to the electronic age, is used to indicate change from the visual and specialized values of the Gutenberg era. But it is used as if it might imply progression. This leads to the paradoxical proposition that as we progress (change) we regress (revert to earlier behavior).

When he discusses media, McLuhan seems unaware that he is describing the witchcraft of our time. Media, in effect, are the irrational elements which motivate part of our irrational behavior. Unfortunately, McLuhan identifies with the irrationality of the media he describes, with a result analogous to Montague Summer's literal belief in magic. The believer, as analyst, is undone by his belief. This acceptance of processes as descriptive models may account in large part for McLuhan's methodological floundering. In dealing with irrational elements one may need both logic and psycho-logic, but one cannot, for descriptive purposes, turn to the things themselves and become like them.

The method of presentation in *Understanding Media* is essentially that of the *Gutenberg Galaxy*. A sequence of insights, as verbal *Gestalten* intended to correspond to the field approach of behavior, are configured into the grand *Gestalt* of a book. In the earlier book, McLuhan said: "Such a mosaic image of numerous data and quotations in evidence offers the only practical means of revealing causal operations in history." This method was used more successfully in the *Galaxy* than in *Understanding Media,* which is primarily concerned with the present, rather than history. *Understanding Media* is too diverse, its content and arguments too sweeping, to stay within the orientation and limits of his mosaic framework. Methodologically, McLuhan seems to be striving for some kind of modular concept: a set of interchangeable, reusable intellectual building blocks which can be used over and over again in a variety of ways and still present bright new faces: rather like a set of alphabet blocks with a different intellectual proposition, instead of a letter, on each surface.

As one reads the book, one wonders whether McLuhan is presenting illuminations or attempting the preliminary model of a system. His letter to Frank Kermode, published by the latter in *Encounter,* shows that at one time he was seriously concerned with problems of form and possibly system construction. However, he might have gained something by treating his material as a continuum rather than in episodic disconnection. Except through artifice, life doesn't really live that way.

For any consideration of "the psychic and social consequences" of media, some psychological orientation is necessary. McLuhan's might be described as broadly eclectic, leaving some questions about its structure and organization. One is never quite certain whether the element of consistency is merely lurking or really lacking in the "mosaic image." His indebtedness to MacDougall has already been mentioned. Not only in the formal organization of the book, but in the text itself, through his insistence on "insight" and his elaboration of field theory, *Gestalt* psychology is given a good run for its money. Consciously, for reasons often obscure, he tends to reject Freudian and post-Freudian psychoanalytic theory except for a brief quotation from C. G. Jung, even though it would serve to bolster his projections more adequately than his numerous literary quotations. He is aware that somehow we have become "conscious of our unconscious," but he fails to apply that awareness where it might lead to a better understanding. In the chapter on money, he rejects the psychoanalytic view of money "since it does not correspond sufficiently to the nature and function of money in society." On the next page he unconsciously writes: "Currency is a way of letting go. . . ."

Similarly, McLuhan rejects value judgments and the idea of "content" in the usual sense. "It is wise to withhold all value judgments when studying these media matters, since their effects are not capable of being isolated." For better or worse, the man deserves to be taken at his word. Unfortunately, it is possible to find statements which seem to be implied value judgments, such as those on the small car, and it is equally possible to misconstrue some of his neutral statements as judgments of "content." McLuhan demands that others be more careful in the role of reader than he was in the role of writer.

Some of these shadowy values are adumbrated in the chapter on the photograph: ". . . Literate man is not only numb and vague in the presence of film or photo, but he intensifies his ineptness by a defensive arrogance and condescension to 'pop kulch' and 'mass entertainment.' . . . The vested interests of acquired knowledge and conventional wisdom have always been by-passed and engulfed by new media."

Nowhere does the haste with which this book was written betray the inclusive view of media more than in the chapters on "Number" and "Clocks." In the "Number" chapter his insights appear and disappear, making one wish he had been able to find time to Do A Little More Reading before meeting that McGraw-Hill deadline. In this chapter and elsewhere, he sees the use of the binary number system by computers and other data-processing apparatus as a return to tribal counting methods. This mystical view ought to have been tempered by the realization that the modern use of the binary system derived from the inherent limitation of electrical switches to the two basic positions: on and off. As a matter of fact, computers do exist which will handle decimal input-output without [195–196] external conversion to the binary.

Like the chapter on "Number," the chapter called "Clocks: the Scent of Time" is little more than diffuse speculation. The time concepts enforced by the era of data processing and information handling systems necessary for space technology are strangely absent from his discussion, except that "the electronic age . . . found that instant speeds abolish time and space and return man to an integral in primitive awareness." Real time, absolute time and relative time, all of which have to do with time as a medium, and with our time relationships in our space ventures, cannot easily be ignored or dismissed as new forms of primitive awareness, if time is to be treated as a medium at all.

Neither *The Gutenberg Galaxy* nor *Understanding Media* is a literary book either in the canonical, scriptural way of the New Criticism, or in the offhand way of those volumes in which English professors give a bookish view of books and the world. Yet reviewers have tended to treat McLuhan as if he were writing literary books instead of descriptions of social and technical dynamics. Unfortunately, McLuhan himself drags in enough odd bits of literary misinterpretation to make a respectable article for the established journals of that business. As soon as one makes the noises of a literary critic or an English professor, the woods become full of literary critics and English professors who can make the same kind of noise, and louder. It is not easy for anyone else to believe that Andrew Marvell anticipated Einstein in precisely the way McLuhan would have him. At another point, misquotation and misunderstanding of Yeats join hands. To believe that *Among School Children* is concerned with movies is as difficult as it is to find the line "a spume upon a ghostly paradigm of things" in the poem.

It is reasonable at this point to advance the theory that the meaning of things, particularly art works such as poems and paintings, is relative and not absolute. McLuhan's interpretations of Shakespeare and Donne are not less or more ridiculous than other perceptions embodied in much literary criticism, but in the light of McLuhan's own approach, they serve only to fog his intended meanings. This literary appeal to authority (his own) to bolster his arguments is methodologically weak and accomplishes little more than space filling. We have stressed methodology throughout this discussion because it is McLuhan's fundamental weakness—not merely the fact that some of his separate insights are erroneous or farfetched.

A further flaw springs from his facile acceptance of a probable good possibly inherent in electronic technology. He is, of course, sound in saying that if we do not understand the nature and effects of the new media we shall lose by default that much control over our environment. Yet his own approach suggests no realistic methods of control and his general air of hopefulness has no sounder basis than a total pessimism might.

While McLuhan relates TV to every cultural phenomenon of our time from seamless stockings to paperback books, he fails, except for passing mention of the Kennedy assassination, to relate it for better or worse to the perverse violence of our time. Long before McLuhan's books, both André Gide and Antonin Artaud, in different contexts, noted the rise of gratuitous crime—which seems to have a higher incidence in America than anywhere else. In our larger cities, no one is quite safe from acts of violence which are most frequently committed by those under thirty. These are crimes in which the gain—sexual or monetary—becomes secondary to the violence itself. To what extent television, with its underlying emotional mode of terror, is related to this phenomenon is a question McLuhan neither raises nor attempts to answer. Tracing back, through McLuhan's own statements, "the medium is the message." And, following his nesting-box concept of media, in which one medium always contains another, we get back to human thought itself. The medium may, in the case of gratuitous violence, reflect the world—but circularly, it may also be implicated in its creation. The dynamics of this area of behavior certainly deserve more consideration than the cool medium and hot issue of the small car or the qualities of a successful TV master of ceremonies.

McLuhan gives a clue when he says: "Everybody experiences far more than he understands. Yet it is experience, rather than understanding, that influences behavior, especially in collective matters of media and technology where the individual is almost inevitably unaware of their effect upon him." His statement hangs in mid-thought, leaving the reader to relate it to something. Here again is the failure, not of concept but of construct, which flaws the whole work. What might have been one of the most important books of its decade has been so poorly put together that its most realistic claim remains that of being a series of highly stimulating speculations. In reading it, one learns as much about McLuhan as about media.   [196]

1. "The believer, as analyst, is undone by his belief," assert the writers of this review (p. 195). Is this a fair assessment of a weakness in McLuhan? Explain.

2. These reviewers (Holmes and Zabriskie) report that McLuhan's

books are not "literary . . . in the offhand way of those volumes in which English professors give a bookish view of the world." (p. *196*) Do you agree that McLuhan's concern is not, essentially, literary? Into what academic discipline would you place his work if you were including it in a college curriculum?

OUR MASS COMMUNICATIONS

C. J. Fox
Review of *Understanding Media*

This is an infuriating book. It offers a number of brilliant insights but mixes them in with some extravagantly turgid incoherencies. Adopting a tone of Machiavellian candor and acquiescence, Dr. McLuhan loftily records the death of the "literary-logical" spirit in Western Man. This results, he says, from the impact of contemporary mass communications such as television and the jet plane. We are passing out of the age of rationalistic individualism and into an era of "tribal" togetherness and oral culture.

The death of "linear logic" would be all the more lamentable if what Professor McLuhan presents as an intelligently conceived argument is any indication of how things will be in the post-logical phase of man's mental development. The book swarms with non-sequiturs, terminological confusion, sweeping statements unbacked by any evidence and a usage of dozens of quotations that does violence to their authors' meaning and sets new records for tendentious reasoning.

It was about time somebody took stock of the new social and intellectual situation caused by our advances in the techniques of mass education and mass hoax. Often Dr. McLuhan throws light on this situation by de-[*105–*

C. J. FOX, a reporter on the staff of a Canadian News Agency, wrote this review of *Understanding Media* for *The Commonweal* by whose permission it is reprinted here. It originally appeared in the issue of October 16, 1964, pp. 105–106. © *The Commonweal*.

106]liberately adopting a new "mosaic" approach which he assumes is called for by the novelty of the futuristic inferno we inhabit. But he seemingly cannot resist going over the deep end with his generalizations on such varied social phenomena as the motor car, baseball and Body Odor. His deep-end plunges, conveniently, happen to suit his over-all theoretical purpose, as in his terming B. O. "The unique signature and declaration of human individuality." What he reads into the statements he attributes to varied authorities like Sir Lewis Namier, John Donne and Lynn White is enough to make one's old-fashioned "logical" flesh creep while his account of nationalism as, purely and simply, "an unforeseen consequence of typography" is grotesquely inadequate.

Everything, and rightly so, is grist to Dr. McLuhan's ideological mill but too often he spoils his case by excessive indulgence of his fired-up imagination. He can be pictured as a prototype of the new "cosmic man" he insists is rapidly inheriting the earth. For him to have written a book (which he contends is a patently anachronistic medium of expression) is obviously a gross inconsistency on his part. Furthermore, the ear is more tolerant of verbal muddle than is the eye—Dr. McLuhan himself suggests as much. Thus, for at least these two reasons, he should have committed his socio-literary speculating to tape and left it at that.

In every physical respect, his book is a credit to the craft of Gutenberg, except for the lack of an appendix. This omission is doubly unfortunate because the intellectual stars mentioned and lavishly quoted almost defy counting. Yet one such Eminence is conspicuously absent: conspicuously so, since he seems to have had a profound influence on Professor McLuhan. Harold Innis was professor of political economy at the University of Toronto and delved deeply into the subject of communications and their effects on human history. By 1950, two years before his death, Innis had published material to which some of Dr. McLuhan's work seems to owe a great deal. In the 1950's the University of Toronto became a center of Innis-like speculations on "mass media" and in these Dr. McLuhan took a prominent part. The superbly far-out magazine *Explorations* reflected the findings of this far-northern think-colony. The professor himself published a manifesto called "Counterblast" in 1954, setting out what have remained his basic views and doing so in the spectacular typographical manner of Wyndham Lewis and the British Vorticists.

The author of *Understanding Media* started his career as a literary critic. Essentially he remains a man of letters rather than an historian or sociologist. This may account for the ring of ingenuous conviction that characterizes his highly questionable reflections on history. For him, man's fate since about 1450 has been determined by the invention and development of printing. That the adoption of printing may itself have been the result of even more profound factors—social, political or economic—never seems to occur to Professor McLuhan; whose eye is dogmatically focused on surface phenomena. His theory of printing as the prime mover of events is very flattering, of course, to a man whose métier is literature.

With an air of almost smug knowingness, the professor conducts his reader, more rattled by the minute, on a lightning tour of the modern Social Scene. He airily dismisses as the work of a "cultural reactionary" Daniel Boorstin's strictures on the "pseudo-event" in journalism and he dispenses with the impossible job of finding evidence for such statements as, "The book reader has always tended to be passive." Theory after technocratic theory is recited to explain phenomena like the denoting by reporters of the ages of individuals featured in news stories—this practice being attributed to the supposed discovery by journalists of "the iconic power of number." As for four-letter words, they are popular because of their "tactile-involving stress." Shakespeare draws patronizing praise for his "intuition of the transforming powers of new media." And so the heavy-handed rigmarole of Dr. McLuhan's argument lumbers on.

He claims to be firmly abreast of our fast-changing times. Yet he sounds peculiarly old-fashioned, indeed fatally so, in expounding the heart of his argument. The radically new thing he calls "electric technology" renders the globe, so he contends, a mere village where people "are involved in all others at all times."

And in one passage that, oddly enough, reflects a nostalgia in this frenetic futurist for an idyllic social arrangement long gone, he perorates, "The human family (under the electric influences) becomes one tribe again." But surely the sense of community inculcated by media like television lacks the flesh-and-blood rapport of the tribal situation or, for that matter, of the village life which he apparently pines after. At most, the vast new forces produce merely two-dimensional sense of "togetherness," as unphysical and novel as an electrically induced trance. The vision of a Golden Age Restored which Professor McLuhan gives as the upshot of his sometimes zany narrative does anything but bear out his pretensions to being hard-boiled and omniscient concerning the nature and direction of our addled age.   [106]

1. C. J. Fox attributes a good deal of McLuhan's message to the influence of the late Professor Harold Innis, a University of Toronto political economist. Following Fox's lead, discover some of Innis's ideas and assess for yourself the extent to which he inspired Marshall McLuhan's theories. Check your view by reading pp. 1–7 in *The Gutenberg Galaxy*.

2. Fox concludes by saying that McLuhan (the "futurist") ". . . reflects a nostalgia—for an idyllic social arrangement long gone . . ." (p. 106). Do you agree that Professor McLuhan is yearning after a return to the past in his social commentaries?

ELECTRONIC MAN

Christopher Ricks

The importance of *Understanding Media* has nothing to do with worth. Marshall McLuhan is now a power in more than one land, and not only as Director of the Centre for Culture and Technology at Toronto. Since a great many people are concerned about the effects of TV, films, advertisements and the press, they will turn more and more to a praised expert. And there is, too, a market for heady prophecies, especially those which skilfully and at the last moment substitute a sermon for a forecast. Like Jacques Barzun, Mr. McLuhan has the suspenseful air of being about to lift the veil. Does Telstar bode? Yes, indeed, and we may expect (excitement mounts), we may expect that

> the time factor in every decision of business and finance will acquire new patterns. Among the peoples of the world strange new vortices of power will appear unexpectedly.

'Unexpectedly' is about right, for all the help we actually get from Mr. McLuhan's clutch of crystal balls. The car has altered everything, 'and it will continue to do so for a decade more, by which time the electronic successors to the car will be manifest.' Nostradamus redivivus? A reader who crosses Mr. McLuhan's palm with two guineas may feel gulled.

CHRISTOPHER RICKS is a regular contributor of book reviews to *The New Statesman*.

This review appeared in that journal December 11, 1964, pp. 925–926, and is reprinted here by permission of *The New Statesman*.

Three themes cohabit, not very fruitfully. First: electronics and 'electric speed' are different in kind from the mechanical (which is linear, typographic, uniform and repeatable). Our present culture partakes of both. The mechanical or typographic culture necessitated sequence, fragmentation and specialisation; but the new electronic culture 'retribalises', makes the world a village, and is organically instantaneous.

> Man can now look back at two or three thousand years of varying degrees of mechanisation with full awareness of the mechanical as an interlude between two great organic periods of culture.

The second theme is 'The Extensions of Man':

> Whereas all previous technology (save speech, itself) had, in effect, extended some part of our bodies, electricity may be said to have outered the central nervous system itself, including the brain.

Third:

> Political scientists have been quite unaware of the effects of media anywhere at any time, simply because nobody has been willing to study the personal and social effects of media apart from their 'content.'

These are important themes, but they are altogether drowned by the style, the manner of arguing, the attitude to evidence and to authorities, and the shouting.

Any medium has an effect *qua* medium, over and above its content. To have said so would have been to have written a sadder and a wiser book (and a shorter one). But Mr. McLuhan's contempt for people who attend to the 'content' leads him to deny that content plays any part at all. 'The medium is the message,' he intones again and again. 'The effects of technology'—and by technology he means all 'extensions of man'—'do not occur at the level of opinions or concepts, but alter sense ratios or patterns of perception steadily and without any resistance.' If he had said 'do not occur *only* at the level of opinions'—but no, for him the sole effect is that of the medium itself. Literacy creates individualism, and 'this fact has nothing to do with the *content* of the alphabetised words.' 'The effects of radio are quite independent of its programming.' TV creates 'total involvement in all-inclusive *nowness*', and 'this change of attitude has nothing to do with programming in any way.'

All of which means that *Understanding Media* cuts off its extension of man to spite its face. How can Mr. McLuhan possibly use the medium of the *book* (typographic, linear, fragmented) in order to speak in this way about the electronically instantaneous? On his own terms, a book cannot but enforce the typographical attitudes which he insists are cramping Western man. If his arguments are true, how silly to annul them by using a medium which has no option but to annul them.

He wriggles in this unmentioned predicament, and does his best to escape by abandoning all the sequential virtues of a book. He says the same thing on every page, and repeats whole chunks when he feels like it—which is perhaps one kind of instantaneity. He praises the Eastern ('oral') mode of thought: 'The entire message is then traced and retraced, again and again, on the rounds of a concentric spiral with seeming redundancy.' But if this 'oral' tradition could be incorporated in a book, his arguments would all collapse. The attempt may be pluckily preposterous, but the outcome is not just 'seeming' redundancy. The moral position, too, is shaky, and not even the quotation from Pope Pius XII about media quite manages to shore it up. Mr. McLuhan may insist that he is 'withholding all value judgments when studying these media matters,' but in fact his terms are about as neutral as a bigot. Who will be found to speak for literacy (which has 'fragmented' and 'mutilated') when the electronic culture is described in these terms—humble involvement and deep commitment, participation, heightened human awareness and unifying the life of the senses? 'Contemporary awareness had to become integral and inclusive again, after centuries of dissociated sensibilities'—does that withhold value judgments? And is it an act of neutrality to give a chapter to each of 26 media, but no chapter to the theatre?

Very well—people were wrong to ignore the nature of a medium. But that doesn't beautify the airy hauteur to which the arguments rise whenever they confront facts, earthy political facts. Possibly radio does inevitably inflame, and TV does cool, but the authorial tone is too epigrammatically Olympian. 'Had TV occurred on a large scale during Hitler's reign he would have vanished quickly. Had TV come first there would have been no Hitler at all.' Vanished? Like a Walt Disney ogre? So confident a magic wand does not like the fact that there are facts. Can we be quite so sure that Nazi TV would have had no choice but to intervene so coolingly and so effectively? Is 'content' (even anti-semitic content) really a matter of total indifference in comparison with 'the medium proper'? Mr. McLuhan may perhaps be right, but Hitler seems to me a subject where too serene a confidence in one's own theories can easily look unfeeling. After all, there are those of us who would have traded all of Pope Pius's words about mass media for just a word or two about the massacre of the Jews.

Mr. McLuhan's confidence, quite without irony, sees the computer as a type of the Holy Ghost: 'The computer, in short, promises by technology a Pentecostal condition of universal understanding and unity.' So much for greed, crowding, hunger, and all the hard facts which make universal understanding and unity a matter of intractable things as well as of language and media. When Mr. McLuhan invokes his Pentecost, there is no doubt about the mighty rushing wind, but where are the tongues of fire?

It seems that we have been fools, but now at last we will be put right about it all, though our patient teacher can't quite prevent his eyelid from drooping disdainfully. 'It is not the increase of numbers in the world that creates our concern with population,' rather it is 'our electric involvement in one another's lives'. Our 'concern' may well have been pricked by the media, but it is not entirely evolved from them, since there remains the glumly objective fact of the increasing population, a fact which to any man who wants to live as something more than 'a student of media' is in itself a cause of concern. Could it be that Mr. McLuhan averts his eyes from the fact because the Catholic Church wishes it weren't a fact? When the facts would be embarrassing, Mr. McLuhan passes by on the other side. It seems that 'literate man' is a warped creature, 'quite inclined to see others who cannot conform as somewhat pathetic.' And then, without a pause: 'Especially the child, the cripple, the woman, and the coloured person appear in a world of visual and typographic technology as victims of injustice.' But in this world, the world of facts as well as of media, coloured people do not merely *appear* (thanks to tricksy typography) to be victims of injustice, they *are* such. Not every single individual, of course, but quite enough for Mr. McLuhan's enlightened detachment to get tarnished. He long-sufferingly tut-tuts—how naive of people to be upset by circumstances, instead of realising that it is all just the built-in preconceptions of media.

Media, apparently, and not moral convictions, get things done: 'the real integrator or leveller of white and Negro in the South was the private car and the truck, not the expression of moral points of view.' Notice 'was', as if it were all a thing of the past, so that now the historian can bask in equanimity. Notice, too, that it isn't said that the truck was in the end the most effective or most important integrator or leveller—no, it was 'the real' one, which leaves 'moral points of view' (a prettily placed piece of phrasing) as merely unreal. As if there weren't enough people willing to be told that justice in the South (a) has been achieved, and (b) is no moral concern of theirs, without our author handing them warrant (don't worry, the truck'll change all that). This may all be unwitting, in which case it is the consequence of Mr. McLuhan's furious rebound. Since everybody else will talk about nothing but 'content', he will talk about nothing but media—nice, neutral, omnipotent media.

There is a similar stoniness when he discusses 'labour-saving' devices, toasters or washing-machines or vacuum cleaners: 'Instead of saving work, these devices permit everybody to do his own work. What the 19th century had delegated to servants and housemaids we now do for ourselves.' Oh no we don't. When we switch on the automatic washing machine, Mr. McLuhan and I are not in any meaningful sense doing the same *work* as servants used [925–926] to do. There is something unimaginative about a deftness that is so very interested in 'devices' and so little interested in how 19th-century servants really did work. 'Today, in the electronic age, the richest man is reduced to having much the same entertainment, and even the same food and vehicles as the ordinary man.' Try telling that to the many ordinary men who live in 'the other America', let alone three-quarters of the globe. Mr. McLuhan may claim the license of a prophet, but even a prophet will be the more humane if he does not state as today's fact what may perhaps one day come to pass.

Such indifference to fact is not always politically disagreeable, but it is always absurd. Literate societies don't like B.O.? That must be because the

odour 'is far too involving for our habits of detachment and specialist attention.' But why shouldn't it just be that we don't like the smell? Ah, but what
about 'the strange obsession of the bookman with the press-lords as essentially corrupt'? That must, it seems, be due to the antagonism of the book to
the newspaper as a medium. Yet what if it weren't a strange obsession, but a
fact, that press-lords are corrupt?

The style is a viscous fog, through which loom stumbling metaphors.
And Mr. McLuhan's subject, after all, is the imagination and the emotions.
Nothing could be less imaginative than all this talk of 'a complex and depth-
structured person', especially as the depth resembles a sump: 'people begin
to sense a draining-away of life values.' What we need is 'the mosaic of the
press' which 'manages to effect a complex many-levelled function of group-
awareness.' Fortunately 'the tactile mesh of the TV mosaic has begun to
permeate the American sensorium'—hence the 'complex togetherness of the
corporate posture'. What makes it all so grisly is that this unfelt, unfeeling and
nerveless style is forever insisting on how media grip, how they touch, how
they create.

The tastes are of a piece with the style. He asserts that ours is 'one of
the greatest ages of music, poetry, painting, and architecture alike.' Later he
comes to think that this was a bit half-hearted, so he steps it up: 'the arts of
this century' have an 'ascendancy over those of other ages comparable to that
which we have long recognised as true of modern science.' And the justification for such a claim? Well, there is the 'extraordinary intensity' of Agatha
Christie's *Labours of Hercules*. And there are advertisements.

> The ads are by far the best part of any magazine or newspaper. More pains
> and thought, more wit and art go into the making of an ad than into any
> prose feature of press or magazine.

Anybody who thought that advertisements have as much ugly lying as witty
art would simply be exposing himself as one of the 'media victims, unwittingly
mutilated by their studies'. 'Ads are ignored or deplored, but seldom studied
and enjoyed'—as if enjoyment could not but follow study, as if it weren't even
a possibility that one might study and then deplore. Since he so admires advertisements, it is not surprising that he uses them as evidence. Is Mrs.
Khrushchev's plain cotton dress an icon of thrift? Yes—a 'very ingenious ad'
has said so. Are the Greeks more sensuously involved? Yes—a travel guide has
said so. *Vogue* proves one fact (and I don't mean about *Vogue*), and *Life*
another, as if they were irreproachable works of history.

Mr. McLuhan uses his authorities about as convincingly as his evidence. No doubt there is still a lot to be said for Bergson and Toynbee, but
it is not now possible to plonk down their names as if they settled a matter.
Mr. McLuhan invokes Lynn White's *Medieval Technology and Social Change*
for its argument that at a particular time the stirrup profoundly affected ways
of life—but he does not mention that there are unridiculous historians who
believe that the arguments are important but the evidence (especially as to

dating) far from complete. Similarly, great play is made with that dread 'dissociation of sensibility' which at some unspecified date overtook Western man —as if any scrupulous cultural historian now thought the phrase anything but a faded bright idea. It is not only those who have been twisted by literacy who will find all these arguments short on evidence. Perhaps Mr. McLuhan's history is more accurate than are his literary quotations. The audacity is impressive, as when he takes E. E. Cummings as a type of the poet whose work is for the ear and not for the eye: Cummings must be 'read aloud with widely varying stresses and paces', since 'people who feel that poetry is for the eye and is to be read silently can scarcely get anywhere with Hopkins or Cummings.' I would like to hear Mr. McLuhan rendering Cummings's '.gRrEaPsPhOs)'. But even so great a vocal skill would not be a substitute for cogency or clarity of argument. Or for an accurate text of Cummings—Mr. McLuhan does not give us Cummings's spelling, capitalisation, hyphenation, lineation or spacing. The masters of the subtle schools are controversial, polymath. Mr. McLuhan shifts from ham to ham, stirring the water in his bath.   [926]

1. McLuhan's "important themes," according to Christopher Ricks, who identifies three of them, ". . . are altogether drowned out by the style, the manner of arguing, the attitude to evidence and to authorities, and the shouting" (p. 925). Is this too extreme an indictment of the McLuhan technique of exposition? How much validity, in your opinion, has Ricks' criticism?

2. Ricks is British. Do you think his reaction to McLuhan's work is attributable at all to his trans-Atlantic perspective? Explain.

THE COOL REVOLUTION

Neil Compton

The typical reader of *Commentary* is living in a numbed and somnambulistic trance, self-hypnotized by his visual, linear bias. As for the magazine itself, it is an extremely hot medium (much hotter than *Playboy*) perversely devoting most of its space to matters which are peripheral to the real problems of modern culture. The ads are the best part of the journal.

These conclusions are forced upon anyone who accepts the main argument of *Understanding Media*. They are not the eccentric maunderings of a madman. On the contrary, Marshall McLuhan is one of the most brilliant socio-cultural theorists writing today. I have been shamelessly pilfering his work for years, and others have been doing it too: it is easy for a practiced eye to discern little bits of McLuhan nestling like fossils in the gritty prose of many a literary critic or sociologist. For all that, McLuhan is a somewhat lonely figure with many admirers but few disciples. His cocksure wisecracking manner, his extravagant generalizations, and his maddeningly repetitive style tend to repel fastidious readers. Even a strong sympathizer is likely to find irritation and illumination fairly evenly blended in his books. *Understanding Media* contains the mixture as before.

NEIL COMPTON is Professor and Head of the Department of English, Sir George Williams University, Montreal, Quebec.

Reprinted from *Commentary* January, 1965, pp. 79–81. Copyright © *Commentary* magazine. Reprinted by permission.

McLuhan, who is a professor of English at St. Michael's College and Director of the Institute of Culture and Technology at the University of Toronto, brings an essentially Thomist and Catholic sensibility to a field of study which has been traditionally dominated by theorists with a Protestant or Jewish background. He acknowledges a considerable intellectual debt to the late Harold A. Innis (a Canadian economist whose contributions to the history and theory of communications have been inadequately recognized), but his recent books have carried him far beyond his mentor and, indeed, outside the main stream of contemporary thought about culture.

He began as a relatively conventional observer of the mass media. *The Mechanical Bride* is a brilliant application of the techniques of iconography and literary criticism to such hitherto neglected phenomena as advertisements, comic strips, and newspapers. Though McLuhan now apparently repudiates its essentially hostile and derisive tone, many will feel that this devastingly witty and high-spirited work is his finest achievement. Between *The Mechanical Bride* and his next book, McLuhan edited *Explorations,* an extraordinary periodical devoted to the study and criticism of all types of communication. In its pages one can trace McLuhan's gradual shift from ironic contemplation to total immersion in the destructive element of modern media. The Old and New Testaments of the faith that followed this baptism are *The Gutenberg Galaxy* (1962) and its successor *Understanding Media.*

Subtitled "The Making of Typographic Man," *The Gutenberg Galaxy* set out to analyze and describe the distortion of human consciousness that has resulted (according to McLuhan) from the domination of Western civilization by the phonetic alphabet and its offspring, the printed book. By translating all human experience into the visual, linear, sequential form of written sentences, and by mass-producing the result with the aid of the printing press, Western man has tended to alienate himself from deep involvement with his environment. "Numbed" into a "hypnotic trance" by his visual bias, "the bookman of detached private culture" cannot cope with reality until it is processed into the linear, mechanical order of print. The orderly, rational eye (in contrast to the muddled, emotional ear) is the individuating organ *par excellence*—such terms as "perspective," "point of view," "outlook" suggest this quality. The visually oriented civilization which reached its apogee early in this century culminated in the hard, lonely, anxious personality of the [79–80] rugged individualist. It also developed techniques and institutions to serve him, all based on the linear rationalization of phenomena: the assembly line, the state examination system, the stock market, suburbia, bureaus of standards, research laboratories, and railway timetables.

The argument that there is some connection between these phenomena and our print-dominated culture is difficult to resist. All the same, in this book and its successor McLuhan faced an insoluble problem of method. How is it possible to diagnose and attack the distortions caused by phonetic literacy while using the very medium one is deploring? He has tried to resolve the dilemma by arranging his books in a "mosaic" of separate chapters which can be read in any order (thus making necessary a good deal of repetition). Since he regards the idea of cause and effect as an illusory linear abstraction, McLuhan tries to avoid making use of it, preferring to suggest the kind of configuration implied by the word "galaxy." Unfortunately, the English language does not lend itself very well to this kind of non-syntactical juxtaposition, so he is forced to fall back on such vague rhetorical flourishes as "That is why . . ." or "In the same way. . . ." His favorite mode of discourse is the enthymeme (or incomplete syllogism) which bookmen of detached private character like myself may be forgiven for thinking a vice rather than a revolutionary method of apprehending the universe. Nevertheless, *The Gutenberg Galaxy* is a most exciting book, full of brilliant insights (if one may risk a visual metaphor) and valuable information about communication habits past and present. McLuhan is immensely well-read for a man with a grudge against print, and he quotes liberally from some fascinating and out-of-the-way writers and scholars.

If the earlier book concentrated on the past and its consequences for the present, *Understanding Media* is mainly devoted to the contemporary revolution in communications and its consequences for the future. It ought to be the fulfillment of the author's career as a cultural prophet. Unfortunately, though there is more than enough to reward persevering readers (one of the publisher's editors complained to McLuhan that 75 per cent of his material is new), the book lacks the concentration and coherence of its predecessor. Perhaps it was produced in haste: there are certainly a great many misprints and errors of fact.

McLuhan calls the media "extensions of man" because they each increase the range and power of one part of the human body. In so doing, they effect a modification of consciousness by altering the ratio between the various senses and faculties. His definition of a medium is broad: he devotes twenty-six separate chapters not only to such obvious media as paper, print, telegraph, and radio, but also to wheels, weapons, clocks, money, and houses.

The half-truth which he wishes to establish is that "the medium is the message." He scoffs at old fogies who fuss over the content of books, newspapers, radio and television programs, but ignore the more radical modifications of sensibility effected by the media themselves. So far as he is concerned, "the 'content' of a medium is like the juicy bit of meat carried by the burglar to distract the watch-dog of the mind." So much for *Commentary*, documentary films, television news, and Walter Lippmann. So much also for *Understanding Media!*

The message of the mechanical media of the past, he says, has been fragmentation and dissociation. By "extending" only one sense or part of the body, print, wheel, and assembly line have made possible explosive increases in knowledge and production, but they have done so at the cost of human wholeness. What we call civilization is, in the West, largely the history of this progressive disintegration of man and his relation to nature. McLuhan argues, however, that the new electronic media such as television and computers are extensions, not just of one part of the body, but of the central nervous system itself. They extend the whole man. [80–81] Electronic technology, instead of exploding and fragmenting the human body, tends to be implosive and integrating. It can make all knowledge instantly available, any event anywhere instantly present, and create factories that will mass-produce products individually manufactured to the taste of each consumer. It is making the world one village.

The crisis of our time is that our visual and fragmented culture is inadequate to the electronic technology with which we have to cope. McLuhan reserves his most mordant wit to jeer at literary intellectuals whom he thinks more remote from understanding the world in which they live than the teen-age fans of any disc-jockey. And so long as the educated remain obstinately wedded to the irrelevant values of print-culture, the danger increases that man will slip back into that "Africa of the mind" from which the alphabet liberated our remote ancestors.

McLuhan confuses his thesis by an abortive—and at times even ludicrous—attempt to categorize media as "hot" and "cool." A hot medium extends one single sense in "high definition" (i.e., well filled with data). Cool media are low in definition and therefore require participation or completion by the audience. Photographs, radio, and print are hot; cartoons, television, and telephones are cool. More exotically, lectures, hard-cover books, waltzes, "city slickers," FDR, the "hot line," and girls with glasses are hot, while seminars, paperback books, the twist, farmers' daughters, Calvin Coolidge, and girls with *dark* glasses are cool. There is the making of a maddening party game here. How would you classify LBJ, nuclear submarines, elephant jokes, or the *Wall Street Journal*?

Hot media are supposed to be explosive, specialist, and individuating, while cool media are communal, casual, and participant. The coolest of all is television. McLuhan is so anxious to distinguish TV from old-fashioned hot media that he tries to deny that it is visual: because the TV screen shows "light through" rather than "light on," and the image is a low-definition shifting mosaic mesh, it has a haptic or tactile quality—in contrast to cinema which is highly visual and therefore hot. Eccentric judgments of this kind seem to arise from McLuhan's apparent compulsion to relate every phenomenon of modern life to his theories. Almost casually he "explains" why Kennedy beat Nixon (what would he have said if a few thousand votes had shifted the election the other way?), why mesh nylons are more sensuous than sheer (are they?), why baseball is declining (is it?), why the guards let Jack Ruby kill Lee Oswald, and why B.O. is unforgivable in literate societies. His critics understandably make fun of this intellectual megalomania.

But no review of *Understanding Media* should close on such a note. In this apocalyptic age, a pusillanimous correctness may be far more foolish than the wildest of insufficiently supported generalizations. While most scholars bury their heads in the private little sand plots they have marked out as their "field," McLuhan obstinately takes all knowledge for his province. Like the great writers that he admires—Rabelais, Cervantes, Pope, Joyce—he strives to be a man of "integral awareness." I expect to be equally inspired and infuriated by his next book.   [81]

1. On a continuum ranging from "altogether favorable" to "completely unfavorable" at what point would you locate Neil Compton's commentary on McLuhan's ideas? Provide specific illustrations to justify your conclusion.

2. Compton notes the McLuhan "dilemma" on p. 80: "How is it possible to diagnose and attack the distortions caused by phonetic literacy while using the very medium one is deploring?" Do you concede that this is an insoluble paradox in McLuhan's method?

3. Compton observes that McLuhan "brings an essentially Thomist and Catholic sensibility to a field of study which has been traditionally dominated by theorists with a Protestant or Jewish background." Can you identify either the Thomist-Catholic strains in McLuhanism or the Jewish-Protestant influences to which Compton implies that McLuhan might be in opposition?

PHILOSOPHY
IN A
POP KEY

Harold Rosenberg

Understanding Media (McGraw-Hill) has a dry, professional-sounding title, suggesting a handbook on magazines and television for advertising men, in particular those charged with buying space and time. It was written, however, by Professor Marshall McLuhan, director of the Center for Culture and Technology at the University of Toronto and author of *The Mechanical Bride* and *The Gutenberg Galaxy,* whose conception of pop culture is no more conventional than an electronic opera. McLuhan is more likely to write a manual for the angels than for Madison Avenue. *Understanding Media* carries the subtitle "The Extensions of Man," which alerts readers at the start that more is at issue in this book than the relative merits of news and entertainment packages. We all know that radio, the movies, the press do things to us. For McLuhan they also *are* us: "They that make them," he quotes the Psalms, "shall be like unto them." So *Understanding Media* is nothing less than a book about humanity as it has been shaped by the means used in this and earlier ages to deliver information.

HAROLD ROSENBERG'S critical writings have appeared widely in leading journals and periodicals. He is the author of *The Tradition of the New*.

"Philosophy in a Pop Key," from *The New Yorker,* February 27, 1965, pp. 129–136, is reprinted by permission. © 1965 *The New Yorker* Magazine Inc.

McLuhan's account of the effects of the media upon the human psyche lies between fact and metaphor. The instrumentalities through which words, images, and other human signals reach us transform our bodies as well as our minds. Our eyes are bulged out by vacuum tubes, our ears elongated by transistors, our skin ballooned by polyesters. ("Clothing and housing, as extensions of skin and heat-control mechanisms, are media of communication.") In his first book, *The Mechanical Bride,* published a dozen years ago and unmistakably inspired by Duchamp's erotic apparatuses, McLuhan dealt with the pop creations of advertising and other word-and-picture promotions as ingredients of a magic potion, "composed of sex and technology," that was populating America with creatures half woman, half machine. "Noticed any very spare parts lately?" he inquired in a subhead of his title chapter. The legs, bust, hips of the modern girl have been dissociated from the human person as "power points," McLuhan claimed, reminding the reader that "the Hiroshima bomb was named 'Gilda' in honor of Rita Hayworth." Man, to McLuhan, often appears to be a device employed by the communications mechanisms in *their* self-development. "Any invention or technology," he writes in *Understanding Media,* "is an extension or self-amputation of our physical bodies, and such extension also demands new ratios or new equilibriums among the other organs and extensions of the body. There is, for example, no way of refusing to comply with the new ratios or sense 'closure' evoked by the TV image."

In McLuhan's *The Gutenberg Galaxy,* the analysis of how the human organism has been remodelled by a single communications medium is turned into a full-scale interpretation of Western history. The outstanding characteristics of life in Europe and America from the Renaissance to the turn of the twentieth century are traced to the invention of movable type and the diffusion of the printed word. The streaming of letters across a page brought into being an "eye culture" that found symbolic representation in *King Lear,* with its blindings and its wanderers stripped naked by the storm. (McLuhan got his Ph.D. in English at Cambridge.) With Gutenberg began the technological acceleration of history that has made constant change the norm of social life. The portability of books, McLuhan says, allowed "alphabetic man" to feed his intellect in isolation from others, thus introducing individualism and the Hamlet-like division between knowing and doing, as well as split personality ("Schizophrenia may be a necessary consequence of literacy") and the conflict between the ego and its environment. The separation of seeing from the other senses and the reduction of consciousness to sight-based concepts were compensated for by the emergence of the world of the unconscious. The fixed position of the reader vis-à-vis the page, says McLuhan, inspired perspective in painting, the visualization of three-dimensional objects in deep space, and the chronological narrative. The uniformity and repeatability of the phonetic bits that make up a line of type strengthened mechanistic philosophies, serial thinking in mathematics and the sciences, and ideals of social levelling, and they were the model for the assembly line. In replacing vernacular with mass media, print generated the centralizing forces of modern nationalism: "The citizen armies of Cromwell and Napoleon were the ideal manifestations of the new technology."

Understanding Media is McLuhan's goodbye to Gutenberg and to Renaissance, "typographic" man; that is, to the self-centered individual. As such, it takes its place in that wide channel of cultural criticism of the twentieth century that includes writers like T. S. Eliot, Oswald Spengler, D. H. Lawrence, F. R. Leavis, David Riesman, Hannah Arendt. *Under-[129–130]standing Media,* McLuhan's most neatly ordered and most comprehensive book, is an examination of how the eye-extended, print-reading individualist of the past five centuries is in our time undergoing metamorphosis under the bombardment of all his senses by new electronic media, the first of which was the telegraph. With the loss of the monopoly of the column of type has come the breakup of its peruser, and with this a landslide of all print-based social and art forms; e.g., the mechanical assembly line gives way to automation, and perspective in painting to two-dimensional, over-all composition. Thus the changeover of media is synchronized with revolutionary phenomena in production and in cultural life and with an extreme crisis of values.

Of all crisis philosophers, McLuhan is by far the coolest. Though his notion of the "externalization" or "numbness" induced in the consumer of today's popular culture accords with Eliot's "hollow men," Riesman's "other-directedness," and Arendt's "banality," he is utterly unsympathetic to any concept of "decline." The collective trance of his contemporaries is to his mind a transitional phenomenon—one that recurs in all great historic shifts from one dominant medium to another. Current unfeeling and anxiety parallel states prevalent in the early Renaissance, when the printed document was replacing the hand-written script. Regarding us all in this light, McLuhan is immune to despair; in his terms, the theory that the modern world is a cultural wasteland is meaningless. What, he might ask, makes the inwardness of yesterday preferable to the shallowness of tomorrow, if both are by-products of more or less effective devices for conveying information? As the phonetic alphabet carried man from tribalism to individuality and freedom, the new electric media are taking him beyond "fragmented, literate, and visual individualism." If man today is part machine, this is not an effect of the Industrial Revolution. Technologies have been a component of human living for three thousand years, and our loftiest feelings have derived from that segment of us that is least ourselves: "By continuously embracing technologies, we relate ourselves to them as servo-mechanisms. That is why we must, to use them at all, serve these objects, these extensions of ourselves, as gods or minor religions. An Indian is the servo-mechanism of his canoe, as the cowboy of his horse or the executive of his clock." In line with Toynbee (the idea of the Eskimo as a merman, the cowboy as a [130–131] centaur, is his), McLuhan has superseded Marx's "fetishism of commodities" with a fetishism of the medium to explain the forms of belief by which men have been governed in various epochs. Societies in which the sacred played a greater role than it does in ours were simply those ruled by media of communication more primitive than the visual. "To call the oral man 'religious,' " McLuhan observed in *The Gutenberg Galaxy,* "is, of course, as fanciful and arbitrary as calling blondes bestial."

McLuhan, then, is a modernist to the hilt; his own "sacred" touch-stones are Cézanne and abstract art, the new physics, *Finnegans Wake*. His is the kind of mind that fills with horror the would-be conservator of values (a Leavis, a Yeats, a Lukács). He is not tempted in the slightest to dig in at some bygone historical moment. Accepting novelty as inevitable, he is not only a modernist but a futurist. In his latest mood, he regards most of what is going on today as highly desirable, all of it as meaningful. His position is to be inside change; he is given over to metamorphosis on principle. The present world-wide clash between the new and the old arouses him to enthusiasm, since "the meeting of two media is a moment of truth and revelation from which new form is born." It is this appreciation of innovating forms that distinguishes McLuhan from other writers on popular culture. Instead of discovering menace in the chatter of the disc jockey and the inanities of the commercial, or relief in New Wave films or in Shakespeare and ballet on TV, McLuhan probes be-yond the content of the media to the impact of each medium itself as an art form. What takes place at any moment in the rectangle of the comic strip or on the screen of the TV set may not be worth serious reflection. But as you look, or look and listen, in the particular way demanded by the comic strip or the television image, something is slowly happening to one or more of your senses, and through that to your whole pattern of perception—never mind what gets into your mind. Hence the first axiom of *Understanding Media* is "The medium is the message." Radio tells us about bargains in second-hand cars, the great books, the weather, but the ultimate effect of radio is that, day after day, it is displacing reading and reintroducing on a new, technological level the oral communication of preliterate societies—or, as McLuhan calls it, "the tribal drum." The effect of a tale differs depending on whether we read it, hear [131–132] it, or see it on the stage. McLuhan therefore ridicules the reformist idea that changes in programming could alter the cultural mix now produced by the popular arts. "Our conventional response to all media, namely that it is how they are used that counts, is the numb stance of the technological by the popular arts. "Our conventional response to all media, namely that it is how they are used that counts, is the numb stance of the technological idiot. For the 'content' of a medium is like the juicy piece of meat carried by the burglar to distract the watchdog of the mind. . . . The effect of the movie form is not related to its program content." In fact, McLuhan suggests that one medium always uses another medium as its subject matter: "The content of the press is literary statement, as the content of the book is speech, and the content of the movie is the novel." Whether or not this is so in every case, it provides a suggestive description of much contemporary art—for example, that of Rauschenberg, who through photographs and silk-screen reproductions makes news the content of painting.

A remarkable wealth of observation issues from the play of Mc-Luhan's sensibility upon each of today's vehicles of human intercourse, from roads and money to games and the computer. After "Understanding Media," it should no longer be acceptable to speak of "mass culture" as a single lump. Each pop form, this work demonstrates, has its peculiar aesthetic features: the comics, a crude woodcut style; TV, a blurred "iconic" image shaped by the eye of the viewer out of millions of dots (in contrast to the shiny completed image of movie film). A further aesthetic complexity of the popular media pointed out by McLuhan lies in their division into "hot" and "cool." The hot medium, like radio and newspapers, is aggressive and communicates much information, while the cool, like TV and the Twist (also open-mesh stockings and dark glasses), is reticent and tends to draw its audience into participation. The varieties of aesthetic influences by which modern man is showered ought to dissolve the belief, prevalent among intellectuals, that today's man in the street, in contrast to the peasant or the bushman, has been cut down to a bundle of simple reflexes.

Responding to the man-made forms that flow continually through our senses, McLuhan arrives at happy conclusions for the future. No, man is not being impoverished by packaged cultural commodities. On the contrary, it was the split personality created by the book who was deprived of sensual self-realization: "Literacy is itself an abstract asceticism that prepare the [132–133] way for endless patterns of privation in the human community." Though the shock of the sudden passage from mechanical to electrical technology has momentarily narcotized our nerves, integral man is in the process of formation. For the first time in history, the media are providing us with extensions not of one or more sense organs but of our sense structure as a whole, "since our new electric technology is not an extension of our bodies but of our central nervous systems." The mechanical age is departing, and with it the division of man within himself and his separation from his fellows. "Synesthesia, or unified sense and imaginative life, had long seemed an unattainable dream to Western poets, painters, and artists in general. They had looked with sorrow and dismay on the fragmented and impoverished imaginative life of Western literate man in the eighteenth century and later. . . . They were not prepared to have their dreams realized in everyday life by the aesthetic action of radio and television. Yet these massive extensions of our central nervous systems have enveloped Western man in a daily session of synesthesia." Instant communication through the electric media, McLuhan goes on to argue, is ending the age-old conflict between city and country; by "dunking entire populations in new imagery" and bringing them together in the "global village," it is eliminating, too, the conditions that make for war.

In sum, McLuhan has built a philosophy of history on art criticism, which he has directed not at styles in literature, painting, or architecture but at the lowly stuff of everyday life. In doing this, he has also sought to recast the meaning of art and literature since the Renaissance by finding in Shakespeare, Pope, or Blake "galaxies" of meaning related to the aesthetics and metaphysics of print. He has experimented with form in his own writings; that is, he has tried to function as an artist. *The Mechanical Bride* was a kind of early pop art, with a layout like a museum catalogue and with headlines, clips of advertising art, comic-strip boxes. *The Gutenberg Galaxy* and *Understanding Media* regard the human habitation as an enormous art pile, a throbbing assemblage of things that communicate, and they try to make it comprehensible by means of a mosaic of exhibits and comments that the author's "circulating point of view" has assembled from widely separated fields; McLuhan is attempting to imitate in his writing the form of the TV image, which he describes as "mosaic." The [133–134] effort to develop an open, expressive social-science investigation in place of the customary learned research report may in time produce important results; McLuhan's version of this new form has the virtue of allowing the author to pick up bits of observation (e.g., that girls in dark glasses are engaged in "cool" communication) that are usually excluded, and it also enables him to bring into focus, a remarkable spread of information (e.g., the measurement of time by smell among the ancient Chinese and among modern brain-surgery patients). McLuhan's concern for style tempts him into discharges of epigrams, wisecracks, and puns. These have abated in *Understanding Media,* but the chapter titles are still haunted by gags ("Money: The Poor Man's Credit Card," "The Photograph: The Brothel-Without-Walls"). Some of this wit is low-grade ("Movies: The Reel World") even if we consider bad puns to be in keeping with the pop spirit. However, formulas like "If it works it's obsolete," to suggest the rate of change in media, and "Today, even natural resources have an informational aspect," more than balance the account.

McLuhan, then, is a kind of artist, and his quick leaps from datum to axiom ("Take off the dateline, and one day's paper is the same as the next") are often aesthetically pleasurable. In his communications-constructed world, the artist is the master figure—in fact, the only personage whom he differentiates from the media-absorbing mass. The artist, McLuhan believes, anticipates the changes in man that will be wrought by a new medium and through his work adjusts the collective psyche to it. Thus the artist provides an antidote to the numbness induced by change-over. Painting has long since gone beyond being a merely visual medium; praising someone for having a "good eye," as if a modern painting were an object to be taken in by a single sense, is tantamount to praising him for being out of date. A Kandinsky or a Mondrian is actually apprehended through a "resonating interplay" of the whole keyboard of sense and consciousness; no wonder that eye-trained people continue to ask, "What does it mean?" One of McLuhan's most valuable contributions is to help dissolve the craft-oriented concept that modern art works still belong in the realm of things contemplated instead of being forces active in "the unified field of electric all-at-onceness" of tomorrow's world community.

Unfortunately, despite his insights [134–135] into form, McLuhan's organization of his own ideas is far from first-rate. As a composition, *Understanding Media* is often out of control; "circular" perspective becomes synonymous with going round in circles. Endlessly repetitious, the book, for all its rain of bright intuitions, creates a total effect of monotony. This repetitiousness probably reflects McLuhan's uneasiness about his ability to make himself clear. For there are in his thesis inherent ambiguities. Given the advanced nature of the electric media, the implication is that older forms, like the book and the stage, are obsolete and that film and comic strip are the art forms of the future. In clinging to a sense extension (the eye) that has been surpassed, the novelist is a reactionary—except for the beatnik who gives readings in coffee-houses. Even being an individual is retrogressive, so turn the dial and slip into the new global kraal. Much as McLuhan lauds the artist, he has pitted the pop media against him, in disregard of the fact that the masterpieces of this century have been paintings, poems, plays, not movies or TV shows. The point is that while McLuhan is an aesthete, he is also an ideologue—one ready to spin out his metaphor of the "extensions" until its web covers the universe; if clothes are media, and trees and policemen are, too—if, in short, all of creation "speaks" to us—McLuhan is discussing as media what used to be called "Nature," and his notion of the "sensuously orchestrated" man of the future is a version of the pantheistic hero. He is a belated Whitman singing the body electric with Thomas Edison as accompanist. Yet to expect Adam to step out of the TV screen is utopianism of the wildest sort. For McLuhan, beliefs, moral qualities, social action, even material progress play a secondary role (if that) in determining the human condition. The drama of history is a crude pageant whose inner meaning is man's metamorphosis through the media. As a philosophy of cultural development, *Understanding Media* is on a par with theories that trace the invention of the submarine to conflicts in the libido or the decline of the handicrafts to the legalization of interest on loans.

"Usury," Ezra Pound wrote in the "Cantos,"

> . . . rusts the man and his chisel
> It destroys the craftsman, destroying craft;
> Azure is caught with cancer.

McLuhan has taken with deadly literalness his metaphors of the media as extensions of the body and of a [135–136] nervous system outside ourselves. "Man becomes, as it were, the sex organs of the machine world, as the bee of the plant world, enabling it to fecundate and to evolve ever new forms." His susceptibility to figures of speech leads him to describe possibilities of technological innovation as if they were already achieved facts. In his world, money and work are things of the past; we live on credit cards and "learn a living" as managers of computers, and the struggle, backwash, surprise of real events are somnambulistically brushed away. The chilly silence of science fiction reigns over a broad band of McLuhan's temperament.

These deficiencies might be decisive were there to arise a McLuhan "school" of cultural interpretation through media analysis. If one judges McLuhan as an individual writer, however, what remain paramount are his global standpoint and his zest for the new. As an artist working in a mixed medium of direct experience and historical analogy, he has given a needed twist to the great debate on what is happening to man in this age of technological speedup. Other observers have been content to repeat criticisms of industrial society that were formulated a century ago, as if civilization had been steadily emptied out since the advent of the power loom. As against the image of our time as a faded photograph of a richly pigmented past, McLuhan, for all his abstractness, has found positive, humanistic meaning and the color of life in supermarkets, stratospheric flight, the lights blinking on broadcasting towers.

In respect to the maladies of de-individuation, he has dared to seek the cure in the disease, and his vision of going forward into primitive wholeness is a good enough reply to those who would go back to it. *Understanding Media* is a concrete testimonial (illuminating, as modern art illuminates, through dissociation and regrouping) to the belief that man is certain to find his footing in the new world he is in the process of creating.   *[136]*

1. Rosenberg recognizes pervasive optimism as a prime character-
    istic of McLuhan's thought and method: "Of all crisis philos-
    ophers, McLuhan is by far the coolest." (p. *136*)
    "The present worldwide clash between the new and the old
    arouses him to enthusiasm." (p. *131*)
    ". . . McLuhan arrives at happy conclusions for the future."
    (p. *132*)
    To what extent does McLuhan's optimism account for the con-
    troversy he generates? Examine a number of his critics, pro and
    con, and measure how much they seem to split on the issue of
    "happy conclusions" for the human race.

2. How does Rosenberg react to the style in which McLuhan writes
    (pp. *134–135*)? Is his dictum here in accord with most other critics,
    or is it a unique and original observation?

PARADISE
REGAINED
OR McLUHANACY?

Jack Behar and Ben Lieberman
Review of *Understanding Media*

DR. BEHAR'S VIEWS

The Gutenberg Galaxy gave us McLuhan's major thesis about the new world of sensibility being created under the aegis of the electronic media, and at the center of this new book are the formulae that figured prominently in it. Briefly, the picture that emerges is something like the following: Pre-literate or tribal man lived in a rich oral-aural world, one structured by myth and ritual, its modes of awareness being "tactile" and "auditory," its values communal and sacred. (Here, of course, McLuhan finds the perfect myth, one centering in collective participation, that so attracts him and us; and from it grows a rather familiar mystique of the organic in the repeated use of the notion of "unified sensibility.") The Gutenberg revolution exploded the world of tribal man, creating via print the open society, modern individualism,

---

DR. BEHAR is a professor of literature at the University of California, San Diego.

DR. LIEBERMAN is a consultant in communications to a number of industrial and other concerns.

From *Teachers College Record*, April, 1965, pp. 645–649. Reprinted by permission.

privacy, specialization, mechanical-repeatable techniques, etc., all at the cost —a very heavy one, for McLuhan—of cutting us off from a rich auditory experience. Hence, fragmented, specialized, impoverished modern man is Gutenberg Man, a necessary victim of the visual emphasis given by printing technology. The electronic revolution, however, once more makes oral-aural experience central, promising liberation from the impoverishing effect of print, demanding participation rather than print-fostered passivity, and restoring us to wholeness and harmony in the reconstituted tribal society. McLuhan apparently believes, then, that the problem of contemporary "fragmentation" is being solved whether we know it or not, that Utopia is unnecessary when we have begun to be projected, via our electronic technology, into an incredibly rich world of auditory experience that begins to wipe out our disabling legacy from the mechanical age of Gutenberg. We may yet find salvation in a happy, active, out-[645–646]going sensorium in Paradise Regained.

Certainly there is an obvious craving in our society for a more richly orchestrated life of the senses, for oral-aural modes of experience and communion with others, and in a somewhat over-popularized way, for a kind of revolt against passive, consumer-oriented roles. We are becoming devoted to the idea of full-time creativity for everyone, to process rather than to product, to "getting with" things rather than imposing oneself on them, to "acting out" rather than "reading up on." But to find, as McLuhan does, the TV image the trigger of all this is going rather far—too far, I would suppose. Some of us may find what McLuhan calls the "tactile mesh" of the TV image a quite maddeningly abstract idea. On the other hand, McLuhan's analysis of newspaper form as "mosaic" is perfectly valid, and here the formula of "simultaneity" and "total field" awareness seems to work, as does the notion that the mosaic of newspaper form tends to neutralize the "hot" point of view reserved for the editorial pages. Perhaps McLuhan presses so hard on the idea of the mosaic-like TV image because he is desperate to come by at least a token reality of "community" and the new "ritual" forms on which it can be based. What he needs to do is to define "involvement" and "participation" so that these large terms are not simply produced on the analysis of perceptual schema. We tend to regard "involvement" as (in part) distinct from the way a person looks at the TV image.

In the drama the book makes of opposing worlds of sensibility, where does McLuhan stand? What is he after in foisting so heavy a load of subliminal work on the backs of the media? On the whole, quite like the literary men whose culture-bound responses to the media he makes light of, he wants collective involvement in a "ritual process," and he sees TV, the newspaper, and radio as providing this at a "magical" communal level. He doesn't want ideas ("point of view") but action, a magical process working itself out, communal awareness restored, participation "in depth" made possible, the "Africa within" released to the sound of the tribal media. And indeed, it is easy to conclude that, for all the many sharp observations McLuhan gives us on the workings of the media, what he finally desires is a kind of religion. He is, like Blake and Lawrence, whose names occur in these pages, a foe of "single vision and Newton's sleep," and logically, then, an advocate of "ritual." But it is odd that McLuhan's proto-religious longings should fasten on the TV image and the electronic revolution.

The large question McLuhan's book raises seems to be this: How can we see to it that the necessary specialist sensibility, fostered by whatever happens to be the form of our media indoctrination, doesn't come to dominate the whole field of our awareness? McLuhan doesn't want us to resemble the teenager caught up in the self-mesmerization of the twist, happily submerged in the trance. He refers to "autonomy," and he says about education that it must be regarded as "civil defense against media fall-out." Yet he is so bound to the idea of the subliminal power of the media to impose their assumptions about the structuring of primary social processes on those who use and are used by them that he can't descend to what is inevitable—some fairly grubby educational programming. We don't want simply a subliminally enjoyable interplay of the sense—a kind of electronic *symboliste* madness, however liberating—or the total triumph of habits print technology has fostered. If we live [646–647] indeed at a moment of crucial cultural change, when the assumptions imposed by print technology begin to strike us as making for some inevitable distortions and a harmful imbalance, then we must assess what resources we have that allow for righting the balance. Righting the balance, however, will not give us anything so comprehensive as "unified sensibility," so it is a rather foolish messianism to talk as McLuhan does about this.

The world which the media have helped to build is inescapably the one in which we live. Keeping watch over the media is one of the ordinary daily chores. It follows, I think, that we cannot help but act as analysts of content, not merely of the apparently unconditioned power of media *forms* to create or to transform the conditions of our lives.

DR. LIEBERMAN'S JUDGMENT

The Cult of McLuhanacy now has its full gospel. Everything is Explained by seeing electric (= instant) information and communication become the whole of matter and energy; the central Mystery that every good cult needs is provided in the phenomenon that the very *form* of the communication media not only creates all change without the slightest regard for *content,* but has this causal effect despite the fact that there is no such thing as causality.

If you do not understand this, at least do not dismiss it as caricature. It is doctrine very seriously laid forth, with a very profuse profusion of printed language (a form the Master seems to deplore). For the details, you will have to read the book if you can. It will be hard enough, here, in limited space, even to cover the main points.

McLuhan's message is that the media aren't what people think they are (especially not what scholars and media people think they are), and we can't understand the vast technological and cultural changes now upon us if we don't understand media. Unfortunately, McLuhan is so full of jerry-built theory, dogmatic overgeneralizations, non sequiturs, disorganized successions of parenthetical observations, and bewilderingly swift and large leaps among high peaks of misconception, that he makes little contribution himself to that understanding. On the contrary. It will take years to unravel a defenseless student who takes McLuhan's "facts" literally.

Nevertheless, and lest this review begin to sound critical, it must be said strongly that the book does perform a useful negative service for the mature reader, and even more for any encrusted communicator who can somehow be brought to plunge into McLuhan's super-souped-up style.

McLuhan is right to thrust out at the pipsqueak communication theories of the academicians and at the smug assumptions of most of the media leaders. We certainly have no communication theory today that is anywhere close to encompassing the realities and ramifications of communication. It is literally appalling to see how little effort is made to study and understand (much less teach) communication *per se* in major colleges and universities. No one can even get his feet wet in *Understanding Media* without at least feeling viscerally that the usual views of communication are utterly superficial and wrong, and that something drastic ought to be done about the matter.

But McLuhan unfortunately does not seem able to organize himself into a coherence that can fit the internal facts of the communication complex itself, much less the relationship of the communication complex to the industrial complex, the educational complex, the *[647–648]* political complex, and all the other polarized but interdependent facets of our total society. It is not enough to say, as he does, that the advent of the electric media has made everything one non-linear whole that needs no delineating. And in any event, as fuzzy a little tail as even McLuhan's ABC (All-Being Communication) trying to wag a dog as big as all mankind Past, Present, and Future really is preposterous.

Nor does it help too much that McLuhan thrusts at the excesses of specialism in our society, including specialist teaching. When he lays the blame at the print media and proclaims that the new electr[on]ic media have already completely changed the situation, he reveals the frail substance of his insight. The specialist phenomenon is a necessary, inevitable development, arising out of and creating our whole technology—not just communication— and it was growing long before the "explosion" of phonetic literacy. It *does* need to be counter-balanced as our society becomes too complex for the innate generalist sense in each of us to keep our total effort a workable whole. And despite McLuhan's dangerous complacency which arises from his mystic generalist role for the "implosion" of electronic media and automation, we *are* in real danger of either splintering into paralysis and doom or else accepting a conformist pattern that will make us into an ant society. A lot of us are going to have to work hard to restore the generalist balance, but McLuhan's faith in radio, TV, and the computer—as media which have already changed the reality and thus eliminated the danger—is not the clarion call to duty.

Unfortunately, as has been perhaps hinted, McLuhan has no real positive contribution to make in this book. He produces a great confusion of aphorisms, striking sentences, arresting allusions, hindsightful insights, and breathtaking inferences. It may well be that some of them are great and will be quoted millenia hence as imperishable truths. But it is possible to suspect also that if so, this will be true simply by the laws of probability invoked in the spewing out of a torrent of statements of one kind or another—just as a pack of monkeys can theoretically, in due time, type out a Shakespearean play. But is it worth the prodigious waste of paper, and even more the staggering work of wading through all those near-miss typings to find the gems?

Not that McLuhan's creative process is sheer probability, like the monkeys. He has what can only be called an eclectic mind, an eclecticism sent skittering over all sorts of facts and artifacts by the electric charge of a neglected truth. Using *Understanding Media* as a fascinating casebook, the process in McLuhan goes something like this:

> —Any straw in a field is a straw in the wind if it happens to have at least one characteristic that is also characteristic of the point being made.
> —Any straw in the wind is the complete clue of a great new condition of the human mind or society.
> —Any clue to a great new condition of the human mind or society that is going to develop from some new communication medium is the evidence that this change has already been effected.
> —(Corollary) Any such change was caused entirely by a new communication medium.
> —(Corollary) Any such change is also revolutionary, permanent, and tied to some great past.

To test all the implications, ramifications, and conclusions which this kind of creativity puts onto even one typical [648–649] McLuhan page would take years. But, to repeat, would it be worth it?

One reason for fearing not is the way McLuhan can base whole chunks of his theory (if that's what it is) on the most simple and yet staggering distinctions based on sheer error. One example must suffice, but it is central: his analysis of TV.

He finds TV different from film, to say nothing of print media, because (p. 164) "From the three million dots per second on TV, the viewer is able to accept, in an iconic grasp, only a few dozen, seventy or so, from which to shape an image. The image thus made is as crude as that of the comics." And from that stems the dichotomy which leads to the whole social change and the complacency mentioned earlier. What an incredible misconception of what the eye sees! Yet one must accept this starting point, and the inferences which follow, or the "understanding" of media throughout the whole book is made meaningless.

The greatest defect of McLuhan's theory, however, is the complete rejection of any role for the content of communication. One can only assume that the irony that his own work creates "content" exclusively is lost upon McLuhan. At any rate, he ignores the power of ideas, of values, of emotions, of cumulative wisdom—to say nothing of the hard facts of geography, economics, politics, and the human glory and tragedy of life and death. "The medium is the message," and there is no other. Just like that. The truth is overwhelming in its pristine simplicity, as great a stroke of genius as Einstein's $E = mc^2$. And the result, unleashed, is a comparable radioactivity that creates horrible mutations. McLuhan bombs a landscape already in critical condition, and then strews his special seed for the growth of the new truths he sees.

Well, let us end ungrudgingly and say that his bombing is useful. Even that his seeding is a prodigious and noble gesture. But let us hope that very few readers believe he has reseeded our land with a viable, useful crop of truth. There will have to be new seed, certainly, and a tremendous amount of patient work to cultivate the new truths that our new technological society needs to replace the old—but glibly Marshalled McLuhanancies are only going to grow weeds that will need pulling if they take root at all.   [649]

1. On page 646, Mr. Behar discloses, according to his own analysis, what McLuhan "wants": ". . . he doesn't want ideas . . . but action, a magical process working itself out, communal awareness restored, participation 'in depth' made possible . . ." etc., and ". . . what he finally desires is a kind of religion." Can you agree that this program of action suggested by Behar is, indeed, what McLuhan is recommending in his work?

2. Lieberman (p. 649) attacks McLuhan's analysis of TV as "an incredible misconception of what the eye sees!" Are you persuaded by McLuhan's explanation of the physiological process of watching television or by Lieberman's sweeping denunciation of it?

THE McLUHAN METAPHOR

The New Yorker Talk of the Town feature

When the Westinghouse people announced that at the end of the World's Fair they will again bury a Time Capsule filled with assorted cultural and technological mementos of twentieth-century man, a friend of ours suggested that they should replace the codes and artifacts with Dr. Marshall McLuhan, who could be counted on to explain us vividly to anybody digging around in Flushing Meadow two thousand years from now. Dr. McLuhan, a professor of English at St. Michael's College of the University of Toronto, is also the director of the university's Center for Culture and Technology and the author of three startling books on Western civilization—*The Mechanical Bride, The Gutenberg Galaxy,* and, most recently, *Understanding Media,* in which he joyfully explores the tribal virtues of popular culture, casts a cynical eye on the "classification traditions" that came in with print, and sees near-mythic possibilities in our computer age. He has compared the Bomb to the doctoral dissertation; discussed the "depth-involving" qualities of sunglasses, textured stockings, discothèques, and comic books; reported on the iconic properties of Andy Warhol's signed soup cans; and predicted a happy day when everyone will have his own portable computer to cope with the

From *The New Yorker,* May 15, 1965, pp. 43–44. Reprinted by permission © 1965, *The New Yorker* Magazine Inc.

dreary business of digesting information. In so doing, Dr. McLuhan has earned a reputation among the cognoscenti as the world's first Pop philosopher.

Last week, Dr. McLuhan flew to New York to deliver a lecture at Spencer Memorial Church (which has its *own* reputation, as the world's first far-out Presbyterian congregation), and we took the subway to Brooklyn Heights to hear him. At the church, an old, oak-beamed building that was bustling with young McLuhan enthusiasts, we found the Professor sitting quietly in the pulpit while a young man in a green corduroy jacket and narrow trousers propped an enormous Rauschenberg painting against it. The young man, who turned out to be Spencer's minister, William Glenesk, explained to us that the poster was "left over from my Rauschenberg sermon." He then told the audience that he had been a fan of Dr. McLuhan's ever [43–44] since 1951, when he attended the Professor's course on Eliot, Joyce, and the Symbolist movement at the University of Toronto. Dr. McLuhan, a tall, steel-haired man given to twirling a pair of horn-rimmed glasses in appropriately professorial style, stood up, thanked Mr. Glenesk, and remarked that the warm May weather was certainly as depth-involving as a good Rauschenberg or a good elephant joke. The new art and the new jokes have no strict, literal content, no story line, he said, and continued, "They are the forms of an electronic age, in which fragmented, dictionary-defined data have been bypassed in favor of integral knowledge and an old tribal instinct for patterned response." Several members of the audience nodded ecstatically, and Dr. McLuhan went on to tackle practically every cultural phenomenon from the tribal encyclopedia to the shaggy-dog story, from Shakespeare to Fred Allen, from the wheel to the electromagnetic circuit. He good-naturedly blamed Plato for writing down Socrates' dialogues and thus inaugurating "codified culture," and he praised the singing commercial for reinstating the old tribal institution of memorized wisdom. Every new technology, according to the Professor, programs a new sensory human environment, and our computer technology has catapulted us right out of the specialist age and into a world of integral knowledge and synesthetic responses. "The computer is not merely an extension of our eyes, like print, but an extension of our whole central nervous system," he explained. He paused, twirled his glasses, and went on to say that every new environment uses as its content the old environment—"the way Plato used the old oral tradition of the dialogue for his books and the way television now uses the story form of the novel and the movies"—but that it is the technological nature of any new medium, and not its borrowed content, that conditions the new human response. Pop Art, he said, glancing affectionately at the Rauschenberg, is merely our old mechanical environment used as the content of our new electronic environment. "One environment seen through another becomes a metaphor," he continued. "Like Andy Warhol's 'Liz Taylor.' Our new, non-literal response to the literal content of that blown-up and endlessly repeated photograph turns Liz into an icon. It takes a new technology like ours to turn an old environment like Liz into an art form."

Dr. McLuhan next suggested the possibility of a new technology that would extend consciousness itself into the environment. "A kind of computerized ESP," he called it, envisioning "consciousness as the corporate content of the environment—and eventually maybe even a small portable computer, about the size of a hearing aid, that would process our private experience through the corporate experience, the way dreams do now." Then he said, "Well, that's enough pretentious speculation for one night," and turned to Mr. Glenesk, who suggested that the audience have "an old Socratic go" at some questions and answers.

Mr. Glenesk thereupon introduced the Professor to some of the McLuhan disciples in the audience.

The first disciple told Dr. McLuhan that he had been amplifying several sounds in one room at the same time, to get the "depth-involving" sound that is part of Dr. McLuhan's brave new world.

"Must make one hell of a racket," Dr. McLuhan said approvingly.

A second disciple, a rather nervous woman from the neighborhood, announced that she could hardly wait to have an experience-processor of her own. "The way things are now, I never can remember anything," she said, and was immediately interrupted by a third disciple, a bearded student sitting next to her.

The student expressed equal eagerness for computerized ESP. "Gee, just think!" he continued. "I could go to sleep a painter and wake up a composer!"

"Terrifying," Dr. McLuhan said.   [44]

In what ways is this author trying to evoke a special kind of response from his readers? Does McLuhan's portrait, presented here performing in the flesh before a live audience, affect one's attitude toward his ideas? Is it intended to?

MARSHALL McLUHAN: CANADA'S INTELLECTUAL COMET

Richard Schickel

Herbert Marshall McLuhan is a tall, gray-haired, enthusiastically eclectic Professor of English at the University of Toronto who, at fifty-four, appears about to join that select circle of intellectual radicals whose members have more or less accidentally had the good luck to advance the right new theory at just the right historical moment. Already a small but vociferous McLuhan cult is beginning to make itself heard. Outside its confines, meanwhile, many leading intellectuals are being forced to take him seriously, even when they find themselves in appalled disagreement with his basic ideas, put off by his methods, and profoundly shaken by a style of discourse that blithely ignores all the conventions of critical-historical exposition. All in all, the intensity of the passions McLuhan has lately generated leads one to think that,

RICHARD SCHICKEL has written two studies of the motion picture, *The Stars* and *Movies;* a social history, *The World of Carnegie Hall;* and a fairy tale, *The Gentle Knight.* He is also coauthor of *Lena,* the autobiography of Lena Horne.

From *Harper's Magazine,* November, 1965, pp. 62–68. Copyright © 1965 by Richard Schickel. Reprinted from *Harper's Magazine,* November, 1965, by permission of the Sterling Lord Agency.

like it or not, he is on his way to becoming one of those annoying "seminal" thinkers whose arguments you must adapt, incorporate, or dispose of before pressing ahead in his field or—as McLuhan clearly believes—into areas well beyond it.

McLuhan's specialty is, for want of a better term, Communications Theory. The instrument of his recent emergence as a force to be reckoned with is his third book, a 359-page volume called *Understanding Media* and subtitled "The Extensions of Man." It was published last year and is already available in paperback. The critic Harold Rosenberg has said that it "takes its place in that wide channel of cultural criticism of the twentieth century that includes writers like T. S. Eliot, Oswald Spengler, D. H. Lawrence, F. R. Leavis, David Riesman, Hannah Arendt." Which may be a polite way of saying that like some of these writers all of the time and all of them some of the time, McLuhan is apocalyptic and dogmatic in tone, egocentric in style (though in person he is none of these things), and utterly untroubled by the usual niceties of scholarship. (The original edition of *Understanding Media* contains no index, bibliography, or notes while most of the supportive historical material is drawn from secondary sources.) On top of that, the author disdains the closely argued, carefully organized argument. Instead, he tends to be at once repetitive and digressive, with a marked tendency to see each new ripple in the cultural sea as a trend of tidal-wave proportions. As a result, the compulsively scholarly or compulsively logical reader has no difficulty in either dismissing his work as a barbaric yawp or in quibbling it to death. Many have done just that.

Yet it is hard to escape the feeling that they are mistaken. Nearly all the writers on Rosenberg's list can be subjected to similar attitudinizing (and have been). Leavis at his most argumentative, Lawrence at his most visionary, Spengler at his most Germanic, are all terrible fellows. But if one does not seek a system of True Belief in their work, or try to organize his entire intellectual life around it, they are most useful fellows as well, rewarding the reader with sudden insights that can, for a moment or two, light up a confused landscape sud-[62–63]den insight that can, for a moment or two, light up a confused landscape and show the odd order underlying seeming chaos. This also is true of McLuhan.

He begins with the simple gesture of overturning all the usual assumptions about communications. "The medium is the message," he cries in the most notorious of his catchy formulations. By this he means that the way information is presented is at least as important as the information itself. The medium, all by itself, with no conscious effort on the part of the people who control or use it, has the power to distort, reinforce, reduce, or neutralize content. Naturally, this makes the creator's role a good deal less significant than we have been led to think in this postromantic era. It also imperils our conventional critical standards, as we have tried to apply them to the mass media. Logic as the organizing principle for the presentation of information is for McLuhan appropriate only to the printed page. It is not to be as highly valued as the "mosaic" style of organization of the electronic media, which may be better suited, in any case, to the way we nowadays perceive and re-spond emotionally. If this seems to imply that the new media may reduce our consciousness to the level of a pre-literate savage, dependent on intuition and feeling rather than logic to make sense of things, so much the better. Mc-Luhan thinks modern communications methods have already reduced our world to the size of "a global village" anyway—also a good thing.

Needless to say, such optimism in the face of revolution is not uni-versally shared. One Oxford don, coming away from a McLuhan lecture, was heard to mutter that the man was dangerous, "for the same reason Hitler was dangerous." And there is no question that in the world which McLuhan predicts a good deal more than the universal primacy of literary values is threatened. Our very vision of man, inherited from the Age of Enlightenment, is threatened, as are our ideas of democracy and progress. That teen-ager with a transistor pressed to his ear as he wanders vacantly down the street, the gang of kids experiencing the tribalism of a frug party—they really could be the wave of the future.

Yet even one of McLuhan's severest critics, communications expert Ben Lieberman, concedes that he is "right to thrust out at the pip-squeak communications theories of the academicians and at the smug assumptions of most of the media leaders." For nearly everyone senses the problem that McLuhan has made manifest—that in communications, as in so many areas, technology has far outreached the development of the critical tools we need to comprehend all its implications, much less control it effectively. It is un-doubtedly a recognition of the fact that McLuhan is at least trying to develop these tools that has caused him to be so enthusiastically greeted by so many people. Whatever else you think about him, his theories are big enough and bold enough to match the revolution he is examining.

WHY WE FAVOR TRASH

Unfortunately, we have been living without adequate summarizing idea about the mass media for quite a long time—as is probably painfully apparent to anyone who has paid any serious attention to the endless, circular, inapposite argument between the critics of mass media and the proprietors. It is not too much to say that no one, other than McLuhan, has brought any-thing new to the discussion within living memory, with the result that one of the really crucial issues of our time has started to become a bore.

Consider, for example, the behavior of literate people when they confront that total communications weapon, television. Most of them know that by the standards they would normally apply to a medium of communi-cation, TV is an unparalleled purveyor of trash; the most extraordinary docu-mentary, for instance, provides less information—in the usual sense of the word—about a subject than a very ordinary article in a slick magazine. Yet we sit there, eyes glued to the set, watching this explication of the obvious in hate-ful fascination and even find ourselves compelled to stay tuned to whatever follows—*The King Family, Gomer Pyle, Bonanza.* Consciously we despise our-selves, yet we are as fascinated, to use an image McLuhan would completely approve, as any savage before his totem. Often, indeed, we reject the documentary show in favor of the trash. Audience surveys tend to bear this out; the very people who claim to desire more elevated fare are also the ones who ignore existing programs which critics regard as the medium's finest hours.

Something, obviously, is so wrong here that all attempts to reform the wayward giant, to bring it more closely into line with our professed [63–64] cultural aspirations, appear foredoomed to failure. By now it must be clear that all the witty poses struck by critics like Marya Mannes or cultural elitists like Dwight Macdonald, very little practical good has come of their work. Television, by their standards, continues to "decline" and none of the other media has improved much. Attempts to get the FCC to act more like a cultural Pure Food and Drug Administration have failed dismally and we have not witnessed any very serious revolt against television by its audience.

Instead of revolt we have Pop Art and Camp, which must be read, in part, as do-it-yourself attempts to resolve the conflict between our pretensions to the finer things and our visceral adoration of the less fine. Pop, as a mode of expression, Camp as a shorthand style of appreciation, are both means of giving some sort of aesthetic-intellectual rationale to the fascinated attention we pay the mass media. It is probably a mistake to impute much depth to these movements—especially Camp—but as symptoms of a desire to move beyond the attitudes of cultural criticism as it is customarily practiced by literary people they are very important.

And so is the reception accorded McLuhan. He has not written a great deal about Pop and he had not heard of Camp until Susan Sontag's now famous definition of it in *Partisan Review** was pointed out to him. But the Poppers and the Camp Followers have heard of him. When he lectures in the United States he is likely to attract people who regard themselves as converts and disciples. They tell him how eager they are for the next steps in the technological revolution which he has predicted—things like personal, computerized ESP devices that would extend consciousness itself into the environment. Or they speak of their own experiments at creating a greater "depth involvement" (one of his catchphrases) with the media, frequently by hooking up a multitude of amplifiers, all broadcasting different sounds, and then sitting in the middle of the cacophony absorbing, absorbing, absorbing—and quite likely getting terrible headaches.

Earlier this year, at the University of British Columbia, a group of professors set up the world's first festival of what the French are already calling *mcluhanisme*. People wandered at random—there was, naturally, no set sequence—through a maze created out of huge plastic sheets while slides were projected, at random intervals, on every available surface (floors and ceilings included). Musicians whacked away at gongs and bells and wood

* Fall 1964 issue, in which she stated, among other things, that "the essence of Camp is its love of the unnatural: of artifice and exaggeration. And Camp is esoteric—something of a private code, a badge of identity even, among small, urban cliques."—*The Editors*

blocks, dancers whirled among the spectators and there was even something called a Sculptured Wall. It consisted of a piece of stretch fabric on one side of which was a squirming girl, whom you were supposed to palpate, through the screen, gaining, presumably, a major lesson in an oft-ignored method of communication—the tactile.

THE FIRST POP PHILOSOPHER?

McLuhan did not attend the festival and does nothing to encourage this sort of thing, although he seems vaguely amused by it. He goes in for no such gadgeteering himself and claims to go to the movies or watch TV (he likes *Perry Mason, The Rogues,* that sort of thing) for the same reasons we all do—to see how the story comes out. He is, indeed, an unchic type who dresses in academically nondescript suits, drinks Manhattans, incessantly twirls his glasses as he talks and is given to chuckly little professional puns and jokes in those rare moments when he is not discoursing on his subject. He treasures his life in Toronto precisely because it is well away from the great communications and fashion centers; he sees them better, he thinks, from the perspective of distance.

In short, he is not the kind of man who consciously set out to earn his journalistically awarded title as "the first pop philosopher" nor, apparently, did he think he would be claimed by people who see in his work the first coherent statement of something they have all been groping for. He did anticipate, however, the severe criticism of literary people who have, he thinks, a vested interest in keeping cultural criticism within its present, literarily defined limits.

The reasons for their antipathy are not hard to find. Set aside, for the moment, his chilling prediction of a media-induced return to a tribal level of consciousness and consider his radical redefinition of the essence of the communicative process: "The medium is the message."

This is, perhaps, self-evident. But very few people take it into account when discussing media. In order to do so intelligently a critic would have to become an expert in the special properties of each medium, and this would be so much more difficult than merely taking an attitude toward them. It is so easy simply to find a television pro-[64–65]gram inadequate by the standards of literary criticism and let it go at that. This may lead to overpraising shows that are excruciatingly bad television or to ignoring programs of merit within their own electronic terms. It may lead to the futile and wasteful efforts to regulate a fundamentally uncontrollable medium, for how do you rationally control something which may make its strongest point in the wink of an eye, with a jump cut or with the tone of a voice, not the content of the words it is speaking?

McLuhan himself has few concrete suggestions for a new public policy or critical strategy for TV or any of the other media of what he likes to call "the electric age." He seems to feel that is work for other hands. He concentrates instead on offering a way of "understanding media" that could bridge this most obvious of the many gaps between literature and science *cum* technology.

His view of history goes something like this: Prior to the invention of the phonetic alphabet, man existed within a "tribal and oral pattern with its seamless web of kinship and interdependence." The chief medium for the exchange of information was speech, in effect a natural resource made equally available to all. No individual, therefore, knew appreciably more or less than the rest of the tribe. Hence there was no individualism, very little specialization, and therefore nothing comparable to that most dreaded and prevalent of modern psychic disorders, alienation. In McLuhan's version of life among the noble savages there was no difference between work and play, the idea of a split between a high culture and a low unheard of. Culture was simply culture in the full anthropological sense of the word. This society may have been low in the amount of abstract information at its disposal, and therefore low in its ability to control its environment, but it had certain advantages over our civilization. It could not have created a *Hamlet* or a *Lear* but, happily, it numbered no real life models for these archetypes among its citizenry. It probably had a sense of community we might envy and, McLuhan implies, an inner life responsive to myth, to the iconic, to the unseen patterns of the natural world, quite a bit richer than our own.

In brief, it was not the prisoner of words or of print and the special logic they impose on our patterns of thought. Written language is, to McLuhan, incomparably less able to communicate the true, non-rational, nonserial nature of human experience than the spoken word. And the primitive had another advantage: He possessed a better, more balanced orchestration of the senses than we, in our "eye culture," are able to achieve. Touch, taste, smell were, of necessity, developed to high degrees by the primitive striving to maintain a state of balance in a state of nature.

For McLuhan, the replacement of the primitive's pictographic and syllabic alphabets by phonetic symbols was a cultural disaster, beginning the process of man's alienation from his environment. In his discussion of this point he introduces the Greek myth of Cadmus, whose dissemination of an alphabet earned him a metaphoric description as the sower of dragon's teeth. As for the invention of a movable type, McLuhan sees it as nothing less than a major trauma, afflicting the development of all civilization since. The hopeful part of his message is that the new technology may speed our recovery from that trauma.

McLuhan believes the printed line became, for Western man, the organizing principle of his life, forcing upon him both the necessity and the virtues, of logic. It may be responsible, for instance, for the assembly *line* as the basis for industrial organization. Worse, printing naturally pushed us toward an overvaluation of abstract thought and caused "much separation of . . . imaginative, emotional, and sense life." If tribal man, with his balanced orchestration of the senses is, classically, the whole man, then alphabetic man is, classically, the fragmented man. Moreover, he is, compared to tribal man, remarkably detached, capable of "specialization by dissociation," of action "without reaction or involvement."

One can understand what McLuhan thinks we have lost by understanding the values he attaches to an object itself, to a picture of it, and to a printed description of it. For example, the flag. In battle, a standard going forward through a hail of shot has the power to make men die for it; a photograph of the same scene has the power to cause a lump in our throats; a written description of it, set down in cold print, is merely history—interesting, full of more information, perhaps, than a photograph, but lacking the power to involve or move us emotionally.

Cold print! To McLuhan there is no more inept phrase. For he has divided—and this is one of his more controversial [65–66] notions—the media into two categories, hot and cold. "A hot medium is one that extends one single sense in 'high definition.' High definition is a state of being well-filled with data." Thus print, directed only at the eye, is far from being cold; it is the hottest of the hot media, imparting much data with great clarity. Speech, on the other hand, is classically cool "because so little is given and so much has to be filled in by the listener." Contrary to popular opinion, McLuhan believes a reader is far more passive than a television watcher. To the former, scanning the neat, logical lines of a well-printed book, much is given; to the latter, peering into the flickering, blurry home screen, very little is given. With more gaps to fill in, he is compelled to work harder, if not intellectually, then in gathering the emotional message. He is a man puzzling out the meaning of an abstract painting, not a man absorbing the information neatly spelled out in a technical drawing. And doing so under previously unimaginable conditions, which create previously unimaginable pressures. *Understanding Media* begins with these words:

> After three thousand years of exploration, by means of fragmentary and mechanical technologies, the Western world is imploding. During the mechanical ages we had extended our bodies into space. Today, after more than a century of electric technology, we have extended our central nervous system itself into a global embrace, abolishing . . . space and time.

In short, our friend peering intently into his television set is in much the same position as the pre-literate. He is getting a very cool (that is, dataless) view of life by direct, firsthand observation. The only difference is that his "village" is the whole world. Like his primitive ancestor, though, "action and reaction occur almost at the same time. We live mythically and integrally."

On one level, of course, this is unfortunate. When we had to depend on purely mechanical methods of communication, information was emotionally defused in the course of its slow journey to us—and our reactions were cooled (in the non-McLuhan sense of the word) as they made a similarly slow trip back. The advantages of this system, particularly to the statesman, were immense. Today he is in the position of a tribal chieftain, confronting his group's enemies directly, exchanging mortal insults face to face. With the populations of both villages looking on, the art of diplomacy becomes very difficult to practice and the strategic withdrawal almost an impossibility. Our leaders perhaps can be excused if they look back with longing on, say, the eighteenth or early nineteenth centuries when, isolated from their constituencies and uninvolved with their neighbors, they could carry out "the most dangerous social operations with complete detachment," playing "the aloof and dissociated role of the literate Westerner."

Indeed, we can all look back on them longingly. But, as McLuhan says, even as we have begun to absorb the implications of electric technology, we are being hurried forward into the new computerized age, an age "of the technological simulation of consciousness, when the creative process of knowing will be collectively and corporately extended to the whole of human society, much as we have already extended our sense and nerves by the various media."

What, one wonders, will the cultural critics make of that age, when they have not even been able to deal intelligently with something as comparatively simple as television? Eric Hoffer, among others, has pointed out that throughout history literate men have reacted hysterically to each new extension of literacy, seeing its growth as a threat to the favored positions their special knowledge has created for them. Certainly there is evidence of this in their response to McLuhan. *Time,* for example, spoke most bluntly for the prosecution when it declared that *Understanding Media* is "fuzzy-minded, lacking in perspective, low in definition and data, redundant, and contemptuous of logical sequence—which is to say that McLuhan has perfectly illustrated the cool qualities he most values in communications." Dwight Macdonald called it "impure nonsense, nonsense adulterated by sense" and joined in the complaint that McLuhan has an unfortunate tendency to push his thesis too far. "Not that he is careless or untruthful, simply that he's a system-builder and so interested in data only as building stones; if a corner has to be lopped off, a roughness smoothed to fit, he won't hesitate to do it."

HE PLEADS GUILTY

McLuhan pleads guilty, with extenuating circumstances, to these charges. In a letter to the critic, Frank Kermode, he has said that the ideal form for his book would be an ideogram or perhaps a film, for he can think of no other way to create "an inconclusive image that is lineal and sequential." The result, Kermode says, is that "with every word he writes he admits his allegiance to the old order and falsifies his report on the new."

Time's charges merely help to make a cute [66–67] point. But there is some truth in what Macdonald and Kermode say. Essentially, McLuhan is a man of insights and his attempts to create a full-scale system out of them is not very successful. He does tend to breathe a little heavily as he tries to drive every aspect of human development into his metaphoric corral. His "tribal man" was apparently created out of the same anthropological innocence as Rousseau's savage and he is just as hard to believe in the scientific sense. Then, too, one could wish that he were a little more concrete when he discusses the media. Just what *is* the mythic quality of *Bonanza* or, for that matter, of Walter Cronkite or a bottle of Listerine? If commercial considerations pollute the literary "truth" of the media, might they not—and even more seriously—pollute McLuhan's mythic and iconic truths? One could, in short, wish that he would come down just a little closer to earth.

To a degree, his failure to do so is an earnest of his intentions and forms a kind of response to Kermode's charge. McLuhan is, by training—though not temperament—a man of letters and there is nothing "reluctant" about his allegiance to literature; it is only that it is partial. He is, however, completely aware that when concern for precise language, for rationality if you will, is downgraded, democracy which is based on the fiction of the rational man, is threatened. "The media are in the process of changing democratic institutions," McLuhan said as he relaxed in one of his favorite seminar rooms, the library of the new Massey College ("instant Balliol") on the Toronto campus. "Now you can start figuring from there. I honestly don't know if the changes will be good or bad, but I think we'd better start thinking about them."

With this, he came close to summarizing the most valuable element of his work. He is not so much advocating a change in the way we perceive and communicate, as trying to describe what he senses, rightly or wrongly, as a historical inevitability. What matters, as Kermode says, "is that we should *get with it*" before we are swept under. In this context, the refusal of his critics to do so seems reactionary indeed. He would not destroy literature; he would only try to make us see that its values are not universally applicable to all forms of communication. Though McLuhan regards C. P. Snow as "a pathetic nineteenth-century middlebrow," he has, on his more sophisticated level, set a task for himself that is similar to Snow's—the creation of a rapprochement between the literary and the scientific communities. To wish to do so is not necessarily the mark of the Philistine.

One of the historical subcurrents he believes to be a constant in human development is a tendency to equate the traditional with art. "People are always perceiving the old environment, and missing the new one, which is why writing is now such a ritzy art form." Our high regard for it has placed us in a "typographic trance," doomed us to "the numb stance of the technological idiot." Perhaps the only way to preserve literary values at all is to give due recognition to the new values, to awaken from our trance and run with the tide instead of standing against it with unwonted stubborness.

INSIDE A PINBALL MACHINE

"I think of art, at its most significant," McLuhan says, "as a DEW Line, a Distant Early Warning system that can always be relied on to tell the old culture what is beginning to happen to it. In that sense it is quite on a par with the scientific." He believes Rimbaud, Joyce, Baudelaire offered just such signals when they ended "the era of literature as such" and founded literary modernism. Abstract expressionism, soft-focus photography, new-wave cinema, even such fad items as sunglasses and women's mesh stockings, are, at their different levels, similarly "cool." All give us little surface data, provocatively hiding "information" to force us to involve ourselves more deeply in order to perceive their hidden depths and meanings. Last spring McLuhan returned from a visit to Houston's new Astrodome stadium convinced that such structures might well be the salvation of baseball, which as he sees it is much too linear, much too "hot" a game to really interest modern man. "But down there, under that roof, it's like being inside a pinball machine. The environment creates a whole new depth of involvement."

If this implies that, despite the single-minded depth of his involvement in his subject, McLuhan is a delightfully surprising conversationalist, one whose most casual thoughts are often full of the excitement of discovery, then one has the essence of his value and some measure of his personality. He is not really a witty man, but as he tries on and discards ideas, like a lady before a hat counter, he comes up with a lot of amusing effects. In the course of one of our conversations, we somehow got to talking about *Pygmalion* and *My Fair Lady*. The former, he noted, had been around for a long time, but it required our age to turn it into a stupendous success. Why? Because the taste-making urban audience is now dominated by thou-[67–68]sands of Eliza Doolittles, people who owe their new eminence, glamour, and prosperity to the fact that, like Shaw's heroine, they have mastered a new language—that of mass people who owe their new eminence, glamour, and prosperity to the fact communications in their case—and see themselves in her. When he learned that the Columbia Broadcasting System had been the chief backer of *My Fair Lady*, McLuhan was delighted with the information. "Oh yeah, Oh yeah," he chortled, using the expression of agreement he most often favors and one which he generally reserves to register his pleasure with his own ideas as they tumble forth.

In brief, conversation with McLuhan is by far the most satisfying means of getting to know his mind. There is a charisma about him, a wayward, egocentric, and disarming charm that is absent from his books. As a medium McLuhan is elliptical, repetitious, given to chasing odd tangents and overstating his case. But his message comes through loud and clear anyway.

Without diminishing the seriousness of his work, perhaps the best way to come to terms with him is to see him as a man conducting a kind of wide-ranging, midnight bull session. As everyone knows, such sessions are rarely productive of the last word on any subject, but they can provide enormously stimulating first words, opening new paths, goading one out of conventional habits of thought and, in general, encouraging one to look at old problems in new ways.

ODD FAITH FOR A RADICAL

McLuhan tends to agree with this estimate of his role and at the same time prefers not to discuss his work autobiographically. As far as he's concerned it has a life of its own and bears little relationship to his own experiences. He concedes that his birth in Edmonton, "rather like your Southwest," may have contributed to his impatience with fine distinctions and that its traditions may account for his preference for oral rather than literary expression. In any case, his graduate degrees are in rhetoric, not literature, and he vividly recalls the excitement with which, as a student at Cambridge, he discovered that the Leavisites were willing to write serious criticism of the language of advertising and the popular media. He is also inclined to believe that his first teaching job, at the University of Wisconsin, had a profound effect on him. "There was a language barrier," he recalls. "Either the students had to learn mine or I had to learn theirs. I decided it would be better if I used their idiom—though not necessarily for their ends."

This early preference for verbal communication within a closely knit community (the small town, the university) certainly created a strong emotional bias, and it is possible to see all McLuhan's work as a rationalization for this bias.

Consider his method of creation: As director of his university's Center for Culture and Technology, he presides over what amounts to an interdisciplinary seminar that is constantly in session. It is here, more than anywhere else, that he tests his ideas and gathers others. He cheerfully admits that the loneliness of the scholar in his library, the writer at his typewriter, is not really for him. "I have to engage in endless dialogue before I write; I want to *talk* a subject over and over and over." He loves to collaborate, too, and claims that whenever he finds a disciple, or merely a like-minded person, his instinct is to work with him on some project or other. At the moment two books are going forward with collaborators and he has gathered together some research teams to try to measure the effectiveness of various kinds of communications processes.

Or consider his personal life: He has six children, almost a small village within his home. And he is a convert to Catholicism, which seems an odd faith for a radical until you consider that a mass, celebrated in a great cathedral, is an almost perfect example of what McLuhan means by an experience of communication in depth, far "cooler" than, say, that festival in British Columbia.

Here is stimulation for all the senses—in the music, in the rich decorations of the altar, in the smell of incense, in the vestments, movements, and voice of the priest. Here, too, are icons and a "data-free" liturgy (so different from a Protestant sermon) which can only yield up its meaning if the communicant refuses to remain psychologically passive and is willing to delve deep into it and himself. Even then, the ultimate mystery will elude him, for, of course, the nature of the religious experience is that it lies far beyond the power of words or logic to explicate it.

One cannot but wonder—is the power of our new media similar, in the most profound sense, to that of religion? Is this why our secular intellectual establishment reacts with such frenzy to it or to someone like McLuhan who tries to comprehend them on their own terms? Is McLuhan, perhaps, creating a new iconography to serve as the basis for a new catholicity, one which will serve modern man as the Church served the men of the Middle Ages? So far, McLuhan has remained silent on these points. But they represent the ultimate implications of his work, and it is in his character for him to speak to them before he is finished.   [68]

1. Schickel quotes an Oxford don's opinion that McLuhan is danger ous "for the same reason Hitler was dangerous." (p. 63) What might be the don's reasoning that prompted such a warning?

2. How fair and unbiased a position does Schickel take, compared with the majority of other commentators, toward McLuhan's thesis? Illustrate your decision with various examples of statements and the tone of different critics.

3. Schickel quotes McLuhan (p. 66): "The media are in the process of changing democratic institutions . . . I honestly don't know if the change will be good or bad, but I think we'd better start thinking about them." From your own observations of his work, is McLuhan as indifferent and noncommittal about what the "media" are doing as this statement suggests?

4. Do the details of McLuhan's personal and professional life, as Schickel describes them (p. 68), shed any light for you on the quality of the ideas expressed in his writings?

REVIEW OF UNDERSTANDING MEDIA

Richard Kostelanetz

Understanding Media. By Marshall McLuhan. (McGraw-Hill. $7.50) It took me three readings to appreciate this badly written, ill-organized essay on the significance of media—electronic means of communication; but Mc-Luhan's originality and brilliance overcome the blocks he puts in their path. If there is meaning in the fact that the two favorable commissioned reviews I wrote on the book—one for an American magazine; the other for an English —both went unpublished, it would be an enormous resistance on the part of literary people to his central idea. The major revolution in the modern sensibility, he says, is a shift from linear forms of organization and comprehension (symphonies; magazines; books) to spatial or disjointed patterns (television; movies; newspapers). As a print man myself, I find this future less congenial than McLuhan does; but one should be grateful to him for identifying what is truly radical in our contemporary culture.

RICHARD KOSTELANETZ is a critic who produces film portraits of American intellectuals for the B.B.C. His book, "The Theatre of Mixed Means," was published in 1967. This review, written for and published in *The Commonweal* of December 3, 1965, p. 286, is reprinted by permission.

UNDERSTANDING McLUHAN

Newsweek: Unsigned Press Dep't. feature

Marshall McLuhan is the oracle of the New Communications. Industrialists travel from as far away as Japan and India for audiences in his disheveled, book-lined office at the University of Toronto. American executives pay him fees of up to $1,000 to come to their luncheons of stringy roast beef and preach his often impenetrable sermons on communications. His last two books, equally arcane, have nevertheless sold more than 55,000 copies so far in hardcover and paperback. And some critics have ranked him with such social commentators as Eliot, Spengler and David Riesman. "McLu is Archimedes," says San Francisco adman Howard Gossage. McLu's mail is just as effusive: "We shall build a new world and our children will stand on the stars," said one recent letter. "You have shown the way—the world will follow."

Just exactly how Dr. Herbert Marshall McLuhan has "shown the way" is never altogether clear. But, unquestionably, more and more advertising men, scientists, journalists and academicians—seeking an explanation for the computerized, instantaneous web of communications they've helped create but are still groping to understand—are willing to follow the 54-year-old Canadian.

'Very Difficult': A Cambridge graduate, literary critic and professor of English at Toronto for 21 years, McLuhan has set down his dizzying vision of the

From *Newsweek*, February 28, 1966, pp. 56–57. Copyright, Newsweek Inc., February, 1966.

world in *The Gutenberg Galaxy* (1962) and *Understanding Media: The Extensions of man* (1964). His irritating contradictions and sometimes preposterous philosophical fiats make him a somewhat unlikely guide. "I don't pretend to understand it," he says. "After all, my stuff is very difficult."

Indeed, McLuhan's reasoning is often so foggy that it has become a cliché to brand him "the communications expert who can't communicate." Reduced to its simplest terms—and they are by no means simple—McLuhan's thesis is that "the medium is the message." By that he means that the impact on society of any medium itself—whether print, radio, television—is as great, if not greater, than the effect of the medium's content.

In *Galaxy*, for example, he argues that the invention of movable type by Johann Gutenberg in the fifteenth century was responsible for the major characteristics of Western life from the Renaissance to the dawn of the "electric age." Print, maintains McLuhan, caused the linear fragmentation of society and thought; this produced everything from the serial thinking in mathematics to the chauvinistic thinking of nationalism. McLuhan also regards print as having traumatized mankind because it ended his natural tribal existence by imposing a special logic alien to the true nature of human experience. **Eye, Not Ear:** In other words, before "typographic man," society communicated verbally and learned by listening. With the invention of print, the eye—not the ear—suddenly became the principal sense. As a result thought and action became separated for the first time—because the act of reading slows down reaction.

In *Media*, McLuhan argues that man is returning to his pre-printing tribal ways because of the electric age. "As electrically contracted," he writes, "the globe is no more than a village. Electric speed in bringing all social and political functions together in a sudden implosion has heightened human awareness of responsibility to an intense degree. It is this implosive factor that alters the position of the Negro, the teen-ager . . . They can no longer be *contained,* in the political sense of limited association. They are now *involved* in our lives, as we in theirs, thanks to the electric media." In short, because of the incredible speed-up in communications made possible by electric technology, the separation between thought and action is narrowing and "retribalizing" the world.

McLuhan attempts to demonstrate all this by arbitrarily labeling media either "hot" or "cool." A medium is hot if it is well-filled with data and requires a minimum of involvement. Thus the book or newspaper is hot. Television, however, is cool because its hazy image provides a minimum of information and thus requires a kind of "tribal" involvement on the part of the viewer. Yet isn't a reader involved in a book? And why is radio hot instead of cool, like television? Such exasperating and unexplained inconsistencies repeatedly obscure McLuhan's work, yet he seems not to care. Once, after a lecture, one of his students rose to say that McLuhan had contradicted himself 28 times. "You're still thinking lineally," the professor replied.

If the bewildered student is "thinking lineally," McLuhan often seems to be talking in circles. "We can program the whole environment as a work of art," he says, adding a Beatle-like "Oh, yeah" for emphasis. Or he may offer: "Pavlov did not condition his dogs by little sounds—I just discovered this—he eliminated all sounds and then tinkled little bells—real cool."

Intellectual Cartwheels: Hot. Cool. The medium is the message. From that shorthand beginning, McLuhan turns intellectual cartwheels, spilling, like so much loose change, eccentric ideas and maddening literary references. ("Francis Bacon never tired of contrasting hot and cool prose" or "Carroll drove a fantasia of discontinuous space-and-time that anticipated Kafka, Joyce and Eliot.")

Recently, seventeen Canadian executives—including two presidents and five vice presidents—paid $150 apiece for the privilege of a two-day seminar with McLuhan in Toronto. Among other things, [56–57] the voluble professor told them that color television will change the environment, that their children would love to learn Chinese because it would allow them to get involved, like in a comic book, and that Bell Telephone doesn't know what a telephone is. "Such seminars," says McLuhan matter-of-factly, "take a great deal out of you because you're dealing with people who don't know what you're talking about."

What McLuhan is talking about, apparently, is his ukase that "the medium is the message." Because they are ordinary mortals, executives at Bell Telephone think the instrument is something on which you call your mother when the rates go down after 6 p.m. But not McLuhan. "Our conventional response to all media, namely that it is how they are used that counts, is the numb stance of the technological idiot," he says. "For the 'content' of a medium is like the juicy piece of meat carried by the burglar to distract the watchdog of the mind." The "truth" about the telephone is that it's cool.

Brush-off: There are no buts. Like a television set, McLuhan transmits a lightning stream of ideas that allows no interruption for elucidation. He doesn't like questions. They get in the way. This brush-off, of course, is part of the McLuhan mystique. During lunch one day last week in Toronto, he mused at one point: "I wonder who's going to be . . ." In mid-sentence he stopped, gazed into his minestrone for a moment and then decided. "No, I'm not going to tell you."

His refusal to play by the logical rules of the literary Establishment infuriates some critics. "He writes like a mad jackdaw," says Canadian writer Lister Sinclair. And after hearing him transfix a group of American businessmen, an observer from Oxford said: "It was rather unpleasant to watch. All that uncritical adulation. He was so hypnotic that their eyes were glazing over." McLuhan is unfazed. "The academic community," he says, "has a huge vested interest in existing knowledge—a discovery is a disaster."

Not all the literary-academic community, however, is so hard on McLuhan. Reviewing *Media* in *The New Yorker* last year, critic Harold Rosenberg concluded that it "is a concrete testimonial (illuminating, as modern art illuminates, through disassociation and regrouping) to the belief that man is certain to find his footing in the new world he is in the process of creating."

Good News: McLuhan is optimistic about the new technology and he accepts pop culture without a sneer. "The ads are by far the best part of any magazine or newspaper," he writes. "Ads are news. What is wrong with them is that they are always good news." This stance has turned him into as much a fad as philosopher.

At the University of British Columbia, the faculty—in the name of McLuhan—set up a sensory fun house in which professors walk through a maze of plastic sheets hung from the ceiling of an armory while slide projectors splashed images on floor and ceiling and loudspeakers blared weird noises. They also rigged up a "sculptured wall"—a frame covered with a stretch fabric behind which a girl writhed. The idea: Touch the girl and learn all about tactile communication. In San Francisco last month, McLuhan was invited (but did not go) to a three-day sensorium at Longshoremen's Hall that included nude projections, a God box and jazz mice (*Newsweek,* Feb. 7). And last week, at the 3rd Rail Time/Space Theater off-off Broadway in New York's East Village, a series of happenings happened under the title, "McLuhan Megillah." "I'm not inclined to favor these things," says McLuhan. "Temperamentally, I'm a stodgy conservative."

Far from the crackle and pop he has created, McLuhan goes quietly about his academic business. Besides teaching three courses (modern drama and poetry, modern literary criticism, and media and society), he finds time to lecture to the alumni association, telling them the same things he tells magazine promotion men in New York. Even the jokes are unaltered. "What is purple and hums?" "An electric grape." "Why does it hum?" "Because it doesn't know the words." No story line. Tribal man to tribal man. Involvement. Cool. Clear?

As director of the University of Toronto's Centre for Culture and Technology, McLuhan is currently overseeing a "sensory profile" of Toronto's citizens to test their sensory preferences. "We'll use quantitative statistical methods because we wish to satisfy the conventional approach of the social scientists—but there are lots better ways of doing it." What are they? "I can't tell you," the professor answers, turning up the mystique. The answer, he says, will be in a book called *Space in Poetry and Painting.* McLuhan is also working on two other books, *The Future of the Book?* and *From Cliché to Archetype,* which he says is an analysis of what happens when a new environment "goes around" an old one.

Poet: "Marshall," says a former colleague, "claims he's a scientist. I've never agreed with that, I think he's a poet. You can't argue with him, just as you can't argue with Tennyson or Browning." Certainly McLuhan's scholarly outlook is poetic. "If you don't have a point of view," he says "you can go around making all kinds of discoveries. People who have a point of view are always in despair. Being without one is much more fun than going around being a nineteenth-century liberal."

Cool? Absolutely. But not nearly so cool as McLuhan's ultimate observation. "I don't agree or disagree," he says, "with anything I say myself." [*57*]

Newsweek points out that McLuhan is attracting some professed disciples, perhaps even some lunatic fringe. Which of his ideas give rise to the "sensory fun house," the "sculptured wall," the "God box," and the "jazz mice" mentioned on page 57 of the article? In your opinion are these "happenings" logical extensions of McLuhan's ideas?

MEDIUM IS THE MESSAGE

Wesley C. Meierhenry

Such statements as "the medium is the message," and suggestions that a medium can be either "hot" or "cold," have been labeled mere nonsense by some, while others feel that they are the words of a genius. There are even more people in the media field who ought to have some idea as to what Marshall McLuhan is writing and speaking, who reject his ideas.

This reviewer would like to suggest that there are a number of things which add credence to McLuhan's theories about communication. In the first place, it has been obvious in such a field as mathematics that the idea of straight lines and right angles taught in Euclidean geometry have greatly retarded both mathematical developments as important scientific developments around the world and particularly in the United States. In other words, the teaching and belief that there are certain fixed ideas in mathematics which are of a straight line variety put mathematical and scientific thinking into a straight jacket.

WESLEY C. MEIERHENRY is Assistant Dean and Professor of Education at the University of Nebraska, and served during 1966 as President of the National Education Association's Department of Audio-Visual Instruction.

From *Educational Screen and Audiovisual Guide*, March, 1966, p. 26. Reprinted by permission.

McLuhan's writings suggest that the same thing has happened with language. We have permitted language structure and word meanings to so freeze and crystalize what is transmitted. Print medium, which is considered "hot" by McLuhan, he considers as presenting a great deal of information but involving the reader little in any kind of intellectual experience. As McLuhan suggests, there is a whole cult which has grown up around maintaining the status quo in verbal symbols even though these symbols are now so far removed from reality that their impact and significance is lost for most persons.

For those of us who have worked in the medium of television, we are aware that a motion picture shown on a screen is quite a different experience from the same motion picture shown via television. The failure to understand this difference has led many educators including media specialists to raise the question as to why utilize television when you can do the same thing with motion pictures. Without trying to explain what McLuhan means when he says that "the medium is the message," it is evident that the television image projected toward the viewer is a different image with different qualities than the reflection of light from a motion picture screen.

One of the most critical problems facing media specialists has been the one of determining which type of medium should be used in order to present a certain experience for a specific purpose. It has been evident for some time that such simple explanations as "you have to have concrete experiences" is an inadequate justification for the use of any media, let alone any specific audiovisual device. Therefore, it seems to many that of all people, media specialists ought to be studying and examining such works as *Understanding Media* in order to determine for themselves if his speculations do not have a great deal of promise. The reader will have to be content with incomplete formulations at this point, but the most important matter is to examine his theories and to arrive at some judgments about their validity. Extensive curriculum formulations using some of McLuhan's ideas, which are underway, indicate the possibility of their practical application to classroom situations.   [26]

This brief critique of McLuhan's theories is almost unreservedly favorable toward them. Are there reasons which make this evaluation (from this source) something you might expect?

McLUHANISMS

Moira Walsh

I was highly entertained for 90 minutes the other night by a program on New York's educational TV channel on which Marshall McLuhan was spouting "McLuhanisms," as a panel of four brainy but frustrated questioners were trying unsuccessfully to pin down his soaring but frequently impenetrable and seemingly contradictory flights of thought. McLuhan is the University of Toronto English professor who is suddenly "in" as a theoretician and prophet of mass communications. His most widely quoted aphorism is: "The medium is the message," by which I presume he means that the existence and widespread use of a medium in themselves exert a greater influence on a society than does the content. McLuhan never explains himself, however, except by unburdening himself of ten more theories each equally in need of explanation. "I don't have a point of view," he says blandly. Or again: "I don't agree or disagree with anything I say myself."

I do not at all mean to deride Mr. McLuhan. I think he is a shrewd showman who is using an effective means to get a widespread hearing for important even if not yet fully distilled ideas. On the program, he furnished a further clue to his method and purpose when he repeated several times: "I merely regard myself as a probe." I believe he also said that our best hope for further illumination is to look to the artists (which would seem to acknowledge the importance of content). As I listened—and I say this at the risk of getting bogged down in a point of view myself—McLuhan suddenly began to make a lot of sense to me, especially with regard to a group of current and upcoming off-beat films that I had been mulling over in my mind.

MOIRA WALSH is film critic for *America*.

From *America: the National Catholic Weekly Review,* May 28, 1966, pp. 784–785. Reprinted with permission from *America: The National Catholic Weekly Review*, 106 W. 56 St., N.Y., N.Y. 10019. © 1967 American Press Inc.

I take it that McLuhan, by his general stance, intends to convey the following points: [784–785]

1. Our communications technology—coupled, I might add, with such other factors as affluence and the failure of theology to keep pace with technology—has changed us and our world to a degree we don't begin to grasp. (For the benefit of any heresy hunters, I am not suggesting that theology should accommodate itself to the modern world; I am suggesting, rather, that it should confront the modern world   instead of the 19th or the 16th century, as it all too often does.)

2. Our best brains had better address themselves to pondering the resulting problems, with McLuhan himself playing the deliberately obscure gadfly and court jester to make sure that nobody settles for facile answers that do not answer.

3. Some valuable insights into today's actualities can be found by observing the works of the mass-media artists.

Like most McLuhanisms, the third observation can be taken at least two ways. For example, we can deduce a lot about today's mass audience, for whom the medium probably is the message, by looking at The Sound of Music or Madam X, or TV's "Batman," "Bonanza" and "Beverly Hillbillies." Or we can watch a few real artists (intermingled, no doubt, with some bogus or would-be ones) struggling to convey some of the new realities of life in "the electric age" (another McLuhan phrase). It was this second meaning of the observation that caught my attention, because I was trying to put into words a common denominator I had sensed in that already mentioned group of odd-ball films.   [785]

AN ARCHITECTURE
FOR THE
ELECTRONIC AGE

John M. Johansen

Most of us for some time have been aware of the field of cybernetics and the vast effects of the current electronic revolution. Norbert Wiener, in his book *The Human Use of Human Beings* (1954), presented these matters most vividly. Since that time electronics has made possible accelerated development of computers for data processing, worldwide communication systems by Telstar, and guidance of weapons and space craft. Already several newspapers have installed computer typesetting; soon we will have three-dimensional TV, and at the Massachusetts Institute of Technology a team is developing a nation wide computer network that will make all knowledge, whether stored or presently recorded, instantly available anywhere. Publishing will almost surely undergo a radical transformation; the book will be replaced by research packages assembled to suit specific needs. The takeover by datamation of traditional methods is borne out by the recent news that the Radio Corporation of America has bought out Random House: a very signifi-

JOHN M. JOHANSEN'S architectural designs include the Robert Hutchings Goddard library at Clark University, the United States Embassy in Dublin, Ireland, and Clowes Hall, the opera house in Indianapolis. He has taught at Yale, Harvard, M.I.T. and Pennsylvania and is now an adjunct professor at Columbia.

From *The American Scholar*, Summer, 1966, pp. 461–471. Reprinted by permission.

cant event. In addition, cybernetics has already had its influence on teaching, psychology, language and mathematics.

In each period of well-established cultural achievement, there is apt to be a consistency in the thinking and experience of the arts, science and philosophy. In his book, *Music, History and Ideas,* Hugo Leichtentritt points out that in the seventeenth century, [461–462] for example, as the concept of infinity became widely accepted for the first time in scientific thinking, it was also expressed in the endless vistas of the Baroque painters and sculptors, and in music by the elaborate and boundless developments by composers of the fugue and concerto. Although it may be disputed whether such consistencies in any time were conscious or unconscious, the fact remains that consistencies are indeed found and that for us today there are likely to be similar consistencies. It is with this background in mind that I am prompted, after reading Marshall McLuhan's *Understanding Media,* to examine the new aspects of experience predicated by the electronic revolution, and find their effects, established or predictable, upon our architecture. While certain of our architects who seem not to be aware of the present need reorientation, other architects, who sense the current change, deserve encouragement, reassurance, and a cause around which to rally their valuable talents.

The effects of the electronic age upon architecture may be felt in the following ways:

First, the overwhelming presence of electronic devices will lead to a degree of imitation in the design of our buildings. We witnessed this happening in the 1920's and 1930's when Le Corbusier romanticized and imitated the machine and industrial products. Mies Van der Rohe expresses the industrial processes or rolled steel in the application of standard sections to the facades of his buildings; and Walter Gropius made his great contribution by bringing design talent to manufacturing and building methods. But with the passing of the industrial age, we may now expect an architecture conceived more as a computer, of components rigged on armatures or chassis connected by circulation harnesses. The use itself of electronic terms conjures up new mental pictures of architecture. There should be a new kinetic quality in this manner of assemblage that will be more convincing than buildings that imitated moving mechanical parts yet did not themselves move. Interchangeability of parts with different circuit patterns for various performances may suggest that very different building types, the house, the high-rise office building and the theater, will be assembled of different combinations of the same components or sub-assemblies.   [462–464]

Habitable chambers may be arranged not for closest physical connection, but according to most practical circuiting. Circuit patterns, whether for public use or mechanical equipment, will be shown vividly coursing through, overlaid or circumventing one another as one now sees them in the rear view of a TV cabinet. Intercommunication systems themselves, although less conspicuous, will be given expression. *Plug-in City,* the science-fiction proposal by Peter Cook in 1964 in England, is certainly a bold effort to state our environment in new terms. In this design, buildings old and new were to be plugged into, or removed, at will from a vast raceway of service conduits providing power, water, sewage and transportation. Here, however, the value of this liberating idea derives from a sense of city organization rather than from imitation. So although this influence through direct imitation may be the most readily apparent visually, it is probably the least significant or valuable.

The second influence will be felt through the use of the computer. Already scaled drawings are made from architectural data. Even perspectives are constructed when a computer is given plan and elevation. However, more influential in the design process will be the instantaneous assembly, organization analysis and conclusion of controlling conditions or determining design factors which can relieve us of endless calculation, research and comparative study. The effect will be to make the building in process of design as malleable as clay, which can be manipulated and recomposed or reorganized before our eyes. The aid then is more in planning; the architect will see alternate solutions of building types, configurations and functional organizations simultaneously and instantaneously, by programming different design data into the computer. This will also free the architect's mind, we hope, for greater aesthetic evaluation and judgment, or intuitive flow of creative ability.

Third, architecture must constantly be thought of in new terms that have force and meaning for us today. Such a term is "Cyborg," which may be defined as the entity resulting from the application of attachments to the human body of any mechanical or electronic device, to extend and enlarge the performance of its [464–465] physical or mental faculties. The computer as an extension of the brain is of course the most revolutionary. But why cannot the buildings we live in be considered "extensions of man"—of their inhabitants? The control of natural or artificial light relieves diaphragm adjustment for the eye. The floor platforms and the elevator assist the legs in setting our position in space. The protective walls and roof supplement the limited and inadequate protection provided by our epidermis. Air conditioning is an addition in extension of the nasal functions of constant air temperature control and the cilia hairs which filter out dust. The concept of "building and man as Cyborg" may well free our thinking architecturally; the extension of man as grafted or as portable equipment and the more fully equipped building may soon be indistinguishable. Then again, as we can already see in terms of self-opening doors and fully programmed temperature control, the building itself will eventually develop into a sensory organism with feedback and consciousness of its own performance.

A fourth influence will be electronic communication itself used within or between buildings. The telephone obviously has already decentralized cities, administrative and government agencies, and much of light industry. In a similar way, the parts of buildings will be decentralized. As McLuhan says, the implosion due to electronic communication will cause an explosion of population and physical plant. Within the building, rooms and departments will be more loosely assembled, as is already true of one college in the West. It is fully equipped for communications, and can provide one hundred and thirty-six lectures simultaneously at any time at any student study on the campus. This arrangement replaces the lecture halls with dormitory rooms or individual student study cubicles possessing total reception. The library will be metamorphosed into a single computer room with limited staff space, which will receive data from its own tape library or from any other library or fact-storage center; it will select, edit, xerox and transmit written and pictorial material.

Generally then, with proximity of building elements no longer necessary for reasons of communication, the building design will be more loosely conceived. The long conduit will replace the short [465–466] corridor. The new functional configuration will be found to be consistent to or sympathetic with the aesthetic configuration, which for satisfaction of our reconditioned psyche will follow its own process.

However, aside from the planning and organizational aspects of our buildings, the architectural expression is of particular interest and concern. The fifth influence will be the most subtle but the most inevitable of all: that of our reconditioned minds and senses. The architect will undergo—has already partially undergone—a retraining of his perceptive habits, his psyche, his methods of thinking, his language, the relative acuteness of his senses and his aesthetic values. The influence upon him will be partially subliminal, the change in his design partially unconscious. He will produce sooner or later, inevitably, a new architecture.

The sixth and last influence, as I see it, will also be upon aesthetic content, but will be governed by conscious awareness of our changing technology and environment. From what has already been said, it is rather unlikely that a number of the fanciful tacks of current architectural expression will find a place. Historic revival—neoclassic and neobaroque opera houses and museums, neomedieval castles to house factories, neo-Gothic dormitories, and the "mono-pitch school"—is out-of-date. The air terminal that looks like a bird: the "architecture of imagery" is out-of-date. And since the mechanical age has been replaced by the electronic age, buildings styled after machines are out-of-date. Those who do not derive their forms from the experience of our present environment upon our changing habits of perception are out-of-date. Those who approach architecture from an academic or fine arts or "master work" point of view, the "beauty seekers" and the formalists, have no place. As Wiener observed, a rigid deterministic world has given over to one of contingency and organic incompleteness and probability. We can therefore assume that perfectionism and rationalism are irrelevant. For architects oriented in these directions offer society no interpretation or reconciliation with our technological environment—instead, merely an escape. For, as Mr. McLuhan says, we must first understand our environment if we are to control it.   [466–467]

In the mechanical age, action and reaction were not closely connected in time, response was slow, involvement limited, consequences of our actions unreal. In the electronic age, action and reaction are almost simultaneous. "We have extended the central nervous system itself in a global embrace, abolishing time and space," writes McLuhan. This separation of action and reaction or consequence formerly meant noninvolvement. Now, with the technological extension of the self including all mankind, we necessarily participate, and in depth, in the consequences of every action. The theater of the absurd dramatizes the dilemma of Western man who appears not to be involved with the consequences of his actions. The electric speed of bringing all social and political functions together in sudden implosion has heightened human awareness to an intense degree; and the partial, specialized or detached point of view will not serve in the electronic age. The "all-inclusive image" prevails. Wholeness, empathy and depth of awareness is of our time.

The images of the electronic world are continuous, simultaneous, nonclassified or noncodified. They run counter to the traditional Platonic compartmentation of ideas and things, and counter to the analytic and rational processes of thought. Images are abstracted and require the viewer's involvement and participation for their complete transference. They represent a continual flow of data, not measured or measurable. This process has been described as a "mosaic" effect of composite impressions producing a total comprehension. Many effects and impressions are absorbed by the viewer instantaneously, involving a fusion of all the senses. The spectator becomes part of the system or process and must supply the connections. He is the screen upon which images are projected. Images as on TV are low definition, therefore require high participation. In this sense, the new experience is anti-"square," since "squares" don't get involved. It is "cool," in that the message is implicit. The new media deal in slang rather than in eloquence, since slang is the outgrowth of firsthand experience and the immediate scene; not restated, refined, edited, but real. No detached point of view, whether of physical position or state of mind, is longer possible.   [467–468]

Now we may attempt to restate these experiences and attitudes in architectural terms. If we have been reconditioned to an intensely heightened awareness of places and events, the viewer will expect all parts and aspects of buildings to be made known, to be immediately comprehensible, not as a composite impression but as an all-inclusive image. Buildings will reveal themselves totally. They will clearly express their elements, functions and processes. The viewer will identify with them, feel an empathy with them. "Package design" is out-of-date, and there will be a conscious attempt to force an expression of elements and processes to the exterior, or by pulling apart the elements to allow the viewer to see in depth within, possibly to inner buildings. We are not interested in the epidermis or skin, only, but insist on knowing the mesoderm and the endoderm; that is, the bones and internal organs.

Intercommunication systems within the building will further allow the pulling apart of elements, relieving the current prosaic and boring compactness and density in favor of a vastly more interesting form—space composition effected by the multiple impact of many parts.

The "facade" in the traditional sense, no matter how richly sculpted or how irregular or bold, will disappear in favor of separate habitable enclosures posed freely in space. If it can be said at all that there will still be a facade, it will be a composite of all facets of all enclosures, their four walls, roof and soffit. To use Mr. McLuhan's words, it will become a "mosaic" of facades, a bombardment of the eye by many images. Already I find among the drawings of my current designs, not only the four exterior elevations, but many more sheets devoted to the interior elevations; the inward and side-facing facets.

In this heightened human awareness which the viewer will be trained to feel, occupants will not be lost from view when in the building, but their infusion through space will be seen from outside as well as in. Or, if occupants themselves are not in view, the loci of their coursing will be felt by the shaping of the habitable spaces and passages; we will feel in the enclosed forms the loci of their movements.   [468–469]

The rational, analytic aspects of architecture will give over to a nonclassified accretion of elements in continuous uninterrupted flow without any particular sequence. As modern physics no longer sees a universe in which everything happens precisely according to law, which is compact, tightly organized and in which everything is governed by strict causality, so too, our impressions will not be ordered, controlled or in sequence. Impact will derive from group effects, and on every view, the mosaic or staccato images will present themselves. Views will not be selected or limited, but will include unplanned peripheral sensations; adjacent, oblique, marginal experiences; adjunct images of other functions, structures or mechanics. Perhaps the view of a stairway, for example, will be inseparable in a composite view of other elements, or may itself be purposely broken into multiple images.

As buildings become looser assemblages, less finite and static, they will become volatile, will reach out and fuse with adjoining buildings and lose their identity in a continual froth of spaceform. It would appear that the current concept of the city as one continuous building is borne out. The individual building appears to be many; the campus, neighborhood or city may in fact be one. The total architectural environment, as McLuhan has said, will be a mythological world in which all things are connected in the human mind and experience, as opposed to the Aristotelian classified world of knowledge and exact definition. We are now closer to the flux, continuous currents, coalescence and change of the earlier philosopher Heraclitus. If architectural elements are not defined or codified, recognizable symbols will not be used, and there will be no fixed architectural language.

The experience we derive from our buildings will be drawn from a fusion of the senses: the impact swift, instant, condensed, total; the message immediate, direct, possibly crude, unedited, unrehearsed, but real. Textures of exposed finishes, for example, allow us to feel with our eyes from a distance; or we see with our sense of touch.

Our designs will use architectural slang. Eloquence in architecture, now so much in vogue, will be out. Slang will be used because as in speech, it is direct, vivid, brash, effective, sometimes inge-[469–470]niously poetic, and has always to do with immediacy in time and situation; with firsthand experience.

This is indeed typical of modern communications. Architects will make known through their design the fact that they have had immediate participation in "pre-living" their buildings, while occupants will in actual "re-living" read back the firsthand experience. Like the computer, the building has "memory," by which previous conditions can be recalled. The architect will reveal his processes of design, and the contractor's processes of construction—may in fact show the building in stages, even incomplete or unresolved in order to allow the viewer to participate in the processes. This is "cool architecture," that is, low definition, high participation, as in electronic communications to-day. The viewer is required or encouraged to extend his powers to "make the connection," as McLuhan says; to fill in that additional content which is only implied. Low definition will mean that the architectural expression is implicit, not explicit, understated, not overstated, suggested, not hammered home.

Akin to this characteristic is the coming insistence that the architect and occupants will not be detached from the realities of architecture, in the sense that they will not take a detached or contrived point of view, be it academic, preciously professional, or one of personal isolation. Since we cannot detach ourselves from conditions and events as they really are anywhere on the world—or off—we are in fact there. We no longer will have patience with the hypothetical, the make-believe, the isolated event out of natural context, with sophistries, stunts or mannered poses. Architecturally this would condemn historic revival, literary reference, moralizing, academic or fine arts attitudes.

As electronic communications have made it possible to assume a station point anywhere in time and space, our way of viewing our buildings will change for all time. Not only is the fixed axial reference point of the Renaissance out-of-date, but so also is the "Space Time," or moving, station point conceived by Siegfried Giedion, which might be said to represent the mechanical age of the wheel. Now I would make the observation that we will have a new station point of the electronic age: one that is multiple and [470–471] simultaneous, a "simul-station." Obviously we don't change our physical position within a building as instantaneously as we follow an intercontinental discussion by Telstar. However, we may now be trained to project ourselves into positions, to identify ourselves with many other stations and circumstances. Buildings then will be designed by architects who can project themselves in this way, and for occupants who will easily respond with this same developed faculty of identification in space. Applied literally, any or all station points, fixed positions or loci of moving occupants will be identified and expressed. Rooms or other spaces can be designed to suggest by scale and form, their use; passages, tunnels, bridges, tubes, troughs, arches, platforms can be so vividly expressed as to make us extend ourselves in space, as it were.

Finally, Mr. McLuhan's observation that "the medium is the message" has its parallel in architecture. This simply means that the influence of the vehicle by which the message is sent is greater than that of the message itself. Correspondingly, the building as an instrument of service has greater effect upon our lives than the functional service itself. To any serious architect this is hardly new. We should expect today, however, that this will be recognized more than ever. Further, we can fulfill our social purpose by designing buildings not as "consumer commodities," or as "diet for the privileged," as McLuhan says, but as instruments for explaining and helping all to understand and adjust to our often bewildering environment of rapid technical change. Great and responsible artists and thinkers in all times both have been affected by their technology, and have helped to find a meaning in it for their society. It should certainly be expected of the architect today that he be aware of the vast growth and influence of the electronic revolution, that his perceptive habits be retrained, and that his architecture in turn be a consistent and valid expression of his times.   [471]

This article is chiefly interesting, perhaps, because it demonstrates the wide acceptance and interest given to McLuhan's theories in unexpected and seemingly unrelated fields. Read Prof. Johansen's discussion with a view toward discovering why an architect (speaking qua architect) finds the message of McLuhan so intriguing.

AGAINST McLUHAN

Benjamin DeMott

A marvy year for Marshall McLuhan, take it all in all. Tom Wolfe compared him with Darwin, Freud and Einstein, Susan Sontag said in public she thought he was swell. London saw him as an epoch maker and intellectual frontiersman (*Encounter* and the *Times Lit Supp*), and *The New Yorker* reviewed him rapt. What is more, academe—after a period of sitting tall but silent on his bandwagon—began talking out loud about his work. (One example: a recent international convocation of savants at Southern Illinois University spent days discussing the "communications revolution" in open session —mainly in McLuhanian terms.) Success being what it is, wasps and carpers were doubtless waiting for the man a piece or two up the road. But no amount of carping could obscure the facts of his rise. Overnight the author of *Understanding Media* had emerged as Midcult's Mr. Big. And ahead of him lay a shot at mass adulation and the title of Everyman's Favorite Brain.

The secret of this ascent isn't instantly visible to casual reportorial eyes. Marshall McLuhan is no literary old pro blessed with a power base and a rich experience at name-making. An English professor for most of his working life (Wisconsin, Assumption, St. Louis), he moved on from teaching only quite recently to his present post as director of Toronto University's Center for Culture and Technology. And despite long years in the classroom, he has no credit reserves in the trade—no stretch of unheralded, scholarly

BENJAMIN DeMOTT is Professor of English at Amherst College; his articles appear frequently in *The American Scholar* and *Harper's Magazine*.

From *Esquire,* August, 1966, pp. 71–73. Reprinted by permission of *Esquire Magazine,* © 1966 by Esquire Inc.

labor of the kind fellow professionals pant to puff. McLuhan avoided book-writing until he was forty. His first work, *The Mechanical Bride* (1951), was an analysis of the sex-power-horsepower ploy by which two generations of ad men have sold us our annual car. (Not much there for the Modern Language Association.) And after the *Bride* appeared, the author resumed his silence as a bookman and maintained it for another full decade and more.

Nor can it be said—still on the mystery of the McLuhanian boom—that here is a case of a late-blooming stylist, somebody who had to turn fifty to turn a slick phrase. In terms of style, this flower has yet to bud. Marshall McLuhan's present reputation rests on two books—*The Gutenberg Galaxy* (1962) and *Understanding Media* (1964); both are sometimes stimulating, but neither is pretty prose. One problem is that of opacity (McLuhan's pages are dense with stoppers like "sense ratios," "interiorizations of alphabetic technology," and the like). Another is that the favored method of organization has a bit too much in common with that of an impresario squirrel. *The Gutenberg Galaxy* looks gathered, not written: a pasteup from a hundred histories of math, political theology, nationalism, and fur-trading, and from a thousand "other authorities." (Walt Whitman and Walt Whitman Rostow, Cicero and Father Ong, de Chardin and de Beauvoir, Rabelais, Riesman and Shakespeare, the Opies, Powys and Poe—name your hero, he surely is here.) The man's work reads for pages at a stretch like a Marlboro clearance ad:

"Clagett [author of *The Science of Mechanics in the Middle Ages*] presents the treatise of Nicholas of Oresme *On the Configurations of Qualities* in which Oresme says: 'Every measurable thing except numbers is conceived in the manner of continuous quantity.' This recalls us to the Greek world in which as Tobias D. Dantzig points out in his *Number: The Language of Science* (pp. 141-2): 'The attempt to apply rational arithmetic to a problem in geometry resulted in the first crisis in the history of mathematics. . . .' Number is the dimension of tactility, as Ivins explained in *Art and Geometry* (p. 7)," etc.

Furthermore, the two leading articles of this thinker's gospel can't be called easy to grasp. The first is a theory of culture which contends that communications media impose a wide range of assumptions "subliminally." (The form of the media, not the content, structures men's values, according to McLuhan; the form also determines the content of the senses and the very look of the world.) The second is an interpretation of history which claims that revolutionary transformations of media occur periodically through the ages, and that one such transformation is in progress right now. (A five-hundred-year-old "typographic and mechanical" era is ending and an "electric galaxy of events" has begun; the new "galaxy" offers experiences of simultaneity and heightened interdependence in which traditional values—privacy, independence and so on—are engulfed.) Neither of these items is wholly lacking in interest, and McLuhan's historical chapters are often enlivened by canny, comprehensible remarks. But the key idea, to repeat—that of the centrality of *form* in the media as the determinant of social structure and individual minds—is to most men unfamiliar and abstract. An author who makes it into his dogma would ordinarily be ill-advised to brood overmuch about fame.

That Marshall McLuhan is now in position (if he chooses) to brood about nothing else owes a little to his skill with the magic of the modern. "Baby, it's what's happening" is a regularly sounded ground theme in his work. The basic language is video-mesh, circuits and data processing. Injunctions to *Think Modern!* appear on page after page. ("We still have our eyes fixed on the rearview mirror looking firmly and squarely at the job that is receding into the nineteenth-century past.") The right names—Cage, Camp, Bond, Van Der Beek, the whole of the switched-on mob— are fingered throughout like sacred medals. The Farthest-out Art—electric landscapes, Pop Happenings or whatever—is treated either as classic or already passé, and idols of the hour are probed intensely, like important neglected codes:

"The Beatles stare at us with eloquent messages of changed sensory modes for our whole population, and yet people merely think how whimsical, how bizarre, how grotesque. The Beatles are trying to tell us by the anti-environment they present just how we have changed and in what ways."

Old times and old-timers do turn up, as indicated—especially in *The Gutenberg Galaxy.* But even they swim into the reader's ken to a definite R-and-R beat. (Who was Christopher Marlowe? The man, says McLuhan, turning dead Kit hummingly on, who "set up a national P.A. system of blank verse." Who was Heidegger? A cat who "surfboards along on the electronic wave." What were the Middle Ages? *The Late Show* for the Renaissance.")

Among other crowd-pleasing elements in the McLuhan equation, the author's literary persona rates a word. At some moments [71–72] this writer plays Inside Dopester (I called the Kennedy-Nixon election, he announces, I knew exactly why Jack would win). At others he's simply a Scrappy Little Professorial Guy. Enemies as various as George Bernard Shaw ("he lost his nerve") and General Sarnoff ("the voice of the current somnambulism") are worked over in his books; Lewis Mumford, Arnold Toynbee and dozens more are patronized, and English profs ("literary brahmins") come off naturally as jerks. The author also does a turn as Kitsch Cynic, mocker of Goodie-good types—and it is here that he shows his best stuff, speaking again and again with the clarity of last night's knowing cabby or this week's issue of *Time.* People who are easily shocked give him the laughing fits. ("The historian Daniel Boorstin was scandalized by the fact that celebrity in our information age was not due to a person's having done anything but simply to his being known for being well-known. Professor Parkinson is scandalized that the structure of human work now seems to be quite independent of any job to be done.") And he likes interrupting the argument to defend the innocent guilty and to lean on moralizing twerps:

"So great was the audience participation in the quiz shows that the directors of the show were prosecuted as con men. Moreover, press and radio ad interests, bitter about the success of the new TV medium, were delighted to lacerate the flesh of their rivals. Of course, the riggers had been blithely unaware of the nature of their medium, and had given it the movie treatment of intense realism, instead of the softer mythic focus proper to TV. Charles Van Doren merely got clobbered as an innocent bystander, and the whole investigation elicited no insight into the nature or effects of the TV medium. Regrettably, it simply provided a field day for the earnest moralizers. A moral point of view too often serves as a substitute for understanding in technological matters."

A literary self that amounts to an amalgam of Bogie and Dr. Huer might not seem everybody's dish; but the thing obviously meets a felt need.*

And the same can be said about McLuhan's gamesmanly ploys as a historian. A specialist in unnoticed causes, this scholar never delves into a historical situation without emerging with "major factors" nobody quite hit on before. The handling in *Understanding Media* of the advent of philanthropy a century ago is typical of his cunning moves. Why did "even the hardiest of the rich dwindle into modest ways of timid service to mankind"? Because of the invention of the telegraph, McLuhan explains—and does not stop for questions. What is the key factor in the Southern civil-rights struggle? The internal-combustion engine. ("The real integrator or leveler of white and Negro in the South was the private car and the truck, not the expression of moral points of view.") Why were the Jews murdered by the million? Because radio came before TV. ("Had TV come first there would have been no Hitler at all.") The talent in question isn't the kind treasured by trad historians, but it is what is called provocative and universally pleasing to wits.

In the end it won't do, though, to pretend that Marshall McLuhan's secret is a matter either of mere wit or mere newsiness or mere literary self-creation. The truth is more complicated—more painful—than that. Grasping it means facing up to the dozen different kinds of stratagem by which this author empties facts and agonies from the world he thinks of as "Now." Some of these stratagems depend on tricks of futuristic projection, displacements of present-day reality which treat desperate hopes as facts. (Write that "the real integrator of the white and Negro *was*," and you imply that the struggle has already been won.) Other tricks include sudden weird tonal abstractions— see the flip comment about TV and Hitler—deadenings of feeling and sympathy that distance holocaust and shame. Still others con the reader into a frankly theatrical view of experience, a vision that insulates him from immediacies and shows forth all life as a production or stunt. Taken singly, needless to say, none of the stratagems would rank as original, amazing or troubling; taken in concert they have powerful and obnoxious effect. The complaint isn't that Professor McLuhan puts together a thoroughly fantastic account of the situation of contemporary man; it is that he sets himself up, speaking bluntly, as the constituted pardoner of this age—a purveyor of perfect absolution for every genuine kind of modern guilt.

Do I chide myself for trivial failings—my laxness as a parent, my sins

---

* There are occasional bad breakdowns or inconsistencies in this public literary mask. McLuhan stands forth usually as a man quite unafflicted by any sense of inferiority. "I am in the position of Louis Pasteur," he tells his reader repeatedly. Yet the word *humility* comes not infrequently to his lips. For example: his address at Southern Illinois, which began with a summary of likenesses between Marshall McLuhan and Plato, ended with the assertion that "I really feel shatteringly humble." It was a sequel that left some alert listeners confused.

of permissiveness, my failure to exact respect from the kids? Do I worry about rearing layabouts incapable of work or thought?—Oh but come *on,* says Marshall McLuhan, a benign forgiving face, the truth is your children are grand:

"Some people have estimated that the young person, the infant and the small child, growing up in our world today works harder than any child ever did in any previous human environment—only the work he has to perform is that of data processing. The small child in twentieth-century America does more data processing—more work—than any child in any previous culture in the history of the world. . . . We haven't really cottoned on to the fact that our children work furiously, processing data in an electrically structured world. . . ."

Do I feel bad about my *own* laziness, say—my own unending belt of mindlessness in front of TV? Situation comedy, secret agents, mean mockeries of domestic life. . . . Has my intellectual appetite gone dead? My mind turned slush?—Forget it, says this Constant Comforter. The medium is the message, and whatever you think you are doing in front of the box, the fact is you're being expanded-extended-improved. "TV has opened the doors of audile-tactile perception to the nonvisual world of spoken languages and food and the plastic arts. . . ." TV has transformed "American innocence into depth sophistication, independently of 'content'. . . ." TV has "changed our sense-lives and our mental processes. It has created a taste for all experience in *depth.* . . . And oddly enough, with the demand for the depth, goes the demand for crash-programming [in education]. Not only deeper, but further, into all knowledge has become the normal popular demand since TV."

Or am I bugged by my pointless affluence, my guilt about having fat on my hide [72–73] at a time when sores of starvation are the rule for hundreds of millions elsewhere?—But don't be *silly,* says my adviser, you're being ridiculous again. You're mired in outmoded thinking, you're the victim of moldy figs. Oh, yes, we've all heard about the underdeveloped nations, the "ascent into history," the necessity of hard labor, the problems of locating resources, building factories, educating work forces, creating credit systems and the like. But *we* know, don't we now, *we* know that we have it within us practically at this instant to do the miracle of our choice whenever we choose:

"The computer will be in a position to carry out orchestrated programming for the sensory life of entire populations. It can be programmed in terms of their total needs, not just in terms of the messages they should be hearing, but in terms of the total experience as picked up and patterned by all the senses at once. For example, if you were to write an ideal sensory program for Indonesia or some area of the world that you wanted to leapfrog across a lot of old technology, this would be possible if you knew in the first place its present sensory thresholds, and, second, if you had established what kind of sensory effect a given technology like radio or literacy had upon sensory life as a whole."

Or suppose I am simply worried about my *natural* self, my condition as part of the creation, my indecencies to the life around me that is coextensive with mine. I deface the garden, Earth, with cigarette butts, billboards, beer cans. I pollute the streams with uncycled wastes from my factory. Should I not then despise myself as a rapist?

Well, do what you like, answers Marshall McLuhan sniffishly, but you are a bit of wag. Men may have been a bit hard on the planet in the past—but full amends are about to be made. If you'll just be patient a minute or two, you'll see us doing a kind of honor to this Little Old Earth that will more than make up for the past:

"If the planet itself has thus become the content of a new space created by its satellites, and its electronic extensions, if the planet has become the content and not the environment, then we can confidently expect to see the next few decades devoted to turning the planet into an art form. We will caress and shape and pattern every facet, every contour of this planet as if it were a work of art, just as surely as we put a new environment around it."

In sum: give it all over, is the message. Give over self-doubt, self-torment, self-hatred. Give over politics. Give over conscience. Relax, go soft and complacent, accept your subliminal perfectability. Before us, almost at hand, is a moment of revelation when it shall be shown that "we are living in a period richer" than that of Shakespeare, that our time is properly thought of as "the greatest of all human ages, whether in the arts or in the sciences." And while we are waiting, there are worthy acts to be done. We can cut ourselves off from our depressions. We can look beyond the trivia of daily life —beyond entanglements with wives and children and employers, beyond neighbors, bond issues, tax bills and the rest. We can overcome the tired sense that there are urgent local and international issues, and learn to see the dropout, the teach-in, even the casualty himself, as part of The Greater Showbiz:

". . . we now experience simultaneously the drop out and the teach-in. The two forms are correlative. They belong together. The teach-in represents an attempt to shift education from instruction to discovery, from brainwashing students to brainwashing instructors. It is a big dramatic reversal. Vietnam, as the content of the teach-in, is a very small, misleading Red Herring. It really has nothing to do with the teach-in as such any more than with the dropout. The dropout represents a rejection of nineteenth-century technology as manifested in our educational establishments. The teach-in represents a creative effort to switch the educational process to discovery, from package to prove."

Thus will we rise to the certainty that Style and Method are all, that the visible—Vietnam or wherever—is not in any real sense *there*. And having done this we can take off absolutely, fly up from the non-world of consciousness into the broad sanctuaries of ecstasy and hope. ("The computer, in short, promises by technology a Pentecostal condition of universal understanding and unity . . . a perpetuity of collective harmony and peace.")

It is here, of course, precisely here—in the gift of oblivion—that the heart of the McLuhanian munificence is found. This writer does bestow on his reader a welcome grant of hip modernity. He stimulates in addition a voluptuous sense of mastery (to say "The Middle Ages were *The Late Show* for the Renaissance" is rather like cornering a Corvette). And whether or not the basis of his sunniness is sheer terror, his work does rank as the strongest incitement to optimism yet produced in this age. But the great gift offered is, ultimately, the release from consciousness itself. Those who accept it have clearly won a deliverance, a free way up and out.

Are they so reprehensible, it is asked? Poor men, the ignorant, the hopeless, have to buy *their* release from pushers. The Professor's enthusiasts spend less and get more. They buy a guarantee that the disorder, chaos and misery around them are but veils and shadows, lies told by the stupid conscious mind—yet they make no sacrifice whatever of their ability to function in the workaday world. In the act of discounting their own senses and anxieties, they rise up to form an elite—men dignified by their access to the knowledge that nobody knows what's what. If they are at bottom blind devotees of the subliminal dogma, they have at least kept their self-respect. And in any case what *is* the compulsion to Gloomsville that makes it shameful to smile with a Happy Prof? By what laws are we obliged to speak and act always as though tragedy, endless tragedy, were the perpetual human lot? Is it really a badge of reason to hold at every hour of day and night that—as Santayana claimed— "the only true dignity of man is his capacity to despise himself"?

The frustration that breathes in these questions, the boredom with canting pessimism, the thirst for a freshening of life, the longing for an inward sense of courage—these are doubtless the deepest secrets known by our new King of Popthink, the deepest needs his elixir is designed to meet. And making light of the needs is no less inhuman than exploiting them. The best that can be done is to repeat the questions that consciousness—were there any of it left around—would probably feel bound to raise, viz.:

How much can be said for an intellectual vision whose effect is to encourage abdication from all responsibility of mind?

Or: what good is this famous McLuhanacy if it makes men drunk as it makes them bold?   [73]

1. Style and tone here are large factors which give DeMott's article its particular effect. Analyze the author's use of words and phrases to create the portrait of McLuhan he seeks. Provide specific examples of this technique.

2. Apart from the patronizing tone, which bathes DeMott's whole article with protest against McLuhan, what are the principal points he raises in definite objection to Professor McLuhan's theories?

UNDERSTANDING McLUHAN

Hugh Kenner

Marshall McLuhan's name flies about these days the way "Technocracy" did in the Thirties: a picture story in *Life;* status as resident sage in the files from which they confect the *Time* Essay; random allusions in the columns of every journal one picks up, from *National Review* to the *National Catholic Reporter,* not to mention *Encounter, Popular Photography,* and the *Times Lit. Sup.* A season ago one of the better-heeled monthlies was phoning about offering a grand or so to the lean hungry free-lancer who'd tool a few thousand words to go under the title, "Against McLuhan." And I've forgotten which magazine writer, reaching for a handy simile, said that to broach a simple topic with so-and-so was "like talking to Marshall McLuhan about the weather": he's achieved eponymous status, like Dr. Fell and Dr. Pangloss and Dr. Einstein. I've even come across his name, misspelled, in a popular novel.

In all of which he resembles the fly that has gotten into the movie projector and overlays, in silhouette, random scenes. For it's understood (1) that no one has, *really,* dug him; (2) that he's nonetheless "in"; (3) that "the medium is the message," and if you don't understand that you are to keep quiet until you'll say that you do.

HUGH KENNER is Professor and Chairman of the Department of English, the University of California at Santa Barbara.

Reprinted by permission from *The National Review*, November 29, 1966, pp. 1224–1225.
© 1966 *The National Review,* 150 E. 35th St., N.Y., N.Y. 10016.

As one of his oldest—ah—fans (we met in 1946, when I was about to take over the teaching job he'd taken over from Wyndham Lewis) I'm willing to claim (1) that I dig him; (2) that he's perhaps the best commentator on his own in-ness; (3) that the medium ain't the message, and if you don't understand that keep quiet till you've been led through Basic McLuhan as follows:

The initial principle is that there are three McLuhans. The first is a genius. The second is a gear-stripper, who tends to believe that what the first tells him is an adequate Ersatz reality. The third is what you imagine the Delphic Oracle must have been like, when you survey the ruins of Greece: a dealer in *appoggiaturas* and *tremolos* that would give the first fits were he not insulated by the machinations of the second.

With these three there cohabits a goblin who unnerves criticism by the paradigmatic force of his routine exercises (performed on every other page, to show that X, the acknowledged expert on Y, has in the larger analysis Missed the Point. It will soon be quite clear that I have Missed the Point, the Whole Point. But I hope to fix a point or two of my own.

To begin with the Genius, whom the *New Yorker* some years back sought to locate by calling him the first Pop Philosopher. He is. Like Andy Warhol, whose works we don't need to see to appreciate their point, McLuhan is the writer his public doesn't need to read. (The same was true of Newton.) He's carved out a topic (he says, The Topic) virtually by naming it—Media. (One secret of genius is timing; Media were ready to be discovered, just as gravitation was.) Once we'd heard that he'd pointed it out, we could understand at once, without reading him, that TV wasn't just a different way of seeing movies, but a different experience, shaping the movie it shows: gregarious, tight, low-definition, casual: as against tranced, alone-in-a-crowc immersion.

Nor are film and book optional ways of giving us *David Copperfield,* film's discrepancies attributable merely to Hollywood tastelessness. Attempts to translate from print to a mass medium tend to ignore the fact that print is itself a medium, and a mass medium (the printed book was the first mass-produced artifact). Print, encountered in silence and solitude, isn't speech; nor, perfectly uniform in its thousands of identical copies, is it writing. It's a freezer and standardizer of language. (McLuhan's former pupil, Walter J. Ong, S.J., has given these insights two decades of patient attention.)

Thus (and much more) McLuhan No. 1, the genius who tells us things we were just ripe to hear, as we know from the fact that we understand them as soon as told. To him enter McLuhan No. 2, whose material is not the substantial intricate world but the insights of McL. No. 1. McL. 2 extrapolates from "this book is the content of this film" to things like "The content of any medium is always another medium. The content of writing is speech, just as the written word is the content of print, and print is the content of the telegraph." (All references are to the McGraw-Hill editions of *Understanding Media.* That one's on page 9.)

Forget about content then, which is an infinite regress, and look at the medium before you. What is the message of movies? The fact that there are movies, with all that *that* entails. And of books? The fact that there are books. And *this* book, called *The Dialogues of Plato,* whose content is writing whose content is speech whose content is thought whose content is the central nervous system, places before our hypotized eyes yet one more sequence of uniform pages stamped with uniform lines made out of permuted uniform symbols; and all copies of this book are [1224–1225] alike, so that an entire freshman class can turn to page 29, line 3, third word; and this fact, which is the message of the medium, is more important than any thought of Plato's.

And before we have a chance to protest that surely Plato counts for something, McLuhan 2 plunges on to enumerate more media than we had thought possible. Railway is a medium, creating new environments, new kinds of cities, in ways "quite independent of the freight or content of the railway medium." (Ignore the content, remember?) "The airplane, on the other hand, by accelerating the rate of transportation, tends to dissolve the railway form of cities, politics and association, quite independently of what the airplane is used for."

If you think it matters whether airplanes carry people or goldfish keep it to yourself and don't bug No. 2, he's away, away. The wheel is obsolescent (this is the electric age). The electric light is a medium, its content whatever is done in its glow—baseball or brain surgery (forget the content). Its message is the human inter-actions it makes possible. And money is a medium and games are media and clocks are media and— . . . And their message is just the difference they make by existing.

And everything, alas, is something else; and if content is negligible so are facts. Though there's much show of factuality: "One of the most advanced and complicated uses of the wheel occurs in the movie camera. . . . It is significant that this most subtle and complex grouping of wheels should have been invented in order to win a bet that all four feet of a running horse were sometimes off the ground simultaneously. The bet was made between the pioneer photographer Edward Muybridge and the horse-owner Leland Stanford, in 1889. At first, a series of cameras were set up side by side, each to snap an arrested movement of the horse's hooves in action. The movie camera and the projector were evolved from the idea of reconstructing mechanically the movement of feet. The wheel, that began as extended feet, took a great evolutionary step into the movie theater."

Now, Muybridge was an agreeable eccentric who spelled his first name Eadweard. He made no bet with Stanford (do photographers make bets with multimillionaires?). He settled the horse's hooves question working on his own, in 1872. What Stanford did was offer facilities for further research, which was finished by 1879. The wheels, with which Muybridge had nothing to do, were means of holding and moving the strip of film, which Muybridge didn't invent, and they never moved Muybridge's pictures of horses' feet. We have here quasi-facts, grouped around the word "feet," an earlier postulation that wheels were extensions of feet having made it seem a bright idea for feet to have inspired further wheels. That's No. 2's problem, he likes a bright idea, and insight breeds on insight in a void through which quasi-facts drift like dust motes.

The point is not to be picky about the facts; no one is going to *Understanding Media* for information anyhow. The point is that McLuhan 2 cares very little for facts' gristly specificity; their function is not to feed the mind but, like dust, to make insight visible. *Understanding Media* is mostly filled with bright ideas, which is why readers wonder if they're digging it or not; it's undiggable.

And the void where the insights cross is agitated by the pneuma of McLuhan 3, not the genius nor the gear-stripper but the Oracle. The Oracle keeps conscripting artists into his chorus, telling us for instance that Shakespeare "understood the Forest of Arden as an advance model of the age of automation, when all things are translatable into anything else that is desired." Any especially plangent vaticination turns out to be what Shakespeare or Joyce or somebody "really" meant, artist being a handy label for the frogman among media (we hear little of works of art).

McLuhan 3 envisages "the golden age as one of complete metamorphoses or translations of nature into human art, that stands ready of access to our electric age." For "The poet Stéphane Mallarmé thought 'the world exists to end in a book.' We are now in a position to go beyond that and transfer the entire show to the memory of a computer." And "if the work of the city is the remaking or translating of man into a more suitable form than his nomadic ancestors achieved, then might not our current translation of our entire lives into the spiritual form of information seem to make of the entire globe, and of the human family, a single consciousness?"

Watch that Teilhardian "spiritual." For explicitly, "We are certainly coming within conceivable range of a world automatically controlled to the point where we could say, 'Six hours less radio in Indonesia next week or there will be a great falling off in literary attention.' Or, 'We can program twenty more hours of TV in South Africa next week to cool down the tribal temperature raised by radio last week.' Whole cultures could now be programmed to keep their emotional climate stable. . . ." This will presumably happen when "the artists move from the ivory tower to the control tower of society," and "the Executive Suites are taken over by the Ph.D.'s." Lawsy, now. *Et quis custodiet?* McLuhan Three?

Understanding Media, a book that immanentizes every eschaton in sight, has moved from McGraw-Hill hardcover ($8.50) to McGraw-Hill paperback ($1.95) to drugstore paperback (95¢), becoming each time a different book though with the same words in it: since format is medium, not packaging. And the medium is the message? Then the message has become that of paperbackery, which is pop eschatology.

And a pity. A brilliant man, a man to whom friends and students owe incalculable debts, a man who has accurately perceived things the implications of which we shall be following up for decades—this man has not only taught us to say, but keeps putting us in the position where we must say, disregard the content, the medium is being spoken through by bad spirits.   [*1225*]

1. Kenner says, "McLuhan is the writer his public doesn't need to read." (p. *1224*) Explain.

2. Along with DeMott ("Against McLuhan"), Kenner is a sharp critic of McLuhan. Compare the approaches of these two anti-McLuhanites and decide which one you find most convincingly sound.

3. Is the three-part subdivision of McLuhan that Kenner proposes a good analysis? Can you recognize clearly the three distinct facets of McLuhan's method?

WHAT NATURE ABHORS

The Nation–Editorial Staff

Marshall McLuhan, the media guru from Toronto, is presently touring the States, speaking before college audiences and businessmen's luncheons, and the press is following him with an avidity that recalls the royal visitation some years ago of Queen Marie of Rumania. Reporters have ever been partial to public figures who deliver remarks designed to make readers sputter over their morning coffee; Queen Marie had a native talent for such utterances and Dr. McLuhan has made a profession of it.

His great insight into the nature of our age is that reality resides solely in the media of communication—the media constitute the message. Thus recently he has been complaining because people persist in assuming that what he says is intended to mean something. It is the fact of his speaking that is significant, and the purpose of his words is not to convey ideas but to encourage people to think—rather as an electric current encourages a frog to jump.

McLuhan is a smiling sort of man who clearly enjoys being thought outrageous. It is not an unusual type—every large dinner party is apt to include one such, and you're [596–597] lucky not to sit next to him. What is remarkable in McLuhan's case is that he can command national coverage for such

Reprinted from *The Nation*, December 5, 1966, pp. 596–597, by permission. © *The Nation*, 1966.

a statement as that color TV will be more involving than black and white because the cone of the eye receives color, while black and white comes in only
at the edges. However, it is on a par with the fact that $100,000 can be raised to
put on in the biggest armory in New York a week of electronic happenings in
which tremendous technological resources are employed to produce effects
so insignificant that the viewer is not certain whether or not they have occurred, or with the fact that the pathetic Dr. Timothy Leary can fill a large
theatre to preach the religion of LSD. We survived the era of the Big Lie only
to enter the age of the Big Hoax. Dr. McLuhan's current tour is sponsored by
the Container Corporation of America, a company interested in selling the
box, not the contents.

> Comment on the quality and usefulness of this capsule critique of
> McLuhan's ideas. Compare it with other criticisms, both favorable
> and unfavorable.

MARSHALL McLUHAN

Richard Kostelanetz

One tends to be content to attribute importance to what is measurable merely because it happens to be measurable—Karl Mannheim

Marshall McLuhan's two recent books are an intellectual necessity, but hardly a critic's delight. They repel the impatient reader. Their sentences are generally clumsy, despite scattered passages of high grace and true wit; the paragraphs are carelessly constructed; his thoughts are so diffusely organized that the book's pages need not be read chronologically. Moreover, the ideas are so original that they often evade immediate comprehension; and McLuhan's presentation of his insights at first seems arbitrary in manner and excessively dogmatic in tone. To make matters more difficult still, *Understanding Media* often inspires an animus (unjustified, I believe) in people excessively committed to the culture of print. Still, since these are books that must be assimilated, it is nothing but scandalous that between the few short reviews and the numerous profiles in the popular press, the anxious puffs and the ill-considered demolitions, truly open and discriminating criticism of McLuhan's hypotheses has been sparse.

RICHARD KOSTELANETZ is a critic who produces film portraits of American intellectuals for the B.B.C. His book, *The Theatre of Mixed Means,* was published in 1967. During 1967–8 he held a Guggenheim Fellowship for a history of Recent American Thought.

Reprinted by permission from *The Commonweal,* January 20, 1967, pp. 420–426.

In his first work, *The Mechanical Bride* (1951), needlessly out-of-print and exorbitantly expensive on the used-book markets, McLuhan explains his "method" as adapting the analytical techniques of modern art criticism to the study of both popular culture and society itself; and like the best art criticism, his original insights are most adept at illuminating forms other eyes have missed—when they literally render the invisible visible.

In the opening pages of *The Mechanical Bride,* McLuhan perceives, "It is on its technical and mechanical side that the front page [of newspapers] is linked to the techniques of modern science and art. Discontinuity is in different ways a basic concept of both quantum and relativity physics. It is the way in which a Toynbee looks at civilization, or a Margaret Mead at human cultures. Notoriously, it is the visual technique of a Picasso, the literary technique of James Joyce." In addition to being indubitably true in its individual perceptions, this passage, as it incorporates a wide range of examples, succeeds in identifying a central overarching characteristic of the contemporary sensibility. I would place it among the most illuminating passages in all modern criticism.

In *The Gutenberg Galaxy,* perhaps McLuhan's most coherently realized book, he offers the following broad insight into the impact of print on the culture of Western man: "The visual [the perceptual mode of the man raised on print] makes for the explicit, the uniform, and the sequential in painting, in poetry, in logic, in history. The non-literate modes are implicit, simultaneous, and discontinuous, whether in the primitive past or in the electronic present." Here McLuhan transcends his earlier insight by explaining why contemporary culture should find discontinuity a more congenial organizing principle than causality.

Unlike *The Mechanical Bride,* realized as just a series of explanatory glosses, the two more recent books embody significant theses about the major causes of historical change and the radical character of contemporary civilization. Adopting a mode of explanation I can only christen, against his objections, "technological determinism," McLuhan suggests that the invention of a certain, crucially relevant tool or machine initiates huge trans-[420–421]formations in the physical environment, man's social relations, and his perception of experience. For instance, McLuhan surmises that the railroad, in centralizing commerce and transportation around depots, historically shaped the structure of the cities, the character of urban social life, and the peculiar sensibilities of city people; however, the automobile initiated similarly widespread changes in developing the suburbs where houses are accessible largely, if not entirely, through private transportation. With the crossing of the new technology with the old environment—when the automobile enters the city—the result is chaos.

Pursuing this principle of technological determinism, McLuhan develops a more specific scheme of historical explanation, which I would call "informational technological determinism." Here he suggests that a radical change in the dominant technology of communication is the prime initiating force behind human change. By weaving a mosaic of examples (which offer a theme), rather than developing an argument (which would offer a thesis), he suggests in *The Gutenberg Galaxy* that the invention of movable type, which made the printing press possible, radically transformed the culture of Western man, producing phenomena as various as the predominantly visual orientation of the man who prefers print, the linear structure that superseded the repetitious forms of medieval art, a kind of music abstractly divorced from the art's origins in speech, a Protestant religion made possible by the book's capacity to induce individual revelation, the psychological mode of inner-direction, the epistemology of causal explanations, and the mechanical technology that created man's sense of alienation from his environment.

As an interpretation of cultural history, McLuhan's scheme contributes to the contemporary quarrel with those traditional methods of historiography which emphasize, for example, politicians or "great men" as the prime movers, economic factors as predominantly determining, and the mind as a stronger force than matter. The theme of technological determinism is hardly McLuhan's invention. What is original is McLuhan's outrageous comprehensiveness—his willingness to interpret so many aspects of experience as shaped by technologies of communication—as he weaves the diverse observations of others (extensively quoted and credited) into a moderately coherent whole.

ELECTRICITY ENDS SEQUENCE

In *Understanding Media,* very much the sequel to *The Gutenberg Galaxy,* McLuhan's theme is that the new electronic communications technologies of the twentieth century are the determining force in shaping modern culture. Telegraph, telephone, radio, television, automation have radically transformed all experience ranging from social organization to human perception of space and time; for just as the telephone significantly speeds the flow of business, so television makes all news current. Whereas the predominant organizing principle of print culture was linear—introduction, development, and conclusion—contemporary culture is characterized by repetition, juxtaposition, overlap and disjunction. "Electricity," writes McLuhan, "ended sequence by making things instant; it is the new mosaic form of the TV image that has replaced the Gutenberg structural assumptions." Electronic media also downgrade the visual capacity by requiring multi-sensory comprehensions—aural and kinetic as well as visual—as in the movies, and now television.

Unlike intellectuals who condemn the mass media completely—the larger the mass the more vehement the condemnation—or look at them only as an occasion to damn them again, McLuhan was among the first North American intellectuals to investigate precisely what the new media implied and how their forms would affect people. Essentially, McLuhan recognizes that the new media represent "extensions of man"; as such, they embody both opportunity and threat. First, they increase the range of man's control and impact over his environment—the telephone extends the voice and ear;

all switches and dials extend the power of thought. Yet they also increase the environment's potential power over him.

Most of *Understanding Media* is devoted to McLuhan's examination of the major electronic media to define the peculiar character of each, which is to say its limitations and possibilities in communication, as well as the ways it characteristically handles experience. Here the techniques of art criticism are crucially useful, because they illuminate forms that might otherwise remain unperceived.

To define, first, the nature of the medium's expression and, second, the interaction of a medium with human attention, McLuhan posits the descriptive terms of "hot" and "cool." The former word identifies media (or experiences or people) with highly defined contents—a considerable amount of detailed information. Instances include a movie screen or a page of print. Low-definition or "cool" media offer only outlines; examples include cartoons and television. Secondly, where a hot medium fosters detachment and skepticism, a cool medium requires that its audience mentally participate to complete the communication. Watching television, for instance, requires more concentration than mere looking, because the dots of the screen offer only outlines of figures; thus our brain literally learns to flesh in the characters on the screen. Similarly, conversation has a low definition—it is "cool"; a lecture is definitely hot.

Although most hot media create hot responses, a hot medium can be used to stimulate the cool, participational quality of television and *vice versa*. Alain Resnais' *Last Year at Marienbad* (1961) offers a cool experience in a hot medium; a play presented on radio has a cooler [421–422] impact than it would in a theatrical performance (because it forces us to visualize the characters); a face-to-face argument creates a hot experience in the cool medium of human talk. Applying this distinction, McLuhan illuminates phenomena that others perceive but cannot explain, such as why the contents and effects of television are so different from those of either radio or movies. Whereas radio requires, for example, a performance of high definition—announcers attempt to develop a distinctive voice that is instantly recognizable—television favors performers of a definition so low they appear almost bland, like Jack Paar, Johnny Carson and Ed Sullivan.

Indeed, perhaps the most extraordinary quality of McLuhan's mind is that it discerns significances where others see only data or nothing; he tells us how to measure, in the Mannheim sense, phenomena previously unmeasurable. "What Parkinson hides from himself and his readers is simply the fact that [clerical staff always increases because] the main 'work to be done' is actually the movement of information." " 'Mass media,' 'mass entertainment' [are] useless phrases obscuring the fact that English itself is a mass medium." Most of his most perspicacious insights stem from considering how differences in the sensory ratios of a culture affect its culture materials. One can imagine a Ph.D. thesis (if not several) slogged out of the following off-hand remark: "In [contemporary] literature only people from backward oral areas had any resonance to inject into the language—the Yeatses, the Synges, the Joyces,

Faulkners and Dylan Thomases." "The printed book will naturally tend to become a work of reference rather than a speaking wisdom." Conversely, the advertising jingle contributes to the return to oral (and aural) guidance. "The unique character of our alphabet [is that, unlike idiograms or hieroglyphs, it] separates all meaning from the sounds of letters." These remarks resemble McLuhan's books; for they are more valuable for their stimulating insights that complement our understanding than for any final definitions of formative forces.

McLUHAN AND BROWN

Because his perceptions penetrate beneath the surface of observations, McLuhan's ideas also have much in common with other radical tendencies in contemporary American thought. Like Buckminster Fuller and Herbert Marcuse, McLuhan recognizes that cybernation (the automation of work processes), as it eliminates work and increases leisure, promises to give nearly every man the opportunity to devote all his energies to the cultivation of his powers; and not only does McLuhan favor a guaranteed income (in Robert Theobald's anthology of that title), but he also envisions that continuous education will become the prime business of a future society.

Also, like Paul Goodman and Edgar Z. Friedenberg, McLuhan argues that today's conventional education hardly engages the interest of young people, largely because it insufficiently equips them for coping with the actualities of their world. "Our classrooms and our curricula," he writes in Charles R. Dechert's (ed.) *The Social Impact of Cybernetics*, "are still modeled on the old industrial environment. What is indicated for the new learning procedures is not the absorption of classified and fragmented data, but pattern recognition with all that that implies of grasping interrelationships." Like Herman Kahn and Norman O. Brown, McLuhan believes in thinking which is exploratory and speculative, rather than substantive and definitive; and the books of all three are products of men who do not necessarily believe in their thoughts. Just as Norman O. Brown insists in *Life Against Death* that he tries "merely to introduce some new possibilities and new problems into the public consciousness," by offering a series of unashamedly outrageous speculations, so Herman Kahn imagines "scenarios" to conjecture about future possibilities; and so McLuhan speculates about the impact of media. Finally, all three men are similar in that they offer not theses but themes.

Particularly in their grasp of the development of civilization, McLuhan and Brown posit similar ideas. In *Life Against Death,* Brown reinterprets the later thought of Sigmund Freud to suggest not only that the repressiveness of civilized society is the prime cause of neurosis but also that mankind, in the course of human history, is slowly eliminating instinctual repressions for a more fully libidinal existence. McLuhan parallels Brown by arguing that while mechanized society, derived in principle from print, alienates man from his environment, electronic media usher in the end of alienation, first, by extending man's senses into his surroundings; secondly, by favoring more participational, low-definition experiences; and, thirdly, by recreating that oral bond that tied primitive society together. In short, by locating the prime source of mental distress not in man but in his environment, both men predict that as changing society becomes more sympathetic to the human essence, most anxiety and neurosis will disappear.

Similarly, both thinkers predict the end of man's slavery to segmented time; for future man will have less [422–423] awareness of past and future. "Both time (as measured visually and segmentally) and space (as uniform, pictorial, and enclosed) disappear in the electronic age of instant information," McLuhan writes; and Brown identifies the connection between timed existence and civilization's repression. "Only repressed life is in time, and unrepressed life would be timeless or in eternity." It follows that as man loses his sense of quantified time (and, thus, his conception of life as a series of stages), he develops a different attitude toward death. "Eternity," Brown writes, "is therefore a way of envisaging mankind's liberation from the neurotic obsession with the past and the future." McLuhan conjectures that the electronic media will return man to the pre-print perspective that views death as not a termination of existence but an extension of life into a different realm—literally, a life after life. (Indicatively, only non-print cultures can accept the idea of reincarnation.)

Most conspicuously absent from *Media* is any discussion of the future of sexual activity; but on this subject, I believe, McLuhan's implications correspond with Brown's ideas. The latter thinker envisions the decline of sexuality focused upon genital contact and a return to the "polymorphously perverse," unfocused, purely libidinal pleasure characteristic of the baby; McLuhan's thoughts suggest, by extension, that the focus upon genital pleasure, particularly upon the genital orgasm, is related to print; for not only does genital sexuality resemble reading in requiring a concentration of attention, but also its conception of pleasure is analogous to the reading of a traditional novel— a progressive heightening of tension to a total release. In contrast, polymorphous, omniattentive sensuality is formally analogous to the constant pleasures afforded by the electronic media, with their diffusion of attention and absence of climax; and just as the child's sexuality is "cool" and unfocused until society teaches him a "hot" genital orientation, so a baby's attention is unfocused until he learns to read print.

Indicatively, the sexual manuals of pre-print cultures, such as the *Kama Sutra,* espouse a notion of sexual pleasure considerably different from the predominantly genital (and orgasmic) preoccupations of Albert Kinsey and Wilhelm Reich. Sex in the future, both Brown and McLuhan suggest, will be more continuous or constant in time and more diffuse in its multiple erotogenic range. In these respects—the proliferation of pleasure, the disintegration of linear time, the increase in diverse libidinal pleasure—both Brown and McLuhan imagine a future similar to, as its participants describe it, the hallucinogen experience on a grand scale; and all together, these radical thinkers and actors suggest a future utopia on earth not unlike our traditional conceptions of heaven.

Not everything in McLuhan's books is true or perceptive; for Mc-Luhan's methods for achieving insights frequently inspire incredible, if not inscrutable, leaps from reality. Some problems stem from his major theme that "the medium is the message," which is to say several things: first, the ultimate content of the medium is the medium itself; that is, people watch movies primarily for pleasures offered by a kinetic screen accompanied by relevant sound, just as people like reading for the joy of watching print pass before their eyes. Second, "it is the medium that shapes and controls the scale and form of human association and action"; that is, communication media are the primary force in shaping a society. Third, the "message" of the medium is its impact upon society—the idea of informational technological determinism; that is, "the message of the movie medium is that of transition from lineal connection to configuration."

In the first sense, I believe McLuhan is largely wrong; for he completely discounts the question of what appears on the screen and speaker. As anyone who has ever watched movies knows, some of them are more interesting—more engaging and stimulating—than others (just as some are more soporific); and much of the difference depends upon the quality of what we traditionally call the program's "content." However, McLuhan is correct in implying that we are more tolerant of bad content in the media we favor; as a writer I can read most anything, whereas a bad movie either puts me to sleep or drives me out of the theater.

The second dimension of "The medium is the message" has considerably more truth. What McLuhan says here is that the medium determines the kinds of experience and information it can most propitiously present and, thus, what kinds of impact it can have. For philosophical exposition, for instance, the book is quite obviously the most viable medium; for it allows each reader to pursue the thought at his own pace as well as to recheck on earlier statement. Moreover, the second corollary says that as media shape the modes and situations of response—continuity or discontinuity; by oneself, or in a group—they influence ("shape" more than "control") human social life. Thus, he conjectures that TV and movies, where large numbers watch the same thing all at once, will institute retribalization; however, since media are often observed alone and since not everyone watches the same program, retribalization through TV alone would be unlikely. In short, then, where McLuhan's thesis of the medium and the message runs false is precisely in its exclusionary determinism. *The medium is not the entire message, just as it does not totally control the message.* What McLuhan does, here and elsewhere, is escalate a real insight into a fantastic iron-clad generalization; so that, only if one takes these grandiose statements with skepticism will one grasp the truths they have to offer.

McLuhan's mind is, by nature, more admissive than exclusionary; not only is it open to experience that other intellectuals either dismiss or neglect, but he also exhibits the tendency to admit all his own thoughts to print. Just [423–424] as some of them are more comprehensible than others, so some are considerably more perceptive. What I fear is that many people impressed with the brilliance of so much will suspect that everything McLuhan says is true—even worse, true in precisely the way he says it.

Since even the author regards his insights as "exploratory probes," the reader must, of necessity, subject these perceptions to the most rigorous critical scrutiny. McLuhan is deeply indebted to James Joyce—indeed, floating around in *Media* is the nucleus of a brilliant critical book on Joyce's work (a task, I understand, he has passed on to his eldest son); and McLuhan has said, "Much of what I talk about is in *Finnegan's Wake*." The trouble is that in addition to taking his love of punning from Joyce, McLuhan adopts Joyce's most indulgent habits of thought. The organizing principle of the *Wake,* one remembers, is that one story is all stories—to put it differently, at the base of the novel's major actions is the tale of familial conflict. Thus, on the same page, Joyce writes about a range of filial relationships—England and Ireland, Eliot and Yeats, Romulus and Remus, Mutt and Jeff, Shem and Shaun, Greece and Rome, etc.

What Joyce did, then, was transcend the metaphoric relations—that one story is like another—for associations that, as they eliminate the metaphoric dimension completely, transform analogies into identities. McLuhan performs similar leaps, as he writes in *Media* that "The electric light is pure information." By this gnomic sentence, he intends a metaphoric meaning—that the electric light resembles an information medium in that it tells us about something else; without the light, we would not recognize the content it illuminates. However, such an elliptical statement obfuscates meaning, and such an inclusive intelligence loses its sense of discrimination—if they are so much like each other, then there would be no discernible difference between them.

This process of converting correspondences into identities (which, indicatively, also informs Norman O. Brown's *Love's Body*) accomplishes, metaphorically, a transubstantiation, a doctrine which generally separates the post-print Protestant intelligence from the pre-print Catholic; where the former says the bread *represents* the body of Christ, the latter rules that, at a certain point in the Mass, that it *is* the body of Christ. What may rationalize McLuhan's inclusive logic, perhaps, is his notion that differentiation and classification are modes typical of the age of print; he quotes, for example, Phillip Aires' observation that the idea of "childhood" as a distinct stage did not arise until the seventeenth century.

In contrast, the contemporary modes, McLuhan feels, are inclusion and unification; and just as the avant-garde in each modern art overlaps into another—theater into dance with *The Brig* and Happenings and music into theatre with John Cage—so newspapers and mass magazines deny traditional difference by homogenizing all experience. Similarly, where uniformity in grammar and definitions is a product of print, the new writing, like much new art (and McLuhan's new scholarship), is less committed to traditional precision; and McLuhan's use of certain abstract words such as "myth" and "archetype" is highly idiosyncratic—perhaps more metaphoric than accurate. ("Printed grammars since the eighteenth century," writes McLuhan, "created a fog based on the concept of correctness.")

The major trouble with, say, the transformations of analogies into identities are, first, that they betray the experience we know—the light bulb is simply not an informational medium in the way television is—and, second, that such statements, as they defy precise analysis, corrupt the language of explanation. Until man ceases to recognize such crucial differences, perhaps (and only perhaps) an inevitable result of the electronic revolution, McLuhan errs in neglecting them. "You can prove nothing by analogy," Ezra Pound says in *ABC of Reading,* incidentally one of McLuhan's favorite books. "The analogy is either range-finding or fumble. Written down as a lurch toward proof . . . it leads mainly to useless argument." Alas, Pound, too, exaggerates his perception.

CONCENTRIC PATTERNS

Likewise Joycean is the circular structure of all McLuhan's books; for the principle he announces in *The Mechanical Bride*—"No need for it to be read in any special order"—is more or less applicable to his other books. McLuhan's rationale for such a procedure is buried in an extraordinary passage on page 26 of *Media*: "The Hebrew and Eastern mode of thought tackles problem and resolution, at the outset of a discussion, in a way typical of oral societies in general. The entire message is then traced and retraced, again and again, on the rounds of a concentric spiral with seeming redundancy. One can stop anywhere after the first few sentences and have the full message, if one is prepared to 'dig' it. [This] redundant form [is] inevitable to the electric age, in which the concentric pattern is imposed by the instant quality, and overlay in depth, of electric speed. But the concentric with its endless intersection of planes is necessary for insight. In fact, it is the technique of insight, and as such is necessary for media study, since no medium has its meaning or existence alone, but only in constant interplay with other media."

This I consider among McLuhan's most disturbing ideas; and although I recognize that presentation and arguments are rhetorically tied to the linear form, I am not sure, as McLuhan is, that insight is instantaneous. A full understanding of any process, whether of complicated mechanisms or complex ideas, requires some form of successive thought; and if the process is to be effectively communicated, the writer (or speaker) should use developmental syntax.

The most obvious criticism of McLuhan's interpreta-[424–425]tions is his rampaging tendency to over-explain. Not only are his ideas too deterministic, not only does he facilely transform analogies into identities, not only does he tend to encompass all other interpretations of experience within his own (rather than arguing against them), but he ties up his materials into a package too neat for their realities. Quite often, he becomes the victim of his own ideas, conjuring his interpretations through highly resistant evidence.

Much of his prophecy stems from the speculation that as man overcomes his slavery to literacy, he will attain a sensibility similar to that of primitive man; thus, McLuhan creates a dialectical vision of history by continually referring to pre-print experience (thesis) for his images of the present and future (synthesis) that contrasts with the age of print (antithesis). He notes in *The Gutenberg Galaxy* that soon after the impact of print, music became divorced from its origins in song (and speech); therefore, by expecting that all important contemporary music will complete the circle, McLuhan asserts in *Media* that not only does jazz have its origins in speech but also that, "Schoenberg and Stravinsky and Carl Orff and Bartok, far from being advanced seekers of esoteric effects, seem to have brought music very close to the conditions of ordinary human speech." This may be true for Orff, it might be somewhat true for Bartok; but as for Schoenberg, the remark has nothing to do with his central contribution to contemporary musical thought. In fact, serial music is so abstract, so divorced from speech, that an accurate description of its methods forbids extrinsic analogies.

At another point, McLuhan conjures that since pre-print art was corporate and anonymous in authorship, so will be post-print art. However, TV is corporate less because of the nature of the medium than the existing practices for making programs, and the greatest films, except perhaps the Marx Brothers, reveal the touch of an individual director. The point is that once society develops a certain mode of conceptual awareness, it will not necessarily disappear when that society (or its communications technology) changes; historical memory persistently survives new situations. In one sense, McLuhan admits this tendency to exaggerate, insisting that as his ideas are just explorations he feels no need to defend them as scrupulously as a Ph.D. candidate would his thesis. On the other hand, as his dogmatic style and messianic tone subvert his more modest intentions, his lack of rigor makes him an easy target for debunking marksmen.

The point is that other forces beside media shape human experience, both contemporary and historical, as well as the experience of media. The drive for money, for instance, seems to be a universal quality, doled out in unequal measure; and McLuhan's ideas are unable to explain why they should be so. His chapter on money, probably the foggiest in *Media*, makes the obvious prediction that the credit card will replace printed money as the "currency" of the new age. However, these remarks fail to cope with the real importance of money in media; after all, as Harry J. Skornia demonstrates in *Television and Society* (1965), a book McLuhan curiously blurbed, the major inspiration behind television practice today, is the possibilities of enormous profits, not the potentialities of the medium; and as McLuhan's commentary eschews the crucial question of media ownership, it cannot explain the vast and real differences between British radio and television and American.

Since McLuhan attempts to downgrade the power of politicians and political structures, he has little awareness of how they can, in fact, shape a considerable portion of our existence, even our relationship to the media. People cannot have television unless their state permits it; and governmental politics, as we note, often influence, if not control, the content of the programs, usually with scant awareness of the nature of the medium. Likewise absent from *Media* is any elaboration of Harold A. Innis' version of "the medium is the message"—that each new form of communication initiates a shift in political power. Furthermore, it is simply preposterous to say, "The Cold War is largely a conflict between cultures where different sense priorities prevail. The U.S. is eye-oriented. The Soviet Union, with its limited traditions of literacy, is ear-oriented." Similarly naive is McLuhan's prediction, perhaps self-ironic, that "If the 'Voice of America' suddenly switched to jazz, the Kremlin would have reason to crumble." In the end, McLuhan's insights into experience are, as I suggested before, more acceptable as a complement to, rather than a replacement for, other interpretations. He is innocent to omit economic activity, sexual desire and political forces in modern society, merely forgetting them will not make them go away.

Although McLuhan eschews political directives, *Understanding Media* strikes me as implicitly a most persuasive polemic for the necessity of communicatarian anarchism. McLuhan continually predicts that the electronic media and cybernation will produce the decentralization of society (perhaps because it fits into his dialectical scheme); however, he never quite explains how, in the age of networks and expanding government power, this "uniqueness and diversity" and "new world of autonomy and decentralization in all human affairs" will occur. Indeed, by implication, particularly in their images of a possible future, his books suggest that the only way to overcome the incipient nightmare of *1984* is through the dismantling of society to its natural boundaries of existing communities—the political separation of cities from their suburbias and both from the rural areas—and the creation of wholly autonomous communications media within each of these enclaves. McLuhan implies this when he writes, "Restraints of electric absolutist power can be achieved not by the separation of powers, but by a pluralism of centers." Such action, it seems to me, is not only a desirable political solution to [425–426] this age of super-powers but also a spiritual necessity in an era of possible global conformity; and McLuhan confirms this prognostication by suggesting that rebellion will not attract sympathy unless it is instigated by a group for the sake of a *community* opposed to unjust authority.

As intellectual endeavors, McLuhan's books merit nothing but highest praise; in spite of their intrinsically high-definitional quality, they invite participation in their processes of thought, initiating not only dialogues between the reader and the book but between one reader and another. They are among the richest books of our time; and I doubt if any intelligent person can read them without being enlightened, if not influenced, in some way—educated to cope better with his present environment. Indeed, precisely because his thought presumes that mankind, by recognizing technology's importance, can overcome its determining power and shape the social environment to his needs, McLuhan is profoundly humanistic.

Amidst all their chaff, McLuhan's books contain much truth; more important, to many of us, they initiate an education—an awareness of insignificant dimensions previously hidden to us—as they make invisible visible and the unconscious conscious. Like other great native thinkers, McLuhan embodies that peculiarly North American capacity to push ideas, often derived from others, beyond conventional bounds to the wildest conclusions—literally levels beyond other minds in the same field—creating a book in which enormous good-sense and outright non-sense are so closely entwined; and in our post-Marxist, most-existentialist, post-Christian age, such exploratory thought is more valuable and necessary to our culture than another serving of time-worn ideas.   [426]

1. Do you agree with Kostelanetz where, in his introductory paragraph, he says: ". . . truly open and discriminating criticism of McLuhan's hypothesis has been sparse" (as of January 20, 1967)? How effectively does Kostelanetz proceed to fill the lack of a "truly open and discriminating" review of McLuhan?

2. What is your reaction to the analysis on p. 422 of today's educational methods and their reception by young people?

3. Refer to Normal O. Brown's *Life Against Death* (discussed on pp. 422–423) for a comparison and contrast analysis of what Kostelanetz regards as parallel contemporary modes of thought along with McLuhan's.

4. Investigate the novels of James Joyce (especially *Finnegan's Wake*) to verify the relationship claimed by McLuhan himself and noted by many of his critics, Kostelanetz very prominently, between McLuhan and James Joyce.

5. On what evidence does Kostelanetz base his analysis of McLuhan's mode of thought?

UNDERSTANDING
McLUHAN
(IN PART)

Richard Kostelanetz

Marshall McLuhan, one of the most acclaimed, most controversial and certainly most talked-about of contemporary intellectuals, displays little of the stuff of which prophets are made. Tall, thin, middle-aged and graying, he has a face of such meager individual character that it is difficult to remember exactly what he looks like; different photographs of him rarely seem to capture the same man.

By trade, he is a professor of English at St. Michael's College, the Roman Catholic unit of the University of Toronto. Except for a seminar called "Communication," the courses he teaches are the standard fare of Mod. Lit. and Crit., and around the university he has hardly been a celebrity. One young woman now in Toronto publishing remembers that, a decade ago, "McLuhan was a bit of a campus joke." Even now, only a few of his graduate students seem familiar with his studies of the impact of communications media on civilization—those famous books that have excited so many outside Toronto.

RICHARD KOSTELANETZ is a critic who produces film portraits of American intellectuals for the B.B.C. His book, *The Theatre of Mixed Means,* was published in 1967. During 1967–8 he held a Guggenheim Fellowship for a history of Recent American Thought.

Reprinted from *New York Times Magazine,* January 29, 1967, pp. 18–19+, © 1967 by the New York Times Company. Reprinted by permission.

McLuhan's two major works, "The Gutenberg Galaxy" (1962) and "Understanding Media" (1964), have won an astonishing variety of admirers. General Electric, I.B.M. and Bell Telephone have all had him address their top executives; so have the publishers of America's largest magazines. The composer John Cage made a pilgrimage to Toronto especially to pay homage to McLuhan, and the critic Susan Sontag has praised his "grasp on the texture of contemporary reality."

He has a number of eminent and vehement detractors, too. The critic Dwight Macdonald calls McLuhan's books "impure nonsense, nonsense adulterated by sense." Leslie Fiedler wrote in Partisan Review: "Marshall McLuhan . . . continually risks sounding like the body-fluids man in 'Doctor Strangelove.' "

Still the McLuhan movement rolls on. Now he has been appointed to the Albert Schweitzer Chair in the Humanities at Fordham University, effective next September. (The post, which pays $100,000 a year for salary and research expenses, is one of 10 named for Schweitzer and Albert Einstein, underwritten by New York State. Other Schweitzer Professors include Arthur Schlesinger Jr. at City University and Conor Cruise O'Brien at N.Y.U.)

What makes McLuhan's success so surprising is that his books contain little of the slick style of which popular sociology is usually made. As anyone who opens the covers immediately discovers, "Media" and "Galaxy" are horrendously difficult to read—clumsily written, frequently contradictory, oddly organized, and overlaid with their author's singular jargon. Try this sample from "Understanding Media." Good luck.

> The movie, by sheer speeding up the mechanical, carried us from the world of sequence and connections into the world of creative configuration and structure. The message of the movie medium is that of transition from lineal connections to configurations. It is the transition that produced the now quite correct observation: "If it works, it's obsolete." When electric speed further takes over from mechanical movie sequences, then the lines of force in structures and in media become loud and clear. We return to the inclusive form of the icon.

Everything McLuhan writes is originally dictated, either to his secretary or to his wife, and he is reluctant to rewrite, because, he explains, "I tend to add, and the whole thing gets out of hand." Moreover, some of his insights are so original that they evade immediate understanding; other paragraphs may forever evade explication. "Most clear writing is a sign that there is no exploration going on," he rationalizes. "Clear prose indicates the absence of thought."

The basic themes in these books seem difficult at first, because the concepts are as unfamiliar as the language, but on second (or maybe third) thought, the ideas are really quite simple. In looking at history, McLuhan espouses a position one can only call "technological determinism." That is,

whereas Karl Marx, an economic determinist, believed that the economic organization of a society shapes every important aspect of its life, McLuhan
believes that crucial technological inventions are the primary influence. Mc-
Luhan admires the work of the historian Lynn White Jr., who wrote in "Medieval Technology and Social Change" (1962) [18–37] that the three inventions of
the stirrup, the nailed horseshoe and the horse collar created the Middle Ages.
With the stirrup, a soldier could carry armor and mount a charger; and the
horseshoe and the harness brought more efficient tilling of the land, which
shaped the feudal system of agriculture, which, in turn, paid for the soldier's
armor.

Pursuing this insight into technology's importance, McLuhan develops
a narrower scheme. He maintains that a major shift in society's predominant
technology of communication is the crucially determining force behind social
changes, initiating great transformations not only in social organization but
human sensibilities. He suggests in "The Gutenberg Galaxy" that the invention
of movable type shaped the culture of Western Europe from 1500 to 1900. The
mass production of printed materials encouraged nationalism by allowing
more rapid and wider spread of information than permitted by hand-written
messages. The linear forms of print influenced music to repudiate the structure
of repetition, as in Gregorian chants, for that of linear development, as in a
symphony. Also, print reshaped the sensibility of Western man, for whereas
he once saw experience as individual segments, as a collection of separate
entities, man in the Renaissance saw life as he saw print—as a continuity, often
with causal relationships. Print even made Protestantism possible, because
the printed book, by enabling people to think alone, encouraged individual
revelation. Finally: "All forms of mechanization emerge from movable type,
for type is the prototype of all machines."

In "Understanding Media," McLuhan suggests that electric modes of
communication—telegraph, radio, television, movies, telephones, computers
—are similarly reshaping civilization in the 20th century. Whereas print-age
man saw one thing at a time in consecutive sequence—like a line of type—
contemporary man experiences numerous forces of communication simultaneously, often through more than one of his senses. Contrast, for example,
the way most of us read a book with how we look at a newspaper. With the
latter, we do not start one story, read it through and then start another. Rather,
we shift our eyes across the pages, assimilating a discontinuous collection of
headlines, subheadlines, lead paragraphs, photographs and advertisements.
"People don't actually read newspapers," McLuhan says; "they get into them
every morning like a hot bath."

Moreover, the electronic media initiate sweeping changes in the
distribution of sensory awareness—in what McLuhan calls the "sensory ratios."
A painting or a book strikes us through only one sense, the visual; motion
pictures and television hit us not only visually but also aurally. The new
media envelop us, asking us to participate. McLuhan believes that such a multi-
sensory existence is bringing a return to the primitive man's emphasis upon
the sense of touch, which he considers the primary sense, "because it consists

of a meeting of the senses." Politically, he sees the new media as transforming the world into "a global village," where all ends of the earth are in immediate touch with one another, as well as fostering a "retribalization" of human life. "Any highway eatery with its TV set, newspaper and magazine," he writes, "is as cosmopolitan as New York or Paris."

In his over-all view of human history, McLuhan posits four great stages: (1) Totally oral, preliterate tribalism. (2) The codification by script that arose after Homer in ancient Greece and lasted 2,000 years. (3) The age of print, roughly from 1500 to 1900. (4) The age of electronic media, from before 1900 to the present. Underpinning this classification is his thesis that "societies have been shaped more by the nature of the media by which men communicate than by the content of the communication."

This approach to the question of human development, it should be pointed out, is not wholly original. McLuhan is modest enough to note his indebtedness to such works as E. H. Gombrich's "Art and Illusion" (1960), H. A. Innis's "The Bias of Communications" (1951, recently reissued with an introduction by McLuhan), Siegfried Giedion's "Mechanization Takes Command" (1948), H. J. Chaytor's "From Script to Print" (1945) and Lewis Mumford's "Technics and Civilization" (1934).

McLuhan's discussions of the individual media move far beyond the trade talk of communications professionals (he dismisses Gen. David Sarnoff, the board chairman of R.C.A., as "the voice of the current somnambulism"). Serious critics of the new media usually complain about [37–40] their content, arguing, for example, that if television had more intelligent treatments of more intelligent subjects, its contribution to culture would be greater. McLuhan proposes that, instead, we think more about the character and form of the new media. His most famous epigram—"The medium is the message"—means several things.

The phrase first suggests that each medium develops an audience of people whose love for that medium is greater than their concern for its content. That is, the TV medium itself becomes the prime interest in watching television; just as some people like to read for the joy of experiencing print, and more find great pleasure in talking to just anybody on the telephone, so others like television for mixture of kinetic screen and relevant sound. Second, the "message" of a medium is the impact of its forms upon society. The "message" of print was all the aspects of Western culture that print influenced. "The message of the movie medium is that of transition from linear connections to configurations." Third, the aphorism suggests that the medium itself— its form—shapes its limitations and possibilities for the communication of content. One medium is better than another at evoking a certain experience. American football, for example, is better on television than on radio or in a newspaper column; a bad football game on television is more interesting than a great game on radio. Most Congressional hearings, in contrast, are less boring in the newspaper than on television. Each medium seems to possess a hidden taste mechanism that encourages some styles and rejects others.

To define this mechanism, McLuhan has devised the categories of "hot" and "cool" to describe simultaneously the composition of a communications instrument or a communicated experience, and its interaction with human attention. A "hot" medium or experience has a "high definition" or a highly individualized character as well as a considerable amount of detailed information. "Cool" is "low" in definition and information; it requires that the audience participate to complete the experience. McLuhan's own examples clarify the distinction: "A cartoon is 'low' definition, simply because very little visual information is provided." Radio is usually a hot medium; print, photography, film and paintings essentially are hot media. "Any hot medium allows of less participating than a cool one, as a lecture makes for less participation than a seminar, and a book for less than a dialogue."

The terms "hot" and "cool" he also applies to experiences and people, and, pursuing his distinction, he suggests that while a hot medium favors a performer of a strongly individualized presence, cool media prefer more nonchalant, "cooler" people. Whereas the radio medium needs a voice of a highly idiosyncratic quality that is instantly recognizable—think of Westbrook Van Vorhees, Jean Shepherd, Fanny Brice—television favors people of a definition so low they appear positively ordinary. With these terms, one can then explain all sorts of phenomena previously inscrutable—such as why bland personalities (Ed Sullivan, Jack Paar) are so successful on television.

"It was no accident that Senator McCarthy lasted such a very short time when he switched to TV," McLuhan says. "TV is a cool medium. It rejects hot figures and hot issues and people from the hot press media. Had TV occurred on a large scale during Hitler's reign he would have vanished quickly." As for the 1960 Presidential debates, McLuhan explains that whereas Richard Nixon, essentially a hot person, was superior on radio, John F. Kennedy was the more appealing television personality. (It follows that someone with as low a definition as Dwight Eisenhower would have been more successful than either.)

The ideas are not as neatly presented as this summary might suggest, for McLuhan believes more in probing and exploring—"making discoveries"—than in offering final definitions. For this reason, he will rarely defend any of his statements as absolute truths, although he will explain how he developed them. Some perceptions are considerably more tenable than others—indeed, some are patently ridiculous—and all his original propositions are arguable, so his books require the participation of each reader to separate what is wheat to him from the chaff. In McLuhanese, they offer a cool experience in a hot medium.

A typical reader's scorecard for "Media" might show that about one-half is brilliant insight; one-fourth, suggestive hypotheses; one-fourth, nonsense. Given the book's purpose and originality, these are hardly bad percentages. "If a few details here and there are wacky," McLuhan says, "it doesn't matter a hoot."

McLuhan eschews the traditional [40–41] English professor's expository style—introduction, development, elaboration and conclusion. Instead, his books imitate the segmented structure of the modern media. He makes a series of direct statements. None of them becomes a thesis but all of them approach the same phenomenon from different angles. This means that one should not necessarily read his books from start to finish—the archaic habit of print-man.

The real introduction to "The Gutenberg Galaxy" is the final chapter, called "The Galaxy Reconfigured"; even McLuhan advises his readers to start there. With "Media," the introduction and the first two chapters form the best starting point; thereafter, the reader is pretty much free to wander as he wishes. "One can stop anywhere after the first few sentences and have the full message, if one is prepared to 'dig' it," McLuhan once wrote of non-Western scriptural literature; the remark is applicable to his own books.

Similarly, McLuhan does not believe that his works have only one final meaning. "My book," he says, "is not a package but part of the dialogue, part of the conversation." (Indeed, he evaluates other books less by how definitively they treat their subject—the academic standard—than by how much thought they stimulate. Thus, a book may be wrong but still great. By his own standards, "Media" is, needless to say, a masterpiece.)

Underlying McLuhan's ideas is the question of whether technology is beneficial to man. Thinkers such as the British critic F. R. Leavis have argued, on the one hand, that technology stifles the blood of life by dehumanizing the spirit and cutting existence off from nature; more materialist thinkers, on the other hand, defend the machine for easing man's burdens. McLuhan recognizes that electronic modes of communication represent, in the subtitle of "Media," "extensions of man." Whereas the telephone is an extension of the ear (and voice), so television extends our eyes and ears. That is, our eyes and ears attended John Kennedy's funeral, but our bodies stayed at home. As extensions, the new media offer both possibility and threat, for while they lengthen man's reach into his existence, they can also extend society's reach into him, for both exploitation and control.

To prevent this latter possibility, McLuhan insists that every man should know as much about the media as possible. "By knowing how technology shapes our environment, we can transcend its absolutely determining power," he says. "Actually, rather than a 'technological determinist,' it would be more accurate to say, as regards the future, that I am an [41–43] 'organic autonomist.' My entire concern is to overcome the determinism that results from the determination of people to ignore what is going on. Far from regarding technological change as inevitable, I insist that if we understand its components we can turn it off any time we choose. Short of turning it off, there are lots of moderate controls conceivable." In brief, in stressing the importance of knowledge, McLuhan is a humanist.

McLuhan advocates radical changes in education, because he believes that a contemporary man is not fully "literate" if reading is his sole pleasure: "You must be literate in umpteen media to be really 'literate' nowadays." Education, he suggests, should abandon its commitment to print—merely a focusing of the visual sense—to cultivate the "total sensorium" of man—to teach us how to use all five cylinders, rather than only one. "Postliterate does not mean illiterate," writes the Rev. John Culkin, S.J., director of the Communications Center at Fordham and a veteran propagator of McLuhan's ideas about multimedia education. "It rather describes the new social environment within which print will interact with a great variety of communications media."

Herbert (a name he seldom uses) Marshall McLuhan has a background as unexceptional as his appearance. He was born in Western Canada —Edmonton, Alberta—July 21, 1911, the son of mixed Protestant (Baptist and Methodist) parents. "Both agreed to go to all the available churches and services, and they spent much of their time in the Christian Science area," he recalls. His father was a real-estate and insurance salesman who, McLuhan remembers, "enjoyed talking with people more than pursuing his business." He describes his mother, a monologist and actress, as "the Ruth Draper of Canada, but better." His brother is now an Episcopal minister in California.

After taking his B.A. and M.A. at the University of Manitoba, McLuhan followed the route of many academically ambitious young Canadians to England, where he attended Cambridge for two years. There, he remembers, the lectures of I. A. Richards and F. R. Leavis stimulated his initial interest in studying popular culture. Returning home in 1936, he took a job at the University of Wisconsin. The following year he entered the Catholic Church, and ever since, he has taught only at Catholic institutions—at St. Louis from 1937 to 1944, at Assumption in Canada from 1944 to 1946 and at St. Michael's College, a Basilian (C.S.B.) establishment, since 1946.

His field was originally medieval and Renaissance literature, and in 1942 he completed his Cambridge Ph.D. thesis on the rhetoric of Thomas Nashe, the Elizabethan writer. As a young scholar, he began his writing career, as every professor should, by contributing articles to the professional journals, and to this day, academic circles know him as the editor of a popular paperback textbook of Tennyson's poems. Moreover, his critical essays on writers as various as Gerard Manley Hopkins, John Dos Passos and Samuel Taylor Coleridge are frequently anthologized.

By the middle forties, he was contributing more personal and eccentric articles on more general subjects to several little magazines; before long, his pieces had such outrageous titles as "The Psychopathology of Time and Life." By the time his first book, "The Mechanical Bride," appeared in 1951, McLuhan had developed his characteristic intellectual style—the capacity to offer an endless stream of radical and challenging ideas.

Although sparsely reviewed and quickly remaindered, that book has come to seem, in retrospect, the first serious attempt to inspect precisely what effects mass culture had upon people and to discover what similarities existed between mass culture and élite art. Copies are so scarce that they now often bring as much as $40 secondhand. McLuhan had the foresight and self-confidence to purchase a thousand copies at remainder prices; he still gives them to friends, as well as selling them to strangers (at far below the going price). The bottom will soon drop out of the "Mechanical Bride" market, however, for Beacon Press plans to reissue it in paperback and Vanguard, its original publisher, in hardcover.

In 1953, the year after he became a full professor at St. Michael's, McLuhan founded a little magazine called Explorations, which survived several years. Along with a coeditor, [43–47] the anthropologist Edmund S. Carpenter, McLuhan collected some of the best material in a paperback called "Explorations in Communication" (1960), which is perhaps the ideal introduction to his special concerns and ideas.

Though McLuhan remains a Canadian citizen, he became, in 1959, director of the Media Project of the National Association of Educational Broadcasters and the United States Office of Education. Out of that experience came a report which, in effect, was the first draft of "Understanding Media." Then, in 1963, the University of Toronto appointed McLuhan to head a newly formed Center for Culture and Technology "to study the psychic and social consequences of technology and the media."

A visitor expects the Center, so boldly announced on its letterhead, to be a sleek building with a corps of secretaries between the corridor and the thinkers. In fact, the Center is more a committee than an institution. It exists, for the present, only in McLuhan's cluttered office.

Bookcases cover the walls, with battered old editions of the English classics on the top shelves and a varied assortment of newer books on Western civilization on the more accessible shelves—6,000 to 7,000 volumes in all. More books and papers cover several large tables. Buried in a corner is a ratty metal-frame chaise longue, more suited to a porch than an office, with a thin, lumpy green mattress haphazardly draped across it.

In temperament, the Center's head is more passive than active. He often loses things and forgets deadlines. The one singular feature of his indefinite face is his mouth. Only a sliver of his lips is visible from the front, but from the side his lips appear so thick that his slightly open mouth resembles that of a flounder. His only visible nervous habits are tendencies to pucker his mouth and push his chin down toward his neck before he speaks, to twirl his glasses around his fingers when he lectures and to rub his fingers down the palms of his hands whenever he says "tactility."

The professor is a conscientious family man. He met his wife, Corrine, a tall and elegant Texan, in Los Angeles, where he was doing research at the Huntington Library and she was studying at the Pasadena Playhouse. Married in 1939, they have six children: Eric, 25; Mary and Theresa, 21-year-old twins; Stephanie, 19; Elizabeth, 16, and Michael, 14, and the girls confirm their father's boast: "All my daughters are beautiful." Every Sunday he leads his brood to mass.

They live in a three-story house with a narrow front and a small lawn punctuated by a skinny driveway leading to a garage in the back. The interior is modest, except for an excessive number of books, both shelved and sprawled. McLuhan likes to read in a reclining position, so across the top of the living room couch propped against the wall, are 20 or so fat scholarly works; interspersed among them are a few mysteries—his favorite light reading. He rarely goes to the movies or watches television; most of his own cultural intake comes in print and conversation. Talking seems his favorite recreation.

McLuhan seems pretty much like any other small-city professor until he begins to speak. His lectures and conversations are a singular mixture of original assertions, imaginative comparisons, heady abstractions, and fantastically comprehensive generalizations and no sooner has he stunned his listeners with one extraordinary thought than he hits them with another. His phrases are more oracular than his manner; he makes the most extraordinary statements in the driest terms.

In his graduate seminar, he asks: "What is the future of old age?" The students look bewildered. "Why," he replies to his own question, "exploration and discovery." Nearly everything he says *sounds* important. Before long, he has characterized the Batman TV show as "simply an exploitation of nostalgia which I predicted years ago." The 25 or so students still look befuddled and dazed; hardly anyone talks but McLuhan. "The criminal, like the artist, is a social explorer," he goes on. "Bad news reveals the character of change; good news does not." No one asks him to be more definite, because his talk intimidates his listeners.

He seems enormously opinionated; in fact, he conjures insights. His method demands a memory as prodigious as his curiosity. He often elevates an analogy into a grandiose generalization, and he likes to make his points with puns: "When a thing is current, it creates currency." His critics ridicule him as a communications expert who cannot successfully communicate; but too many of his listeners, say his admirers, suffer from closed minds.

The major incongruity is that a man so intellectually adventurous should lead such a conservative life; the egocentric and passionately prophetic qualities of his books contrast with the personal modesty and pervasive confidence of a secure Catholic. What explains the paradox is that [47–50] "Marshall McLuhan," the thinker, is different from "H. M. McLuhan," the man. The one writes books and delivers lectures; the other teaches school, heads a family and lists himself in the phone book. It was probably H. M. who made that often-quoted remark about Marshall's theories: "I don't pretend to understand them. After all, my stuff is very difficult."

And the private H. M. will say this about the technologies his public self has so brilliantly explored: "I wish none of these had ever happened. They impress me as nothing but a disaster. They are for dissatisfied people. Why is man so unhappy he wants to change his world? I would never attempt to improve an environment—my personal preference, I suppose, would be a preliterate milieu, but I want to study change to gain power over it."

His books, he adds, are just "probes"—that is, he does not "believe" in his work as he believes in Catholicism. The latter is faith; the books are just thoughts. "You know the faith differently from the way you 'understand' my books."

When asked why he creates books rather than films, a medium that might be more appropriate to his ideas, McLuhan replies: "Print is the medium I trained myself to handle." So, all the recent acclaim has transformed Mc-Luhan into a bookmaking machine. Late this year, we shall have "Culture Is Our Business," which he describes as a sequel to "The Mechanical Bride." Perhaps reflecting his own idea that future art will be, like medieval art, corporate in authorship, McLuhan is producing several more books in dialogue with others. With Wilfred Watson, a former student who is now an English professor at the University of Alberta, he is completing a history of stylistic change, "From Cliché to Archetype." With Harley W. Parker, head of design at the Royal Ontario Museum, he has just finished "Space in Poetry and Painting," a critical and comparative survey of 35 pairs of poems and pictures from primitive times to the present.

In tandem with William Jovanovich, the president of Harcourt, Brace and World, McLuhan is writing "The Future of the Book," a study of the impact of xerography, and along with the management consultant Ralph Baldwin he is investigating the future of business in "Report to Management." As if that were not enough, he joined with the book designer Quentin Fiore to compile "The Medium Is the Massage," an illustrated introduction to Mc-Luhanism that will be out this spring; the two are doing another book on the effect of automation. Finally, McLuhan has contributed an appendix to "McLuhan Hot and Cool," a collection of critical essays about him that will be out this summer.

On another front, McLuhan and Prof. Richard J. Schoeck, head of the English Department at St. Michael's, have recently produced two imaginative textbooks, "The Voices of Literature," for use in Canadian high schools. And with Professor Schoeck and Ernest J. Sirluck, dean of the graduate school at the University of Toronto, McLuhan oversees a series of anthologies of criticism being published jointly by the Toronto and Chicago University Presses. Obviously, despite the bait from the worlds of media and advertising, McLuhan is keeping at least one foot planted in academia. Only this past December, he addressed the annual meeting of the Modern Language Association on the confrontation of differing sensory modes in 19th-century poetry.

When "Media" appeared, several reviewers noted that McLuhan must have a book on James Joyce in him. That task he passed on to his son Eric, who is writing a prodigious critical study of "Finnegans Wake." Among McLuhan's greatest desires is establishing the Center for Culture and Technology in its own building, with sufficient funds to support a reference library of the sensory experience of man. That is, he envisions methods of measuring all the "sensory modalities" (systems of sensory organization) in all cultures, and of recording this knowledge on coded tapes in the Center. Assistant Professor of Design Allen Bernholtz, one of McLuhan's colleagues, foresees a machine that will, following taped instructions, artificially create a sensory environment exactly similar to that of any other culture; once the subject stepped into its capsule, the machine could be programed to simulate what and how, say, a Tahitian hears, feels, sees, smells and tastes. "It will literally put you in the other guy's shoes," Bernholtz concludes. So far, the projected

Center has not received anywhere near the $5-million backing it needs to begin.

Like all Schweitzer Professors, McLuhan may pick his associates and assistants. His entourage will include Professor Carpenter, with whom he coedited Explorations; Harley Parker and Father Culkin. In addition to teaching one course and directing a research project, McLuhan and his associates plan to conduct numerous dialogues and to publish a son of Explorations. "Once you get a lot of talk going," he said recently, "you have to start a magazine." Because he believes that "I can better observe America from up here," he had rejected previous lucrative offers that involved forsaking Toronto, and as Schweitzer professorships are formally extended for only one year (although they are renewable), McLuhan will officially take only a sabbatical leave from St. Michael's.

McLuhan has always been essentially a professor living in an academic community, a father in close touch with his large family and a teacher who also writes and lectures. When some V.I.P.'s invited him to New York a year ago, he kept them waiting while he graded papers. Although he does not run away from all the reporters and visitors, he does little to attract publicity. His passion is the dialogue; if the visitor can participate in the conversation, he may be lucky enough, as this writer was, to help McLuhan write (that is, dictate) a chapter of a book.

"Most people," McLuhan once remarked, "are alive in an earlier time, but you must be alive in our own time. The artist," he added, "is the man in any field, scientific or humanistic, who grasps the implications of his actions and of new knowledge in his own time. He is the man of integral awareness."

Although his intention was otherwise, McLuhan was describing himself—the specialist in general knowledge. Who would dare surmise what thoughts, what perceptions, what grand schemes he will offer next?   [50]

1. This N.Y. Times Magazine article (January 29, 1967) and the Commonweal article (January 20, 1967) were both published by the same author on the same subject almost during the same week. Write a comparison of the two (be as McLuhanesque as you like) in which you examine how the two media (The Times Magazine vs. Commonweal) seem to have influenced this author's messages as he approached the job of analyzing McLuhan for each of them.

2. What does Mr. Kostelanetz say about McLuhan's writing style?

3. Do you agree with Kostelanetz' description of McLuhan's view of history?

MARSHALL McLUHAN: COMMUNICATIONS EXPLORER

Neil P. Hurley, S.J.

The history of human thought is seeded with master insights that have drastically revised man's view of himself in the universe: Copernicus' theory of a heliocentric cosmos, Darwin's theory of natural selection, Marx's dialectical materialism, Freud's psychoanalytic hypothesis of infantile sexual repression. An addition to this pantheon might well be Marshall McLuhan's statement, which has stirred so much comment, that the medium is the message.

McLuhan, a venturesome "explorer navigator" in the philosophy of communications, has experienced a vision of uncharted seas and exotic lands. Like all pioneers, he has had to "rough out" a course for subsequent generations, aware that his parameters are crude and open to revision. The sweep of McLuhan's thesis not only touches the deepest levels of man's psychic life —his senses, thoughts and decisions—but also leads us across the realms of science, art, history, philosophy and theology. It is the pan-optic nature of his writings that delights the generalist and piques the specialist—and makes them

NEIL P. HURLEY, S.J., who teaches the sociology of communications at the Catholic University, in Santiago, Chile, directs a communications research group at the Jesuit Center for Social Research and Action in Santiago. This article appeared in *America* for February 18, 1967, pp. 241–243.

intensely controversial. One thing seems certain—as Euclid in Edna St. Vincent Millay's poem was the first to see geometric "beauty bare," so McLuhan has been the first to see the dynamics of communications media stripped bare of their message-contents. It is this insight that he is trying to share with a mankind in the throes of an unprecedented communications revolution characterized by transistor radios, home TV play-back recorders, facsimile reproduction, audio- and videotape, satellites, computers, lasers and masers.

The best way to explain McLuhan's seminal thought is by way of an anecdote. The story is told of a feudal polyglot king who was accustomed to boast that he spoke *platt deutsch* to his stable hands, *hoch deutsch* to his infantry, English to his officers, French to his courtiers, Italian to nobility, and to God—"Ah! When I pray to God, I speak Spanish." What this tale does, apart from praising Cervantes' mother tongue, is to disengage the message from the medium to show that the medium is not like a pipeline but necessarily affects the "through-put." A language permits nuances, accents and tone-feelings that are unique.

In other words, there is a thematic message of which we are conscious and, compounded with it, there is a nonthematic message. The latter is the precondition for the former and sets the range for all possible messages. Thus, to speak *platt deutsch* to an empress would be a breach of tact, because that is the communications matrix reserved ideally for less diplomatic, more functional situations.

Since the thematic content, after all, has a dynamic structure of its own, it would be more accurate to say that the medium is the co-message. Understanding McLuhan's thesis in this way, we can readily appreciate the implications for the behavioral sciences. Social patterns of emotion, thought, aspiration and behavior will naturally change as one goes from a culture dominated by one medium to that influenced by another. We still find in the world today people socialized in different communications matrices: oral, pictograph, alphabetic, typographic, electronic. To explain the socio-psychological effects of living in these cultures. McLuhan likes to quote William Blake:

> "If Perceptive Organs vary, Objects
>   of Perception seem to vary:
> If the Perceptive Organs close, their
>   Objects seem to close also."

Man sees what he has been socialized to see, and one of the most forceful agents of socialization is media. Thus, adrift at sea, a typographic person such as an Englishman seeks visual bearings in the stars and land-markers, while an auditory type such as the Eskimo listens to the waves and winds. Media conditioning serves to equip man with an unconscious filter for sifting experience's "inputs." Art offers us some cogent examples of this. As blindness reorganized Milton's inner world, thus co-creating the message known as *Paradise Lost,* so Beethoven's deafness served as a catalyst for the new musical sensibility evident in the *Eroica Symphony.*

McLuhan has applied his telescopic vision to all branches of knowledge. He casts up hypotheses about Plato's fear of poets, the dependence of the Roman empire on written reports, the oral tradition of the schoolmen, the contrast between the "letterpress" bias of Newton and Descartes and the electron-[241–242]ic quality of Einstein and Heidegger, Gutenberg's influence in mass-produced art, about nationalism, capitalism, individualism, urbanism, the Reformation, the American way of life, the Industrial Revolution, the scientific method and the influence of electronics on politics, the military and education. He has divided media into "hot" and "cool," according to the way they invite audience participation. TV and radio are "cool," exciting spectator initiative, while movies, photos and books are "hot," leaving little to the observer's creative imagination.

With the Renaissance fervor of a Pico della Mirandola, McLuhan has been rioting in the meadows of his original insight, attempting to synthesize entire disciplines. His discoverer's zeal to suggest all future areas of possible research is quite understandable, and yet his impressionistic methods and journalist jargon lay him open to such contradictory charges as vulgarization and obscurantism. This fact is a regrettable one, for the McLuhan message does not depend on McLuhan. The message may be McLuhan, but McLuhan is certainly not his message. The "de-McLuhanized" message withstands scientific scrutiny and remains a monumental *aperçu* with revolutionary implications for the system of world-wide communications now developing.

At the root of the divergence between economically developed and backward areas are not only differences in gross national product and per capita income, but differences relating to modes of perception. The nonliterate peoples of Asia, Africa and Latin America configure reality differently than the literate inhabitants of Russia, Europe and North America do. Industrialization has long been recognized as a function of literacy. J. C. Carothers, a psychiatric specialist in nonliterate cultures, maintains that Western man enjoys a visual bias that accounts for his empiric, rational and organizational tendencies. By contrast, the nonliterate inhabits a magical auditory world that inclines him to be passionate, mystical and cunning.

The sharp differences between the "oral-aural" type and the "typographic-visual" kind were clearly portrayed in *Zorba the Greek,* the novel of Kazantzakis, which was later made into a film. McLuhan would describe Zorba as "cool"—an intriguing personality, a rhetorician and poet, myth-prone, communal, unconscious of time and with a low index of information. His English employer and colleague corresponds to McLuhan's terminology of "hot"—a sharply delineated character, verbal and visual, rational and solitary, time-bound and well-informed.

Recalling that the medium is the co-message, we find that every culture has a dominant communications matrix that imparts a perceptual bias that, in turn, validates the point of view of its members. That is why the movie of Zorba struck Latin Americans differently than it struck Anglo-Saxons. For Latin Americans, Zorba is a hero-type, integrated and resourceful, while for Anglo-Saxons, he is not a model of behavior but a parasitic, vain, amoral person. McLuhan's insight brings the subliminal operations of media into conscious awareness, and shows how cultural values depend on the prism of the communications system. In its efforts to design some social system for a world environment, it is indispensable that contemporary mankind should become aware of the assumptions of culture and the misunderstandings due to media forms.

In one of his least known essays on myths and media, McLuhan calls media "macro-myths," since they make believable the contents they transmit. Thus we can speak of the "macro-myth" of print, with its stress on lineal thought processes: the book made up of chapters, which are made up of paragraphs, themselves made up of sentences, which in turn may be broken down into subject, predicate and object. Children raised in "book cultures" become subject to a process of psychic automatism that leads to a privileged point of view, so that their drawings soon surrender a primitive quality to one of perspective—the scene as I see it from where I stand. They are "inner-directed."

On the other hand, children exposed to electronically moved information cultivate a "field-view" of reality, with a sympathy for multiple points of view. These are more "outer-directed." The radio disc-jockey show, the TV news documentaries, the picture magazine, the LP record—all make demands on the consumer: he is not passive, but a co-producer of the particular communications experience involved.

The electronic tide is sweeping over the world, triggering a post-literate revolution that will have varying degrees of impact on different cultures. The auditory sectors of the world will react in ways other than the print-dominated areas will. Western man, for one thing, is being "de-tribalized" to the extent that he sees interdependence in a global social system as a condition of survival. With an electronic membrane of "picture-voice-data" signals around the world, we can anticipate the decline of the "letterpress" bias in favor of efficient and instrumental causality ("What can I use that for?") and a new preference for attitudes based on final and formal causality ("What is that for?").

The implications of McLuhan's writings are far-reaching. Western man's thinking is starting to run along the new perceptual grooves of electronic media without completely surrendering the typographic modes of perception. While the newer media were pioneered in the developed sector of the world, they promise to find revolutionary applications in the nonliterate cultures: mass literacy programs, universal primary education, political socialization, vocational training, and regional economic integration. To the degree that electronic media develop in the "Third World," their assumptions will clash with those of print. Two macro-myths will clash, and that of print will be reluctant to relinquish its 500-year hegemony in the West.

Similarly, the developing nations are feeling the full impact of the conventional media: printed matter, the lecture and the classroom blackboard. The pressures to modernize are linked with literacy, challenging in this manner the assumptions of persons like Zorba. In short, contemporary man is trying to focus into one single kaleidoscopic vision two distinct perceptual ratios: that of the visual coded symbol and that of the "voiced image." Much of the anxiety in this transition period we find ourselves in is due to the myopic conflict of two reconcilable, but not yet reconciled, perceptual points of departure.　　[242–243]

That the medium is the co-message and that a change in any "media mix" will affect collective habits of sensing and judging is a detaching insight. It gives one a confidence in history's workings, relieves one of polemical intentions and bestows on man a power to understand and control his own destiny. This explains McLuhan's own Olympian composure—a far cry from the days of The Mechanical Bride, when, menaced, he felt obliged to unmask the nonrational contents of mass media. Since that time, he has been interested in macro-myths (the formal structure of media) and not micro-myths (the content of media).

McLuhan has brought imaginative power and philosophical acumen to truths that are implicit in Claude Shannon's earlier mathematical theory of communication, with its unconventional but fertile definition of information. Today mankind need no longer be like the turtle, condemned to live within a shell that limits the horizon of conscious experiences. Man will always need media and thus be subject to their macro-mythic influence. Today, however, he can reflect on the assumptions that hitherto were smuggled into his unconscious psyche. The contraband of perceptual biases and emotionally charged values can now enter the customs gate of our conscious mind, and this fact represents no small achievement in man's search for greater auto-determination.

Many myths are being eroded in our "nuclear-space" age, such as belief in a crystal-clear rationality, a world of logical rigor, a univocal universe without irony or humor. We know—or should know—that all instruments, including our senses and minds, are fallible and demand correction. The insight of Marshall McLuhan is fraught with significance for decision makers in every field, for it tells us that culture, as man's second nature, necessarily contains media biases. This implies a healthy skepticism in policy matters, a realization that the conclusions emerging from any macro-myth are no more self-evident than the postulates of Euclid were to the founders of non-Euclidean geometry.

As the electronic wave gathers greater momentum with the help of satellites and new forms of energy, it is hastening the era of civilization in the singular, when men and institutions will be in immediate "sight-and-sound" contact with each other. This tele-civilization promises to put an end to the succession and clash of macro-myths on earth. Those who share the vision of Marshall McLuhan that the medium somehow creates the message are not pessimistic, for they realize that perhaps history is the arch-medium that molds the human race and its destiny in terms not of the absurd but rather of some statement of meaning discernible even to man.　　[243]

1. Father Hurley credits McLuhan with "master insights that have drastically revised man's view of himself in the universe" and calls him a peer among Darwin, Copernicus, Marx, and Freud. (page *241*) He maintains that McLuhan's insight is "fraught with significance for decision makers in every field." Place this analysis of McLuhan in relation to some of the other critics—e.g., Kostelanetz, Kenner, Culkin. In view of the evidence they all present can you see why their evaluations of McLuhan vary? To what relative degrees do these men accept McLuhan uncritically? In what different ways do they bring warnings, reservations, interpretations to bear on his pronouncements? Can you perceive reasons for their various critical viewpoints?

2. Father Hurley says, ". . . the McLuhan message does not depend on McLuhan. The message may be McLuhan, but McLuhan is certainly not his message." Studied in the context in which it appears, what does this statement mean? (page *242*)

ARCHITECTURE IN THE ELECTRONIC AGE

Jonathan Barnett

Some months ago John Johansen sent us a copy of a review he had written for the *American Scholar* which took Marshall McLuhan's theory that the new electronic means of communication are going to make a tremendous change in the nature of our society, and set about projecting the kind of changes he thought were in store for architecture. We had been noticing for some time that almost every architect who came into the office had the paperback edition of McLuhan's *Understanding Media* tucked into an overcoat pocket, or nestling among the model photos in his briefcase, and we began to think that it was time to see whether McLuhan himself was willing to relate his theories of communication directly to the problems of architecture and planning.

A recent trip to Canada provided an opportunity to arrange an appointment at the University of Toronto's Center for Culture and Technology, of which Professor McLuhan is the director. The center occupies part of a wood frame house on a street that is clearly doomed to make way for the University's expansion program. McLuhan and an associate, Harley Parker,

JONATHAN BARNETT, an associate editor of *The Architectural Record*, publishes frequent articles on the subject of architecture.

were seated at a large wooden table covered with neatly arranged manila file folders. They were, McLuhan explained, embarked on a historical survey of concepts of non-visual space and had just gotten as far as E. E. Cummings and Paul Klee.

Non-visual space seemed a good point at which to begin, and McLuhan obligingly elaborated. The printed word, in his view, had fostered a linear and sequential view of reality, in which ideas seemed to follow each other in order. Electronic communication, however, was so close to instantaneous that several ideas could be received simultaneously. The architect, he continued, still encounters the world in visual terms, "but the spaces created by an age of electronic technology are not visual spaces." Visual space, in McLuhan's terminology, is uniform, continuous, and connected; and associated with traditional concepts of reason, order, and civilization. To explain non-visual space, McLuhan reverts to the kind of reasoning by analogy that pervades both his conversation and his writing; "to a blind man, the most significant space is the gap: for him, as for the Oriental, it is the interval that is important—not the connection; and the interval is tactile and auditory, not visual. Electronic space is also tactile and auditory; the boy who holds a transistor radio to his ear is creating an acoustic space bubble, which is like an aqualung."

It is McLuhan's argument that, in what he calls "the electric age," visual continuity is replaced by a simultaneous field. A McLuhan analogy: "In a space capsule there is no right-side-up." Another, more elaborate sample of analogic reasoning: "The slum is the most *avant garde* space in our society; it includes all the senses; and *avant garde* art creates spaces which are exactly like a slum."

McLuhan accounts for the obscurity of his theories with an aphorism: "The future of the future is the present; but the present is so obvious that it is invisible." The corollary of this concept might well be the most convincing explanation yet devised for the history of architecture over the last 200 years: "A new environment does not reveal itself until it has been superseded. The old technologies become today's art forms, so that what appears as today is always yesterday."

Using an analysis of the present to discover the shape of the future might be called McLuhan's basic methodology, and he takes aspects of contemporary culture—that others might consider passing fads—and treats them with enormous seriousness. For example, the new improvised dances of the discotheque strike McLuhan as a response to the simultaneity of a primarily aural environment, whereas traditional ballroom dancing ("uniform, continuous, connected") is a relic of the visual world of print. Similarly, he looks at the cacophony of the city today and concludes that its future is "a showcase of new technologies." He also observes that the railroad established the spacing of today's cities (a linear sequential pattern) whereas the airplane has made "all cities suburbs of each other," (simultaneity).

McLuhan, however, does not view with alarm. Indeed it could be said that he views with delight. The environment, he remarks cheerfully, is a teaching machine; and he looks forward to man's complete mastery over his teacher: "In the world of space technology, the planet becomes a human artifact, not a natural habitat. In the new satellite environment, the planet becomes Williamsburg: we are going to deal with it tenderly as a cherished archaeological exhibit."

McLuhan foresees that the role of the architect and other creative people will be a primary one in the situation he describes: "The artist leaves the ivory tower for the control tower, and abandons the shaping of art in order to program the environment itself as a work of art."   [151–152]

A happy thought on which to end, and McLuhan is a convincing speaker; but somehow, in retrospect, it all seemed to become a great deal less simple and straightforward. We therefore decided to send a transcript of McLuhan's remarks to a group of architects and planners across the country, to see what their reactions would be.

In general, the architects' comments showed considerable interest in McLuhan's ideas, and considerable dismay over the way they are expressed. Atlanta architect Fred Bainbridge said that McLuhan's style reminded him of the items that the New Yorker magazine runs under the heading "The Mysterious East." John Hedjuk, chairman of the department of architecture at Cooper Union, suggested that perhaps McLuhan had modeled his discourse on Gertrude Stein's, while Memphis architect Roy Harrover remarked wryly that McLuhan's mode of expression was not uniform, continuous or connected.

Most of the architects contacted, however, agreed with McLuhan's basic premise. Gyo Obata, of the St. Louis firm of Hellmuth, Obata and Kassabaum, said that he agreed completely with McLuhan's view that our environment will be changed drastically by electronic technology; and Roy Harrover stated that "McLuhan seems to me generally to have constructed a vision of our current environment which is quite valid. Although this vision is based upon a study of media in the extremely broad sense of the term, I do feel that it is pertinent to architecture and planning, since any philosophy which affects our attitude to the world around us will automatically affect our architecture."

The concept of non-visual space won a great deal less acceptance. Robert Anderson, a partner in the office of John Andrews, architect in Toronto, pointed out that one could infer "that McLuhan himself encounters the world in visual terms, for the evidence that architects are aware of more than visual form is less apparent, and somewhat difficult to find, but extant nevertheless."

John Hedjuk's dissent was much sharper: "as long as men have eyes, there will be space that a man can see, and this is visual. We now still live in a visual environment, and I suspect that we will continue to do so for some time; nor is visual space necessarily uniform, continuous and connected. As for the comment that, for the blind man, the most significant space is the gap, I would remind Mr. McLuhan that Leonardo da Vinci said that 'Blindness is the sister of death.' " Boston architect Earl Flansburgh added that, just as no amount of phonograph recordings will diminish the need for live performance, in the same way "man is only willing to accept illusionary space— the acoustic aqualung—if he cannot embrace the more complete experience."

John Johansen, in his review in the *American Scholar,* had postulated a translation of McLuhan's non-visual approach into architectural terms: "If the images of the electronic world are continuous, simultaneous, non-classified or noncodified, . . . the viewer will expect all parts and aspects of the building to be made known, to be immediately comprehensible, not as a complete impression but as an all-inclusive image. Buildings will reveal themselves totally. They will clearly express their elements, functions and processes. The viewer will identify with them, feel an empathy with them. . . . The facade in the traditional sense, no matter how richly sculpted or how irregular or bold, will disappear in favor of separate habitable enclosures posed freely in space. . . .

"As modern physics no longer sees a universe which is compact, tightly organized, and in which everything is governed by strict causality, so too, our impressions will not be ordered, controlled, or in sequence. . . .

"Not only is the fixed axial reference point of the Renaissance out of date; but so also is the 'space-time,' or moving station point, conceived by Siegfried Giedion—which might be said to represent the mechanical age of the wheel. . . . We will have a new station point of the electronic age; one that is multiple and simultaneous, a 'simul-station.' . . . The total architectural environment, as McLuhan has said, will be a mythological world in which all things are connected in the human mind and experience, as opposed to the Aristotelian classified world of knowledge and exact definition."

West coast architect Sim Van der Ryn found such an architectural interpretation of McLuhan much too optimistic: "Has it ever occurred to McLuhan that extending man through media can have, and does have, dehumanizing effects? For example, McLuhan does not touch on the steady erosion of privacy through electronic penetration or the ever-increasing bombardment of urban man's sensory equipment."

There is no doubt that McLuhan takes a much more sanguine view of the future than most of the people who make predictions about the environment. Gyo Obata considered such optimism an implied criticism of the prevailing professional attitude: "I think McLuhan's point about the planet becoming a Williamsburg and a cherished archaeological exhibit is a dig at our professional environmental planners and architects, which, hopefully, will cause us to readjust our thinking to the changing world."

Others, however, could not agree. Earl Flansburgh pointed out that any attempt at environmental control must still take place "within the friendly parameters of the earth's basic properties." Roy Harrover observed that the ability of the architect to be an interpreter of society was weakened by the contradictory pressures of being in control. Robert Anderson put the same thought in even stronger terms: "If we are to 'program the environment,' it must not be 'as a work of art,' for art admits of no imperatives. Programing infers an ever-increasing knowledge of the sources of human behavior and implies an ever-increasing temptation to control it. Architects must be governed by strong moral imperatives to resist this temptation."

Whether or not McLuhan's view of the future promises the kind of specific architectural results that John Johansen foresees (and it is questionable whether McLuhan sees the future this way himself), most of the architects contacted seemed to feel that McLuhan's attempt to assess the future impact of communications technology deserved to be taken seriously. The aggregate effect of recent technological inventions is still incalculable, and any and all prophecies should be gratefully received.   [152]

1. The difference between "visual space" and "non-visual space" is a key concept in Barnett's discussion. Can you clarify this distinction with illustrations that make each of them stand out in sharp, separate relief?

2. Carefully catalogue the reactions of all the architects Barnett mentions having consulted, and tally them according to their "pro" or "con" positions regarding McLuhan. How do McLuhan and his ideas seem to fare among this representative group of leading North American architects?

3. Recognizing that Mr. Barnett is an architect, do you find that his comments about McLuhan's style are any different from those of the professional writers and English teachers who have written most of the other articles?

THE MESSAGE OF MARSHALL McLUHAN —SPECIAL REPORT

Newsweek
Unsigned Press Dept feature

McLuhan, right or wrong?

The Oracle of Toronto thinks big—his theory of communications offers nothing less than an explanation of all human culture, past, present and future. And he excites large passions. "McLuhan's teaching is radical, new, animated by high intelligence, and capable of moving people to social action," writes the novelist George P. Elliott. "If he is wrong, it matters." "He's swinging, switched on, with it and NOW," says Amherst Prof. Benjamin DeMott. "And wrong." "He makes us question all the shibboleths of Western culture," counters critic Gerald Stearn. "He can only be considered a stimulating thinker on a scale quite similar to Freud and Einstein."

Freud, Einstein—Marshall McLuhan?

On first inspection, there are some rough similarities. Freud and Einstein, each in his turn, offered propositions about the psyche and the universe that were plainly contradicted by the senses of all right-thinking men (Sex drives in infants? Space is curved?). And now McLuhan proclaims equally barmy notions to contradict the eye and bend and boggle the mind.

Reprinted from *Newsweek*, March 6, 1967, pp. 53–57. Copyright, *Newsweek, Inc.*, March, 1967.

He firmly avows, for instance, that watching television is a tactile rather than a visual experience; that man goes through life looking through the rear-view mirror, aware of his environment only after he has left it, and that what is communicated doesn't count as much as how it is communicated. This last, of course, is expressed in the aphorism that is McLuhan's trademark: "The Medium Is the Message."

If these propositions are correct, the implications of McLuhanism are staggering. In his world view, wars are obsolete and so are political dogmas, the assembly line and white supremacy; the age of the individual is over, and a new man is emerging.

"I explore, I don't explain," McLuhan explains. Yet he offers himself to the world as a kind of Dr. Spock of pop culture. Are the children alienated? McLuhan has the answer there—somewhere. From Marshall's McClues, Camp Followers supposedly can tell which fashions will sell, and politicians which candidates will go over big. A girl can even read McLuhan's notion of why she makes herself more provocative when she wears dark glasses and fishnet stockings.

LSD and Needles: Naturally enough, McLuhan himself is viewed through a rear-view mirror, darkly. To critics he is, at best, obscure; at worst, a charlatan. But the McLuhanite tong around the country is enthusiastic enough to have made him courted by industry, and to have made the paperback edition of his major work, "Understanding Media: The Extensions of Man," the fastest-selling nonfiction book at Harvard and at Ann Arbor. At Columbia, a coed likens reading McLuhan to taking LSD. "It can turn you on," she says. "LSD doesn't mean anything until you consume it—likewise McLuhan." Fordham has tapped McLuhan next semester for the Albert Schweitzer Chair, a New York State-supported sinecure with a $100,000 per year fund to cover salary and research.

In "Understanding Media," McLuhan needled Bell Telephone's research department for being "oblivious to the real meaning of the telephone." Stung, the Bell people recently journeyed up to Toronto for a séance. McLuhan has an office at Time Inc. and an arrangement to write articles for Look. And last year he signed—-at a handsome fee—with the Container Corp. of America to give a lecture to Container executives and selected customers. In the lecture, McLuhan told his audience they were engaged in the business of mass production at a time when the age of mass production was coming to an end.

'Mysterioso': Already apotheosized in a score of publications ranging from the New Mexico Quarterly to Life magazine, McLuhan is the subject of a new anthology, "McLuhan, Hot and Cool," edited by Gerald Stearn and due out in May from the Dial Press. This week, Bantam Books will bring out McLuhan's latest treatise, "The Medium Is the Massage" *(160 pages. $1.45).* The pun is intended: "Massage" is a once-over-lightly kneading of the idea contained in McLuhan's "Understanding Media." On March 19, he will be the subject of an hour-long NBC television documentary that eschews the usual sequential reporting in favor of quick cuts, overlapped images and out-of-focus shots of McLuhan. "Mysterioso," explains Ernest Pintoff, the producer. And in the ultimate accolade, McLuhan's name has passed into the language. The French apply the term *mcluhanisme* to the mixed-media world of pop art; more invidiously, "McLuhan" has become a synonym for impenetrable prose, as when one columnist accused George Romney of reading too much McLuhan.

Most literary critics tend to favor this second usage. "It is not possible to give a rational summary of McLuhan's ideas," George Elliott declares. "His writing is deliberately antilogical: circular, repetitious, unqualified, gnomic, outrageous." McLuhan, as one not unsympathetic crit-[53–54]ic says, is too "messy and journalistic" for the academic-literary Establishment. And Jerome Agel, an early McLuhan booster and the publisher of the non-Establishment tabloid Books, claims McLuhan was "discovered by young people and the artists, not by the literary crowd. Most of the critics panned him," he adds, "and they still do not understand his books." Nevertheless, the harshness of the reviews didn't hinder sales too much. "Media" has sold more than 9,000 in hardcover—not bad for a serious $7.50 work—and more than 100,000 in soft.

Even more than style, the critics abhor McLuhan's message. McLuhan, it is whispered, actually *likes* television. He is accused of electronic chiliasm, of being an evangelist on behalf of the whole ad-wracked, meretricious pop kingdom-to-come of the media. He has become, as Elliott puts it, "a double agent" who "went out among tribalizing Media as a spy from civilization but stayed there too long." As the CIA knows, however, the intelligence agent's position is always an ambiguous one, and Madison Avenue tends to treat McLuhan gingerly. San Francisco advertising man Howard Gossage proclaims McLuhan is "an Archimedes who has given the ad industry levers to move the world." But Doyle Dane Bernbach president William Bernbach says he "has read only bits and pieces of McLuhan and our agency has not been influenced by him."

Whose Miasma? That McLuhan should be indicted for treason to scholarship and accused of shilling for pop culture, constitutes perhaps the greatest paradox of all about this paradoxical man. As it happens, he is an Establishment figure himself; his doctorate is from Cambridge University, and for two decades he has been writing serious textbooks and straight prose for such scholarly media as the Sewanee Review and the Journal of Economic History. He is a devout Roman Catholic by conversion, and far from selling out to the brave new media world, McLuhan may have a means of coming to grips with it.

Just possibly, then, the miasma about McLuhan may reside in the eyes of his critics. Just possibly, the new environment that McLuhan discerns should be studied as carefully as the O_2 system in the Apollo spaceship. Just possibly, understanding McLuhan may help ensure that earth's environment sustains rather than destroys the crew. Right or wrong, then, it matters to understand McLuhan, his media and his message.

Oar No. 3: McLuhan was born in Edmonton in 1911. "My mother was Baptist, my father [an insurance salesman] was Methodist," McLuhan recalls. "Spiritually, I shopped around as a student." At the University of Manitoba, he started out by studying engineering and reading G. K. Chesterton, later switched to English literature and the more weighty Catholic writers, such as Maritain and Gilson. As an undergraduate at Cambridge University from 1934 to 1936, he rowed for Trinity Hall and his varnished No. 3 oar now hangs in his office in a converted town house on the campus of the University of Toronto's St. Michael's College, along with a large photograph of beat poet Allen Ginsberg and a portrait of James Joyce. At Cambridge, McLuhan came under the influence of Wyndham Lewis, one of the first literary figures to study popular culture seriously.

At Cambridge, too, McLuhan acquired the galaxy of heroes that shaped his later message: Edgar Allan Poe ("He was the inventor of the detective story," McLuhan says. "He made his readers work, made them do-it-themselves"); James Joyce ("He starts with language as the ultimate medium; the whole of 'Finnegan's Wake' is a study of the effects of technology on all of human society"); Gustave Flaubert ("He pointed out that style is a way of perception"); T. S. Eliot and Ezra Pound ("Their poems are full of jazz idioms and pop cult forms"); and Rimbaud, Baudelaire and Mallarmé ("I learned my style from the symbolists—they suggest but do not say all . . .").

McLuhan returned to Cambridge again as a graduate student in 1939, to write his thesis on the poet Thomas Nashe—and, incidentally, to take his honeymoon with Corinne Lewis, a young Texas-born actress he had met the year before at California's Pasadena Playhouse. A strikingly handsome woman, Corinne McLuhan occasionally edits her husband, chauffeurs him around town in the family Toronado and keeps track of their two sons and four daughters.

By his own account, McLuhan's first practical encounter with popular culture occurred in 1936, when he arrived to teach freshman classes at the University of Wisconsin. "I was confronted with young Americans I was incapable of understanding," he recalls. "I felt an urgent need to study their popular culture in order to get through."

Subliminal Sex: The eventful result of this confrontation with pop culture was McLuhan's "The Mechanical Bride" (1951). The Bride is subliminal sex in the service of technology, particularly as revealed by the way some advertising tries to move goods. McLuhan wants to know what mass media have done to American culture; to find out, he looks at ads for autos, caskets and deodorants.

The targets were familiar enough; in the early '50s, sociologists like David Riesman and Reuel Denney, among others, were looking at similar topics. But McLuhan went about his analysis in a jazzier, elliptical manner. In "Bride," his Ph.D. dissertation prose gave way to provocative headlines or glosses. "Does the American immigrant have to reject his father?" asks McLuhan in introducing a discussion of Maggie and Jiggs. There were Joycean puns and word plays; with Life Buoy and Lysol, "Little B.O. Peep Has Lost Her Sheep."

Though well-received by his peers, "Bride" has long been out of print. But a Daughter of the Bride will soon appear; [54–55] McLuhan, aided by his 24-year-old son Eric, is just finishing up and sending to his editors at McGraw-Hill a series of some 140 ads and glosses he has been collecting over the last ten years. The new collection is entitled "Culture Is Our Business," and is full of his re-joycings and probes of such new cultural manifestations as the Jolly Green Giant, Muzak and the Television Information Office.

Coming of Age: After "Bride" came "The Gutenberg Galaxy" (1962) and "Understanding Media" (1964), which examine not only the pop objects of the new technological age but how the age itself came into being. As McLuhan tells it, he has a box seat. Canada and Catholic-supported St. Michael's —the public University of Toronto went ecumenical long before Vatican Council II—provide him with a quiet nineteenth-century vantage point to view the frantic twentieth-century to the south.

McLuhan says he is fond of Canada because it is "a backward country. There are no interruptions and distractions and yet it is close to the center of the world." Also, his light teaching load, together with his disinclination to play the academic climbing game, provide him with time to go with his perspective. McLuhan has been Director of the University of Toronto's Centre for Culture and Technology since 1964, but the imposing name is misleading; actually the Centre consists of McLuhan, his secretary and the down-at-the-heels office they share. No computers, no labs and no staff. Instead, various Toronto professors attach themselves from time to time to collaborate with McLuhan.

In his two decades at Toronto, McLuhan used his time to remain a student. In the 1950s, it was a case of informally but assiduously supplementing his literature major with a strong minor in science and art. With designer Harley Parker and anthropologist Edmund Carpenter, a student of Eskimo culture, he put out Explorations, a magazine modeled after Wyndham Lewis's Dadaesque venture BLAST. McLuhan plans to use some of his Fordham money to bring Parker and Carpenter to New York.

"The Gutenberg Galaxy" and "Understanding Media" reflect the synthesis of literature and science. Both books show off McLuhan's appallingly encyclopedic erudition, his exasperating method and the scatter-shot sweep of his theory of culture and communications. The whole is so chaotic that even friendly critics despair. Many of the sources he uses to build his theory, as Prof. Raymond Waddington has pointed out, are "eccentric and simplistic." He cites, for example, an economist who believes trading can be traced to the monkey's habit of swinging from tree to tree.

Leaving aside most of the monkeyshines, McLuhan in short-course form goes like this:

The basic premise is that there have been three Ages of Man—the Pre-literate or Tribal, the Gutenberg or Individual and the present Electric or Retribalized. Each age, says McLuhan, is shaped by the form of the information available. And by information McLuhan means not only the standard media such as print and TV, but also clothes, clocks, money and any artifact that conveys meaning.

Triple Play: McLuhan's claim is that these information modes or media alter our sensory life—that is, what we see, hear, feel, taste and smell, and, therefore, know. For example, the development of such "media" as tools and language among the low-browed hominids led to the explosive development of the brain and to man's differentiation from other species—and not the other way around. McLuhan sees each medium as a similar extension and modifier of man; just as the caveman's ax is an extension of the hand, so the book is an extension of the eye, and so electric circuitry—the telegraph, telephone and television—is an extension of the central nervous system. Each such extension, McLuhan maintains, changes the balance among the five senses—making one sense dominant and altering the way man feels, thinks and acts toward information. As a result, a new environment is created, spatial relations are reconceptualized. It is a triple play; new media to new sensory balance to new environment. This, he says, is why the medium is the message, why the effect is important, why the fact that the TV image is composed of phosphor dots is more important than whether the dots are carrying the Smothers Brothers or Uncle Vanya.

Bomb: Thus in the pre-alphabet age, the ear was dominant; "hearing was believing." Man lived in acoustic space—a world of tribes, emotion, mystery and communal participation. Beginning with the Greeks, the new medium of the phonetic alphabet forced the magic world of the ear to yield to a new sensory balance centered on the neutral world of the eye. Later, Gutenberg's invention of movable type forced man to comprehend in a linear, uniform, connected, continuous fashion. A whole new environment—the Gutenberg Galaxy—emerged. The portable book was like a hydrogen bomb dropped on the tribal world; for the first time, man could read and think in isolation. Individualism was born, and it became possible to separate thought from action (*vide* Hamlet). Politically, the newly discovered privacy of the reader made a point of view possible; economically, linear thought produced the assembly line and industrial society; in physics, it led to the Newtonian and Cartesian views of the universe as a mechanism in which it is possible to locate a physical event in space and time; in art, linearity produced perspective; in literature, the chronological narrative.

Then, in the nineteenth century man entered the Electric Age with the invention of a new medium, the telegraph. The Gutenberg galactic explosion that had shattered the old tribal unity of the ancients gave way to a huge implosion; [55–56] electric circuitry bound up the world in a web of instant awareness and brought all the fragmentary pieces back together. The old, linear visual connections were severed, and the aural and tactile senses emerged once again. With Telstar and other high-speed communications annihilating space and time, an "all-at-once" environment has taken shape. Tribal man has returned and the world has contracted into a global village in which everyone is involved with everyone else—the haves with the have-nots (foreign aid, war on poverty), Negroes with whites (sit-ins and rights marches) adults with teen-agers (Sunset Strip riots).

'Hot' and 'Cool': Thus, to McLuhan, the key word in the new Electric Age is "involvement." His second major insight (or outrage, if one disagrees) is that the old print medium involves one sense (the visual) while the new electric media, particularly television, involve all the senses simultaneously. This is why he says that some media are "hot" and some "cool." Print, McLuhan insists, is a hot medium: the printed page projects plenty of information; it comes in as high definition for one sense—but does not involve all the senses. By contrast, he says, TV is a cool, low-definition medium; that is, it provides a minimum of information—but involves all the senses all at once. This means there is high participation and involvement.

To the man who has stared for hours on end at the little black box this simply doesn't make sense—to him, quite naturally, TV seems visual. McLuhan would reply: that's eye thinking. In reality, he says, with television *you* are the screen; the TV image is not a still photo but a ceaselessly forming contour or mosaic projecting all those little Seurat-like dots onto you, the screen, at the rate of 3 million impulses a second. You have to fill in the mosaic, connect all the dots. "You have to be 'with it'," McLuhan admonishes, adding Delphically that "the phrase 'with it' came in since TV."

McLuhan also holds that the same messages come over differently via different media. As a prime example, he cites the 1960 debates between Nixon and Kennedy. To those who simply concluded that Kennedy looked and spoke better, McLuhan's theory seems absurd. The public Richard Nixon, he says, was a hot, forceful, high-definition type, while the public Kennedy was a cool, nonchalant low-definition figure. During the later debates, Nixon became more forceful—hot and definite in McLuhan's terms—and many of the political sages thought he was catching Kennedy. But for McLuhan it was the end of Nixon. In a newspaper interview which appeared on Oct. 15, 1960, McLuhan gave the nod to Kennedy. (Yet when McLuhan watched Nixon in another context on TV—talking in a relaxed manner on the "Jack Paar Show"— he knew that *that* Nixon could have won the Presidency.)

Television brings not only the voting booth into the living room but also the civil-rights march along Alabama's U.S. 80 and the bulldozing of a village in Vietnam—and involves the audience intimately. "Without television, there would be no civil-rights legislation," McLuhan declares, sweepingly. Moreover, "a hot war like Vietnam over a cool medium like TV is doomed. The young oppose the war not out of pacifism but out of their pain of involvement."

Ending—eventually—the war in Vietnam is only one of the effects McLuhan claims for television. McLuhan holds that the changes in the environment "since TV" are so pervasive that he despairs of presenting them. All he is able to offer is an "inventory" of effects that includes:

Sex. Among the first victims of television that McLuhan counts are his own views in "The Mechanical Bride" emphasizing the visual nature of advertising, particularly the sexual come-on. "There has been a dimming down of the visual," he says. "We are now in the all-involving tactile mode." That's why discothèques are loud and dark. It is also why a girl is sexier in cool media like dark glasses and fishnet stockings: these things invite involvement.

Morals. There will be more sleeping around among single young people, McLuhan says, but married couples will be models of rectitude—because that's how it is in tribal culture.

Fashions. The shift from the visual to the tactile also is signaled by boys and girls who dress alike and cut their hair alike—gender differentiation now comes with touch. Miniskirts, topless waitresses and the trend toward nudity on beaches and in films are also signs of the TV times: as the visual becomes less important no one minds a show of skin.

Sports. Baseball is linear, individual—the pitcher stands on the mound, the batter waits. By contrast football is like the TV mosaic itself—action occurs simultaneously, with the entire team involved and scattering all over the screen. So football has supplanted baseball as the most popular U.S. sport.

The politics of consensus. McLuhan claims TV is killing off the voting bloc and elevating the leader who tries to be the all-inclusive image; instead of offering a political viewpoint, politicians now will take inclusive political postures.

The generation gap. The young TV generation has a completely different sensory life than the adult generation which grew up on hot radio and hot print. Hence, young people today reject jobs and goals—that's linear thinking. They reject the consumer life—that's fragmented and specialist. They want roles, that is, involvement.

Business reorganizations. The mosaic mesh of TV is driving out lineality in industry. Since TV, McLuhan declares, the assembly line has disappeared and staff and line structures have dissolved in management. In fact, all lines are disappearing: stag lines, receiving lines and pencil lines from the backs of nylons.

Some of this looks—sounds, feels—plausible; some, preposterous. Pencil lines have disappeared from nylons, but have assembly lines disappeared from Detroit? Certainly they have, McLuhan would reply. What then are the autoworkers doing in those plants? Beginning to make custom cars, McLuhan says, like the "basic" Mustang which comes with a score of optional accessories. Why then don't we all realize this? The trouble, says McLuhan, is that people are still looking through the rear-view mirror.

The idea of rear-view mirrorism is the [56–57] newest McLuhanism. When faced with a new situation, McLuhan writes in "The Medium is the Message," "we always tend to attach ourselves to the objects, to the flavor of the most recent past." Contemporary society is like a driver who sees neither ahead to the future nor outside his side window to the present but looks only at the past in the rear-view mirror. U.S. adult society, he says, exists imaginatively among the Cartwrights of Bonanza-land, closing off its life—like so many wagons drawn in a circle—unaware of what's happening outside.

DEW-liner: But a few people are alert. Mostly they are the avant-garde poets, artists and sleuths—McLuhan includes himself in these categories—who have consciously sharpened their perceptions, realized the phoniness of the rear-view mirror and forced themselves to look ahead and see the environment as it really is. The artist, McLuhan says, serves like Canada's Distant Early Warning (DEW) Line; his job is to alert society.

From this short—and considerably glossed over—course on McLuhan, several judgments can be drawn.

First, none of his basic ideas is in itself startling or even original. Discussions about form as content date to Aristotle; Buckminster Fuller, and Henri Bergson before him, explained how tools of man can become extensions of man, and sociologists long ago gave the designation "cultural lag" to situations in which social organizations fall behind technological development. Even the aphorism about the medium and the message is not wholly new; the late Canadian economic historian Harold Innis pointed out the role of print in the transformation of culture more than a decade ago—a priority McLuhan has graciously acknowledged.

Reply: Second, McLuhan is a synthesizer. He has gathered amorphous and scattered ideas, thought them through with force and vivacity, and opened up new areas of awareness. "He has joyously enriched the scope of what is relevant," says the English critic George Steiner. "He has made the jungle of the world more interesting." And Harvard's David Riesman lauds McLuhan as "a reply to the solemn commentators who look with alarm on the rise of pop culture."

Third, McLuhan himself isn't a very good DEW Line. The essence of a DEW Line is to discriminate between the radar scope blips of real incoming enemy planes and the patterns caused by flights of geese and the northern lights. But in his books and in his conversations, McLuhan lets everything through, no matter how outrageous or exaggerated or contradictory. He often takes the good insights that he has hit upon and pushes them too far. The U.S. may still be largely a visual culture just emerging from the nineteenth century. The Soviet Union may be an aural-tactile culture, just emerging from the Middle Ages. But is that why the CIA sends U-2 reconnaissance planes over the Soviet Union while the KGB plants bugs in U.S. embassies? Everything becomes grist for his mad, mod mill. Is the subject the youthful Red Guards? That's easy. China is still a tribal environment, says McLuhan, and, of course, this permits participation of children in adult affairs.

Fourth, the leaky DEW Line and the impossibly broad argument are the inevitable consequences of McLuhan's own beliefs. He is delivering his message via a medium—the printed page—which he has stated is no longer adequate to command the attention and involvement of modern electric man. McLuhan's solution in "Galaxy" and "Media" is to invent a "mosaic writing" that attempts to simulate the disconnected, low-definition coolness of television—and thus capture the reader. The result is deliberately repetitious, confused and dogmatic. In McLuhan's new picture book, "The Medium Is the Massage," he attempts to go further toward mosaic presentation but in shorter, less repetitive takes.

Tailor-made: Despite his dilemma, McLuhan doesn't plan to abandon the book form. He and Toronto Prof. Richard Schoeck are collaborating on a series of volumes of poetry and prose for high-school seniors and college freshmen (written non-mosaically but with accompanying tapes); there is "Culture Is Our Business" as well as "Space in Poetry and Painting," with Harley Parker and "A Message to the Fish," with management-consultant Ralph Baldwin. "The Fish," explains McLuhan, "are the corporation heads moving about in media they know nothing about." Finally, he is writing "The Future of the Book," with William Jovanovich, the president of Harcourt, Brace & World. The *future* of the book? Yes, thanks to photocopying and computers, McLuhan allows that books have a future; they will no longer be assembly-line products, they will be services, tailor-made (like the car of the future) to meet specific demands phoned to the information retrieval center.

But neither does McLuhan plan to abandon his methods of presentation. "Unless a statement is startling," he says candidly, "no one will pay any attention; they will put it down as a point of view." He considers statements in his books and his speeches as tentative probes—disposable as Kleenex. "I don't necessarily agree with everything I say," he adds.

"Most of my work in the media is like that of a safecracker," McLuhan says in the introduction to Gerald Stearn's "McLuhan, Hot and Cool." "In the beginning I don't know what's inside. I just set myself down in front of the problem and begin to work. I grope, I probe, I listen, I test—until the tumblers fall and I'm in."

Jokes: But does he really want to get in—or stay out? His attitude about the media is a little like the punch line in one of his after-dinner jokes: a man went out on a date with Siamese twins and the next day a friend asked if he had a good time; his answer: "Well, yes and no."

Sometimes he seems to be saying the media threaten man. Education, he says, must serve as civil defense against the media fallout; the Ivory Tower must become the control tower. And he likens modern man to the mariner in Edgar Allan Poe's story, "A Descent Into the Maelstrom." The mariner is caught in a whirlpool; but he figures out the relative velocities of currents and saves himself. The sailor's strategy, McLuhan suggests, is his own: understand our predicament, our electrically configured whirl, and save ourselves from drowning.

On the other hand, McLuhan describes, with obvious approval, cool men in a tribal world of full sensory involvement and group participation. It is a situation that the Catholic McLuhan finds not unlike the rich liturgical services of his church. Further, the scholar McLuhan acknowledges that a world where the Ivory Tower is so important can't be too bad.

McLuhan isn't specific about his future strategy of social action; he speaks instead in science-fiction terms about learning how to control the thermostat of the environment in order to shape the new world to come. The thought of just such a thermostat, manipulated by technicians or hidden persuaders, chills many of McLuhan's readers. But he says, optimistically, that the futurists will use their thermostats rationally, for "who would want to turn up the heat to 150?"

McLuhan, right or wrong?

Well, yes and no.   [57]

1. This thoroughgoing and conscientious review of McLuhan's ideas was published in March of 1967, some three years after the ap-

pearance of *Understanding Media* and the rush of criticism and controversy that it provoked. Read the article carefully, compare it with its predecessors, and report on what, if anything, this 1967 analysis offers that is new and important.

2. In what ways, according to this article, is the creative artist analogous to the Canadian DEW Line system of North American military defense? Is this an analogy McLuhan has used elsewhere?

3. On p. *57* we read that McLuhan ". . . often takes the good insights that he has hit upon and carries them too far." What are some specific examples of the McLuhan testament to which this judgment might refer?

LIKE YOGA, NOT LIKE THE MOVIES

Forbes: Unsigned Feature

When the late Fred Allen referred drily to radio as "furniture that talks," he said about all that was to be said. But today's home electronics cannot be so lightly dismissed. It is not only changing society and the economy, it is changing people themselves. The social philosopher of the electronic age is Canadian scholar Marshall McLuhan, co-author of the recently published book, *The Medium is the Massage.* Perhaps fittingly, he speaks in a language that is as obtuse and rambling as Allen's was sharp and witty. In spite of this, businessmen, especially in advertising and publishing, listen to him even if they don't agree—or even understand him.

Interviewed in his University of Toronto office last month by a *Forbes* researcher, McLuhan talked about what electronics means to business and society. Here are some of the things he said:

"The satellite means, among other things, the end of 'news.' It can zero in on any part of the globe at any time and give you direct participation in whatever you want to see going on. No more news reports; they're just a momentary, passing thing of the recent decade. With the satellite, news be-

From *Forbes* Magazine, March 15, 1967, page 40. Reprinted by permission of *Forbes* Magazine.

comes so total, so complete that reports are meaningless. The electronic age is organic, total.

"Closed circuit, for example, makes books available from any library in the world, anywhere in the world. Right now we could have complete access to all the books in the Sorbonne without moving ten feet. There's this same kind of total access to entertainment.

"Entertainment used to mean visiting odd spots in the world. *The Bridge on the River Kwai* is a nice example of an exotic spot and an exotic event. It's entertainment in the old sense, something that takes you out of yourself.

"Entertainment in the future may have quite different patterns and functions. You'll become a yogi, you'll do your self-entertainment in yoga style.

"It's natural, of course, that businessmen should look at the old entertainment patterns. But in fact, I'm pretty sure the whole thing will flip into something like the LSD pattern. The TV companies are playing it wrong. All they're doing is projecting the immediate past into the future.

"Businessmen think of TV as a movie form; it isn't. Children who have never seen movies in theaters but only TV have a very different response to TV than their parents. The TV generation is introverted in the sense of inner tripping. In depth. Profound. Business isn't living in this age. It's living in Bonanza-land, in the past.

"The fact is, the TV images come at you. They go inside you. It's a total reverse of the movies. The industry is striving for photographic images. Trying to make TV like a photograph or movie is utter nonsense. The whole dynamic of TV is to go inside the viewer.

"Research studies show that people who look at ads are the ones who already have the product. Yet the advertisers think of ads as a way of alerting people to the existence of products. The fact to learn is that advertising is a service industry that provides its satisfactions quite independent of the product and that people are increasingly tending to get their satisfactions from the ad rather than the product.

"Businessmen think of work as something you can see people doing. The great work of the world has always been done mentally by people making insights.

"It's always been this way with business. 'Who could have predicted?' is their pet phrase. When they look at the future, they consult the rear-view mirror, so they see the immediate past.

"The future is *now*, but people don't know how to look at it. You know the old saying, 'We don't know who discovered water, but we're sure it wasn't a fish.' How could a fish know something that was so completely environmental? This is true of any business.

"Electronic technology dooms all the old mechanical technology. The rug's been pulled out from all Western forms, all the achievements of the past.

"The sort of thing Xerox is doing is the trend of the present and future, except that Xerox is behaving in the usual rear-view style, buying up old publishing companies. This buying up whole textbook companies is hilarious. They're trying to buy markets, not books. What a bunch! Today with satellite cameras you simply participate in events anywhere in the world. You're involved in world events directly. You just go where it's happening. [RCA Chairman David] Sarnoff's notion that technologies are neutral tools is bunk. Technologies are like cannibals that eat alive all existing populations. The first person to get swallowed is the consumer. There's nothing neutral about any technology.

   "Gutenberg was a cannibal but Xerox is a much more potent one; it will swallow us all."

   What's McLuhan talking about? The point is: Obviously he doesn't really mean that Americans are all going to become yogis. But he *is* talking about a change in man's whole orientation. What's he predicting? Possibly he himself isn't sure except he's convinced that the new electronic technology is going to do what the automobile did: change not only the way people live, but people themselves. People once thought of the car as simply a substitute for the horse. But in the end it changed the whole pattern of America—its sex life, its economics, its family life and business. McLuhan seems to be saying that electronics is going to do the same thing; he's probably right. [*40*].

   This is another instance, like the architects' reactions, of McLuhan's influence being felt and reported on from sources that are unexpected and seemingly unrelated to his message. What is the audience normally aimed at by *Forbes* magazine? What interest does its reading public have in McLuhan, as you interpret it from the column that appears in the March 15, 1967, issue?

A SCHOOLMAN'S GUIDE TO MARSHALL McLUHAN

John M. Culkin, S. J.

Education, a seven-year-old assures me, is "how kids learn stuff." Few definitions are as satisfying. It includes all that is essential—a who, a what, and a process. It excludes all the people, places, and things which are only sometimes involved in learning. The economy and accuracy of the definition, however, are more useful in locating the problem than in solving it. We know little enough about *kids,* less about *learning,* and considerably more than we would like to know about *stuff.*

In addition, the whole process of formal schooling is now wrapped inside an environment of speeded-up technological change which is constantly influencing kids and learning and stuff. The jet-speed of this technological revolution, especially in the area of communications, has left us with more reactions to it than reflections about it. Meanwhile back at the school, the student, whose psyche is being programed for tempo, information, and relevance by his electronic environment, is still being processed in classrooms operating on the postulates of another day. The cold war existing between these two worlds is upsetting for both the student and the schools. One thing

JOHN M. CULKIN, S.J., is director of the Center for Communications, Fordham University.

This article, reprinted by permission, was published in *Saturday Review,* March 18, 1967, pp. 51–53+.

is certain: It is hardly a time for educators to plan with nostalgia, timidty, or old formulas. Enter Marshall McLuhan.

He enters from the North, from the University of Toronto where he teaches English and is director of the Center for Culture and Technology. He enters with the reputation as "the oracle of the electric age" and as "the most provocative and controversial writer of this generation." More importantly for the schools, he enters as a man with fresh eyes, with new ways of looking at old problems. He is a man who gets his ideas first and judges them later. Most of these ideas are summed up in his book, *Understanding Media*. His critics tried him for not delivering these insights in their most lucid and practical form. It isn't always cricket, however, to ask the same man to crush the grapes and serve the wine. Not all of McLu is nu or tru, but then again neither is *all* of anybody else. This article is an attempt to select and order those elements of McLuhanism which are most relevant to the schools and to provide the schoolman with some new ways of thinking about the schools.

McLuhan's promise is modest enough: "All I have to offer is an enterprise of investigation into a world that's quite unusual and quite unlike any previous world and for which no models of perception will serve." This unexplored world happens to be the present. McLuhan feels that very few men look at the present with a present eye, that they tend to miss the present by translating it into the past, seeing it through a rear-view mirror. The unnoticed fact of our present is the electronic environment created by the new communications media. It is as pervasive as the air we breathe (and some would add that it is just as polluted), yet its full import eludes the judgments of commonsense or content-oriented perception. The environments set up by different media are not just containers for people; they are processes which shape people. Such influence is deterministic only if ignored. There is no inevitability as long as there is a willingness to contemplate what is happening.

Theorists can keep reality at arm's length for long periods of time. Teachers and administrators can't. They are closeted with reality all day long. In many instances they are co-prisoners with electronic-age students in the old pencil box cell. And it is the best teachers and the best students who are in the most trouble because they are challenging the system constantly. It is the system which has to come under scrutiny. Teachers and students can say, in the words of the Late Late Show, "Baby, this thing is bigger than both of us." It won't be ameliorated by a few dashes of good [51–52] will or a little more hard work. It is a question of understanding these new kids and these new media and of getting the schools to deal with the new electronic environment. It's not easy. And the defenders of the old may prove to be the ones least able to defend and preserve the values of the old.

For some people, analysis of these newer technologies automatically implies approbation of them. Their world is so full of *shoulds* that it is hard to squeeze in an *is*. McLuhan suggests a more positive line of exploration:

> At the moment, it is important that we understand cause and process. The aim is to develop an awareness about print and the newer technologies of

communication so that we can orchestrate them, minimize their mutual frustrations and clashes, and get the best out of each in the educational process. The present conflict leads to elimination of the motive to learn and to diminution of interest in all previous achievement: It leads to loss of the sense of relevance. Without an understanding of media grammars, we cannot hope to achieve a contemporary awareness of the world in which we live.

We have been told that it is the property of true genius to disturb all settled ideas. McLuhan is disturbing in both his medium and his message. His ideas challenge the normal way in which people perceive reality. They can create a very deep and personal threat since they touch on everything in a person's experience. They are just as threatening to the establishment whose way of life is predicated on the postulates he is questioning. The establishment has no history of organizing parades to greet its disturbers.

His medium is perhaps more disturbing than his message. From his earliest work he has described his enterprise as "explorations in communication." The word he uses most frequently today is "probe." His books demand a high degree of involvement from the reader. They are poetic and intuitive rather than logical and analytic. Structurally, his unit is the sentence. Most of them are topic sentences—which are left undeveloped. The style is oral and breathless and frequently obscure. It's a different kind of medium.

"The medium is the message," announced McLuhan a dozen years ago in a cryptic and uncompromising aphorism whose meaning is still being explored. The title of his latest book, an illustrated popular paperback treatment of his theories, playfully proclaims that *The Medium Is the Massage*—a title calculated to drive typesetters and critics to hashish and beyond. The original dictum can be looked at in four ways, the third of which includes a massage of importance.

The first meaning would be better communicated orally—"The *medium* is the message." The *medium* is the thing to study. The *medium* is the thing you're missing. Everybody's hooked on content; pay attention to form, structure, framework, *medium*. The play's the thing. The medium's the thing. McLuhan makes the truth stand on its head to attract attention. Why the medium is worthy of attention derives from its other three meanings.

Meaning number two stresses the relation of the medium to the content. The form of communication not only alters the content, but each form also has preferences for certain kinds of messages. Content always exists in some form and is, therefore, to some degree governed by the dynamics of that form. If you don't know the medium, you don't know the message. The insight is neatly summed up by Dr. Edmund Carpenter: "English is a mass medium. All languages are mass media. The new mass media—film, radio, TV—are new languages, their grammars as yet unknown. Each codifies reality differently; each conceals a unique metaphysics. Linguists tell us it's possible to say anything in any language if you use enough words or images, but there's rarely time; the natural course is for a culture to exploit its media biases. . . ."

It is always content-in-form which is mediated. In this sense, the medium is co-message. The third meaning for the M-M formula emphasizes the relation of the medium to the individual psyche. The medium alters the perceptual habits of its users. Independent of the content, the medium itself gets through. Pre-literate, literate, and post-literate cultures see the world through different-colored glasses. In the process of delivering content the medium also works over the sensorium of the consumer. To get [52–53] this subtle insight across, McLuhan punned on message and came up with massage. The switch is intended to draw attention to the fact that a medium is not something neutral—it does something to people. It takes hold of them, it jostles them, it bumps them around, it massages them. It opens and closes windows in their sensorium. Proof? Look out the window at the TV generation. They are rediscovering texture, movement, color, and sound as they retribalize the race. TV is a real grabber; it really massages those lazy, unused senses.

The fourth meaning underscores the relation of the medium to society. Whitehead said, "The major advances in civilization are processes that all but wreck the societies in which they occur." The media massage the society as well as the individual. The results pass unnoticed for long periods of time because people tend to view the new as just a little bit more of the old. Whitehead again: "The greatest invention of the nineteenth century was the invention of the method of invention. A new method entered into life. In order to understand our epoch, we can neglect all details of change, such as railways, telegraphs, radios, spinning machines, synthetic dyes. We must concentrate on the method in itself: That is the real novelty which has broken up the foundations of the old civilization." Understanding the medium or process involved is the key to control.

The media shape both content and consumer and do so practically undetected. We recall the story of the Russian worker whose wheelbarrow was searched every day as he left the factory grounds. He was, of course, stealing wheelbarrows. When your medium is your message and they're only investigating content, you can get away with a lot of things—like wheelbarrows, for instance. It's not the picture but the frame. Not the contents but the box. The blank page is not neutral; nor is the classroom.

McLuhan's writings abound with aphorisms, insights, for-instances, and irrelevancies which float loosely around recurring themes. They provide the raw materials of a do-it-yourself kit for tidier types who prefer to do their exploring with clearer charts. What follows is one man's McLuhan served up in barbarously brief form. Five postulates, spanning nearly 4,000 years, will serve as the fingers in this endeavor to grasp McLuhan:

1) 1967 B.C.—*All the senses get into the act.* A conveniently symmetrical year for a thesis which is partially cyclic. It gets us back to man before the Phoenician alphabet. We know from our contemporary ancestors in the jungles of New Guinea and the wastes of the Arctic that preliterate man lives in an all-at-once sense world. The reality which bombards him from all directions is picked up with the omni-directional antennae of sight, hearing, touch,

smell, and taste. Films such as *The Hunters* and *Nanook of the North* depict primitive men tracking game with an across-the-board sensitivity which mystifies Western, literate man. We mystify them too. And it is this cross-mystification which makes inter-cultural abrasions so worthwhile.

Most people presume that their way of perceiving the world is *the* way of perceiving the world. If they hang around with people like themselves, their mode of perception may never be challenged. It is at the poles (literally and figuratively) that the violent contrasts illumine our own unarticulated perceptual prejudices. Toward the North Pole, for example, live Eskimos. A typical Eskimo family consists of a father, a mother, two children, and an anthropologist. When the anthropologist goes into the igloo to study Eskimos, he learns a lot about himself. Eskimos see pictures and maps equally well from all angles. They can draw equally well on top of a table or underneath it. They have phenomenal memories. They travel without visual bearings in their white-on-white world and can sketch cartographically accurate maps of shifting shorelines. They have forty or fifty words for what we call "snow." They live in a world without linearity, a world of acoustic space. They are Eskimos. Their natural way of perceiving the world is different from our natural way of perceiving the world.

Each culture develops its own balance of the senses in response to the demands of its environment. The most generalized formulation of the theory would maintain that the individual's modes of cognition and perception are influenced by the culture he is in, the language he speaks, and the media to which he is exposed. Each culture, as it were, provides its constituents with a custom-made set of goggles. The differences in perception are a question of degree. Some cultures are close enough to each other in perceptual patterns so that the differences pass unnoticed. Other cultural groups, such as the Eskimo and the American teen-ager, are far enough away from us to provide esthetic distance.

2) *Art imitates life.* In *The Silent Language* Edward T. Hall offers the thesis that all art and technology is an extension of some physical or psychic element of man. Today man has developed extensions for practically everything he used to do with his body: stone axe for hand, wheel for foot, glasses for eyes, radio for voice and ears. Money is a way of storing energy. This externalizing of individual, specialized functions is now, by definition, at its most advanced stage. Through the electronic media of telegraph, telephone, radio, and television, man has now equipped his world with a nervous system similar to the one within his own body. President Kennedy is shot and the world instantaneously reels from the impact of the bullets. Space and time dissolve un-[53–70]der electronic conditions. Current concern for the United Nations, the Common Market, ecumenism, reflects this organic thrust toward the new convergence and unity which is "blowing in the wind." Now in the electric age, our extended faculties and senses constitute a single instantaneous and coexistent field of experience. It's all-at-once. It's shared-by-all. McLuhan calls the world "a global village."

3) *Life imitates art.* We shape our tools and thereafter they shape us. These extensions of our senses begin to interact with our senses. These media become a massage. The new change in the environment creates a new balance among the senses. No sense operates in isolation. The full sensorium seeks fulfillment in almost every sense experience. And since there is a limited quantum of energy available for any sensory experience, the sense-ratio will differ for different media.

The nature of the sensory effect will be determined by the medium used. McLuhan divides the media according to the quality or definition of their physical signal. The content is not relevant in this kind of analysis. The same picture from the same camera can appear as a glossy photograph or as a newspaper wirephoto. The photograph is well-defined, of excellent pictorial quality, hi-fi within its own medium. McLuhan calls this kind of medium "hot." The newspaper photo is grainy, made up of little dots, low definition. McLuhan calls this kind of medium "cool." Film is hot; television is cool. Radio is hot; telephone is cool. The cool medium or person invites participation and involvement. It leaves room for the response of the consumer. A lecture is hot; all the work is done. A seminar is cool; it gets everyone into the game. Whether all the connections are causal may be debated, but it's interesting that the kids of the cool TV generation want to be so involved and so much a part of what's happening.

4) *We shaped the alphabet and it shaped us.* In keeping with the McLuhan postulate that "the medium is the message," a literate culture should be more than mildly eager to know what books do to people. Everyone is familiar enough with all the enrichment to living mediated through fine books to allow us to pass on to the subtler effects which might be attributed to the print medium, independent of the content involved. Whether one uses the medium to say that *God is dead* or that *God is love* (--- -- ----), the structure of the medium itself remains unchanged. Nine little black marks with no intrinsic meaning of their own are strung along a line with spaces left after the third and fifth marks. It is this stripping away of meaning which allows us to X-ray the form itself.

As an example, while lecturing to a large audience in a modern hotel in Chicago, a distinguished professor is bitten in the leg by a cobra. The whole experience takes three seconds. He is affected through the touch of the reptile, the gasp of the crowd, the swimming sights before his eyes. His memory, imagination, and emotions come into emergency action. A lot of things happen in three seconds. Two weeks later he is fully recovered and wants to write up the experience in a letter to a colleague. To communicate this experience through print means that it must first be broken down into parts [70–71] and then mediated, eyedropper fashion, one thing at a time, in an abstract, linear, fragmented, sequential way. That is the essential structure of print. And once a culture uses such a medium for a few centuries, it begins to perceive the world in a one-thing-at-a-time, abstract, linear, fragmented, sequential way. And it shapes its organizations and schools according to the same premises.

The form of print has become the form of thought. The medium has become the message.

For centuries now, according to McLuhan, the straight line has been the hidden metaphor of literate man. It was unconsciously but inexorably used as the measure of things. It went unnoticed, unquestioned. It was presumed as natural and universal. It is neither. Like everything else it is good for the things it is good for. To say that it is not everything is not to say that it is nothing. The electronic media have broken the monopoly of print; they have altered our sensory profiles by heightening our awareness of aural, tactile, and kinetic values.

5) 1967 A.D.—*All the senses want to get into the act.* Print repressed most sense-life in favor of the visual. The end of print's monopoly also marks the end of a visual monopoly. As the early warning system of art and popular culture indicates, all the senses want to get into the act. Some of the excesses in the current excursions into aural, oral, tactile, and kinetic experience may in fact be directly responsive to the sensory deprivation of the print culture. Nature abhors a vacuum. No one glories in the sight of kids totally out of control in reaction to the Beatles. Some say, "What are the Beatles doing to these kids?" Others say, "What have we done to these kids?" All the data isn't in on what it means to be a balanced human being.

Kids are what the game is all about. Given an honest game with enough equipment to go around, it is the mental, emotional, and volitional capacity of the student which most determines the outcome. The whole complicated system of formal education is in business to get through to kids, to motivate kids, to help kids learn stuff. Schools are not in business to label kids, to grade them for the job market or to babysit. They are there to communicate with them.

Communication is a funny business. There isn't as much of it going on as most people think. Many feel that it consists in saying things in the presence of others. Not so. It consists not in saying things but in having things heard. Beautiful English speeches delivered to monolingual Arabs are not beautiful speeches. You have to speak the language of the audience—of the *whom* in the "who-says-what-to-whom" communications diagram. Sometimes the language is lexical (Chinese, Japanese, Portuguese), sometimes it is regional or personal (125th Street-ese, Holden Caulfield-ese, anybody-ese). It has little to do with words and much to do with understanding the audience. The word for good communication is "Whom-ese"—the language of the audience, of the "whom."

All good communicators use Whom-ese. The best writers, filmmakers, advertising men, lovers, preachers, and teachers all have the knack for thinking about the hopes, fears, and capacity of the other person and of being able to translate their communication into terms which are *relevant* for that person. Whitehead called "inert ideas" the bane of education. Relevance, however, is one of those subjective words. It doesn't pertain to the object in itself but to the object as perceived by someone. The school may decide that history is *important for* the student, but the role of the teacher is to make history *relevant to* the student.

If *what* has to be tailored to the *whom,* the teacher has to be constantly engaged in audience research. It's not a question of keeping up with the latest slang or of selling out to the current mores of the kids. Neither of these tactics helps either learning or kids. But it is a question of knowing what values are strong in their world, of understanding the obstacles to communication, of sensing their style of life. Communication doesn't have to end there, but it can start nowhere else. If they are tuned in to FM and you are broadcasting on AM, there's no communication. Communication forces you to pay a lot of attention to other people.

McLuhan has been paying a great deal of attention to modern kids. Of necessity they live in the present since they have no theories to diffract or reflect what is happening. They are also the first generation to be born into a world in which there was always television. McLuhan finds them a great deal different from their counterparts at the turn of the century when the electric age was just getting up steam.

A lot of things have happened since 1900 and most of them plug into walls. Today's six-year-old has already learned a lot of stuff by the time he shows up for the first day of school. Soon after his umbilical cord was cut he was planted in front of a TV set "to keep him quiet." He liked it enough there to stay for some 3,000 to 4,000 hours before he started the first grade. By the time he graduates from high school he has clocked 15,000 hours of TV time and 10,800 hours of school time. He lives in a world which [71–72] bombards him from all sides with information from radios, films, telephones, magazines, recordings, and people. He learns more things from the windows of cars, trains, and even planes. Through travel and communications he has experienced the war in Vietnam, the wide world of sports, the civil rights movement, the death of a President, thousands of commercials, a walk in space, a thousand innocuous shows, and, one may hope, plenty of Captain Kangaroo.

This is all merely descriptive, an effort to lay out what *is,* not what should be. Today's student can hardly be described by any of the old educational analogies comparing him to an empty bucket or a blank page. He comes to the information machine called school and he is already brimming over with information. As he grows his standards for relevance are determined more by what he receives outside the school than what he receives inside. A recent Canadian film tells the story of a bright, articulate middle class teenager who leaves school because there's "no reason to stay." He daydreams about Vietnam while his teacher drones on about the four reasons for the spread of Christianity and the five points such information is worth on the exam. Only the need for a diploma was holding him in school; learning wasn't, and he left. He decided the union ticket wasn't worth the gaff. He left. Some call him a dropout. Some call him a pushout.

The kids have one foot on the dock and one foot on the ferryboat. Living in two centuries makes for that kind of tension. The gap between the classroom and the outside world and the gap between the generations is wider than it has ever been. Those tedious people who quote Socrates on the conduct of the young are trying vainly to reassure themselves that this is just the perennial problem of communication between generations. 'Tain't so. "Today's child is growing up absurd, because he lives in two worlds, and neither of them inclines him to grow up," says McLuhan in *The Medium is the Massage.* "Growing up—that is our new work, and it is *total.* Mere instruction will not suffice."

Learning is something that people do for themselves. People, places, and things can facilitate or impede learning; they can't make it happen without some cooperation from the learner. The learner these days comes to school with a vast reservoir of vicarious experiences and loosely related facts; he wants to use all his senses in his learning as an active agent in the process of discovery; he knows that all the answers aren't in. The new learner is the result of the new media, says McLuhan. And a new learner calls for a new kind of learning.

Leo Irrera said, "If God had anticipated the eventual structure of the school system, surely he would have shaped man differently." Kids are being tailored to fit the Procrustean forms of schedules, classrooms, memorizing, testing, etc., which are frequently relics from an obsolete approach to learning. It is the total environment which contains the philosophy of education, not the title page in the school catalogue. And it is the total environment which is invincible because it is invisible to most people. They tend to move things around within the old boxes or to build new and cleaner boxes. They should be asking whether or not there should be a box in the first place.

The new learner, who is the product of the all-at-once electronic environment, often feels out of it in a linear, one-thing-at-a-time school environment. The total environment is now the great teacher; the student has competence models against which to measure the effectiveness of his teachers. Nuclear students in linear schools make for some tense times in education. Students with well developed interests in science, the arts and humanities, or current events need assistance to suit their pace, not that of the state syllabus. The straight line theory of development and the uniformity of performance which it so frequently encourages just don't fit many needs of the new learner. Interestingly, the one thing which most of the current educational innovations share is their break with linear or print-oriented patterns: team teaching, non-graded schools, audio-lingual language training, multi-media learning situations, seminars, student research at all levels of education, individualized learning, and the whole shift of responsibility for learning from the teacher to the student. Needless to say, these are not as widespread as they should be, nor were they brought about through any conscious attention to the premises put forward by McLuhan. Like the print-oriented and linear mentality they now modify, these premises were plagiarized from the atmosphere. McLuhan's value is in the power he gives us to predict and control these changes.

There is too much stuff to learn today. McLuhan calls it an age of "information overload." And the information levels outside the classroom are now higher than those in the classroom. Schools used to have a virtual monopoly on information; now they are part-time competitors in the electronic informational surround. And all human knowledge is expanding at computer speed.

Every choice involves a rejection. If we can't do everything, what priorities will govern our educational policies? "The medium is the message" may not be bad for openers. We can no longer teach kids all about a subject; we can teach them what a subject is all about. We have to introduce them to the form, structure, gestalt, grammar, and process of the knowledge involved. What does a math man do when a math man does do math? This approach to the formal element of a discipline can provide a channel of communication between specialists. Its focus is not on content or detail but on the postulates, ground rules, frames of reference, and premises of each discipline. It stresses the modes of cognition and perception proper to each field. Most failures in communication are based on disagreement about items which are only corollaries of a larger thesis. It happens between disciplines, individuals, media, and cultures.

The arts play a new role in education because they are explorations in perception. Formerly conceived as a curricular luxury item, they now become a dynamic way of tuning up the sensorium and of providing fresh ways of looking at familiar things. When exploration and discovery become the themes, the old lines between art and science begin to fade. We have to guide students to becoming their own data processors to operate through pattern recognition. The media themselves serve as both aids to learning and as proper objects of study in this search for an all-media literacy. Current interest in film criticism will expand to include all art and communication forms.

And since the knowledge explosion has blown out the walls between subjects, there will be a continued move toward interdisciplinary swapping and understanding. Many of the categorical walls between things are artifacts left over from the packaging days of print. The specialist's life will be even lonelier as we move further from the Gutenberg era. The trends are all toward wholeness and convergence.

These things aren't true just because Marshall McLuhan says they are. They work. They explain problems in education that nobody else is laying a glove on. When presented clearly and with all the necessary examples and footnotes added, they have proven to be a liberating force for hundreds of teachers who were living through the tension of this cultural fission without realizing that the causes for the tension lay outside themselves. McLuhan's relevance for education demands the work of teams of simultaneous translators and researchers who can both shape and substantiate the insights which are scattered through his work. McLuhan didn't invent electricity or put kids in front of TV sets; he is merely trying to describe what's happening out there so that it can be dealt with intelligently. When someone warns you of an oncoming truck, it's frightfully impolite to accuse him of driving the thing. McLuhan can help kids to learn stuff better.   [72]

1. Father Culkin quotes (p. 51) a rather well-known McLuhan aphorism: "There is no inevitability as long as there is a willingness to contemplate what is happening." Can you explain, preferably with some concrete illustrations, just what this statement means?

2. Culkin claims that it is today's ". . . best teachers and best students who are in the most trouble because they are challenging the system constantly." (p. 51) Do you agree? Explain.

3. Again, at this late date (March 18, 1967), what did this fairly long and detailed article add that was new and important to the body of McLuhan commentary that had already accumulated? Is it essentially favorable or unfavorable toward McLuhan? Are there reasons you can deduce for the position Father Culkin assumes?

PLUGGED-IN GENERATION

Arthur M. Schlesinger, Jr.

Devotees of the prophet will not find much that is new in his latest communiqué; but, to do Professor McLuhan justice, *The Medium Is the Massage* is intended not to offer new illuminations but to sum up the present status of the revelation. As for the unanointed, they will find here the McLuhan argument in its simplest form, stripped of the historical and sociological patter which filled *The Gutenberg Galaxy* and *Understanding Media*. In preparing this primer of McLuhanism, the leader has enlisted the ingenious assistance of the designer Quentin Fiore, who does his best through the manipulation of type and image to simulate electronic effects in a print medium and thereby to facilitate our escape from the bonds of typographical culture.

What then is McLuhanism? It is a chaotic combination of bland assertion, astute guesswork, fake analogy, dazzling insight, hopeless nonsense, shockmanship, showmanship, wisecracks, and oracular mystification, all mingling cockily and indiscriminately in an endless and random dialogue. It also, in my judgment, contains a deeply serious argument. After close study one comes away with the feeling that here is an intelligent man who, for reasons of his own, prefers to masquerade as a charlatan.

ARTHUR M. SCHLESINGER, JR., historian, is Albert Schweitzer Professor of the Humanities at the City University of New York.

This article of his reviewing *The Medium Is the Massage*, reprinted by permission, was first published in *Book Week*, March 19, 1967, pp. 1–2.

His contention is that the emergence of electronic technology is confronting modern man with a crisis of consciousness. Societies, he suggests, have always been "shaped more by the nature of the media by which men communicate than by the content of the communication." Hence the medium is not only the message but, in a typical feeble McLuhan joke, the [1–2] massage: "All media work us over completely. They are so pervasive in their personal, political, economic, aesthetic, psychological, moral, ethical and social consequences that they leave no part of us untouched, unaffected, unaltered." Where Marx located the motive force of history in changes in the means of production, McLuhan locates it in changes in the means of communication.

Thus when talk was the primary form of communication—or, as he has put it elsewhere, when "speech, drum and ear technologies" prevailed—man lived an organic life, at one with his fellow, his community, and his environment. Then Gutenberg came along, and the print technology split the human sensibility, opening up a breach between visual experience on the one hand and auditory and tactile experience on the other. The typographic culture produced the modern world and committed western man to logic, to precision, to specialization, to detachment, to individualism, to privacy.

But every new technology creates a new environment; and today "the instantaneous world of electric informational media," McLuhan argues, is beginning once again to alter the presuppositions of life. Where the print culture gave experience a frame and viewed it in sequence and from a distance, electronic communication is simultaneous and collective; it "involves all of us all at once." All this means a tremendous strain on inherited modes of perception. "We are witnessing," he observes with relish, "a clash of cataclysmic proportions between two great technologies."

The print culture, fighting a rear-guard action, is doing its best to absorb the electronic culture, "to force the new media to do the work of the old." So respectable critics apply literary criteria to television and overlook what is really vital in the new medium—commercials, for example. But the old technology, McLuhan assures us, is doomed; electric circuitry irresistibly generates involvement and unification. The west is being orientalized; "the contained, the distinct, the separate—our Western legacy—are being replaced by the flowing, the unified, the fused." The electric age, McLuhan indicates in one of his rare lapses into value judgment, thus promises mankind liberation from the tyranny of typography, restoration of the splintered human sensibility, and a vast extension of human consciousness.

As the electronic revolution gathers momentum, McLuhan warns, it will overturn all traditional patterns of thought and behavior. This situation accounts, for example, for the peculiar urgency of the current generational conflict. One generation has mistrusted another since Adam; but the gap between generations has rarely been so intensely perceived as today. The first generation to be reared in an electronic culture, McLuhan notes, instinctively understands the new environment, shucks off the rational-visual past, lives "mythically and in depth." Young people do not look for "detached patterns—for ways of relating themselves to the world, à la nineteenth century;" they demand, instead, a *"participation mystique."* It is this situation, too, according to McLuhan, which has created the contemporary assault on privacy and the "very serious dilemma between our claim to privacy and the community's need to know." Indeed, we are reaching the point, he concludes somewhat obscurely, where "remedial control, born out of knowledge of media and their total effects on all of us, must be exerted."

But how to precipitate our official culture, so hopelessly enslaved by the Gutenberg galaxy, into an awareness of the new environment? Humor, in McLuhan's view, provides "our most appealing anti-environmental tool." I am sure he is right and only wish that his own jokes were better. He plainly sees himself as a card, but his experiments in wit end up as wheezes and sub-joycean plays on words: not only the medium as massage but in a pleased description of his new book, for example, as "a collide-oscope of interlaced situations." His better weapon is simply his vivid, and generally exaggerated, account of the way in which electric technology is shaping "patterns of social interdependence and every aspect of our personal life."

One may read McLuhanism as perspective or as prophecy. The perspective enables him to say many things—some subtle and impressive, as on privacy or on the generational conflict, some forced and dubious, as on TV commercials—about contemporary culture. The prophecy is less lucid and, I think, entraps him in inherent contradictions.

He thus suggests that the electronic world will replace Gutenbergian analysis and specialization by a new environment of all-at-once organic communion. He apparently means two very different things by this: one is the ability of the computer to handle a mass of variables in a single motion; the other is, so to speak, the ability of the young to study while the radio is on. The first is technical, functional, and precise; the second is subjective and intuitive. Yet he seems to confuse them—or at least to fuse them into a single order of perception. "The future of language," he has even said in one of his more rhapsodic moments, "will not be as a system of classified data or meanings. . . . The future of language presents the possibility of a world without words, a wordless, intuitive world, like a technological extension of the action of consciousness."

This vision of a wordless utopia is not highly convincing. For what he has elsewhere called the "mosaic pattern of simultaneous projection" cannot, I think, solve other than technical problems. I doubt that the best computer will ever make decisive political or moral judgments; or that the wholly cybernated society will ever divest itself of the need for exact statement and sequential logic; or that the great issues of politics or ethics will be solved by the impressionism of the subliminal drama. For the medium is only part of the massage; the message is the massage too. While electric circuitry will unquestionably affect—and may in time revolutionize—our modes of perception and communication, it cannot abolish the need for consecutive reason and systematic analysis without, in the end, sapping its own foundations.

But I am sure it is wrong to read McLuhanism as prophecy. One suspects, indeed, that he is indulging his vision of the future primarily for the shock of the thought and the pleasure of the scandal. Underneath the hyperbole and the vaudeville there remains a significant and fertile truth. If one cannot explain history entirely as a result of alterations in the means of communication any more than one can explain it entirely as a result of alterations in the means of production, we nevertheless stand in debt to McLuhan for a marvelously stimulating insight into the dynamics of change—and for the gaiety and aplomb with which he conducts his campaign to heighten our awareness of the processes taking place in the depths below consciousness.   [2]

1. On p. *1*, Professor Schlesinger mentions "bland assertion, astute guesswork, fake analogy, dazzling insight, hopeless nonsense, shockmanship, showmanship, wisecracks, and oracular mystification" in McLuhan's writing. Can you point to specific passages in McLuhan's writing which might be examples of those sins?

2. Besides these general charges which are not supported by examples, Professor Schlesinger spells out some specific criticisms of McLuhan—and illustrates them. Does he convince you?

3. What is the evidence that Schlesinger presents to prove his belief that McLuhan is "an intelligent man"?

GET
THE
MESSAGE?

Marvin Kitman

Sam Goldwyn once said, "If I want a massage, I go to Luxor Baths." For messages today, all the in-people go to Marshall McLuhan's books. Characteristically, there is a message in his latest book. It is such an important message that McLuhan, co-author Quentin Fiore, and "co-ordinator" Jerome Agel broke with publishing tradition by having the paperback edition published before the cloth one. "We didn't have the time to wait a year to get Marshall's message into the hands of the people, so they could know what is really happening today," Agel explained to this reviewer. Agel identifies himself as "the first co-ordinator in publishing history, which means I played the David Merrick, bringing together the sound and the music." Packager Agel added, "For the first time, Marshall puts his message in terms everyone can understand. He is a genius."

The book arrives at a time when public opinion is sharply divided on McLuhan's ideas. That is, some people think he is right; others think he is wrong. As a member of a third group, which public opinion analysts sometimes call by the technical term "don't knows," I was especially eager to get my hands on the message.

MARVIN KITMAN, author of "The Number-One Best Seller," is TV reviewer for The New Leader and an editor of Monocle. This review of The Medium Is the Massage appeared in the New York Times Book Review, March 26, 1967, p. 7.

First I read Bantam's paperback version. It took 27 minutes. Then I read an advance copy of Random House's hardcover edition, containing the same text and pictures, only one-and-three-quarters times larger and more than seven times more expensive. It also took 27 minutes. When the media had finished working me over completely, I found that I couldn't agree more with everything McLuhan has been saying all these years. We differed on one point: I naively thought the commercial was the message.

With all the zeal of a convert, I would like to urge everybody not to buy this book, in either the paper medium or cloth medium. McLuhan argues forcefully that the invention of television makes books obsolete. Anybody who purchases a McLuhan book is playing into the hands of McLuhan's enemies in the intellectual establishment; high sales figures can only tend to discredit him as a modern thinker. Besides, the invention of the Albert Schweitzer professorship, a $100,000 chair in the humanities McLuhan is to occupy at Fordham next semester, makes the need to buy his books obsolete. (If I'm wrong about any of the theories in this review so far, Mr. McLuhan, please understand that I'm only probing. By that I mean, I'm trying to think linearly. Before I fell under your influence, I reasoned circularly.)

The proper way to study McLuhan's ideas is to watch the television show based on the book, which unfortunately went on the air last week. This is no problem for the "now" people who have video-tape-recorder rigs at home. Screen the tape right now. You won't be able to put it down until you've finished viewing the last frame. For those who lack the patience to wait until the TV summer re-runs to get the message, your medium is the telephone.

If the wheel is an extension of the foot, as McLuhan correctly observes, and the book is an extension of the eye, then the telephone must be an extension of the ear. But to have a really meaningful communication experience, it is necessary to establish a connection. Marshall McLuhan's telephone number at the University of Toronto is 416-WA 8-3328.

Random House is charging $10.95 for McLuhan's message in its laughably 15-century media. Bantam is charging $1.45 for its likewise pitifully dated media. But the swinging people at A.T. & T. are charging only 80 cents for a long-distance message, the station-to-station rate from New York. Serious students of McLuhan should call him after 6 tonight. "He's very available," co-ordinator Agel assured me, when I asked for the phone number. Tell Mr. McLuhan that I suggested you call.

This would have been an absurd proposal in 1964, when the theorist first ran his message up the antenna to see if anyone was listening. Apparently he has been rendering the fat out of the definitive work, "Understanding Media." In the current rendition, I have it on good authority that he has boiled down the message to 17 words. "The message, and why it had to get out now, is on page 25," advises co-ordinator Agel. "But pages 26 and 148 are very important, too."

In three minutes on the phone, McLuhan can easily give you the whole message, and still have time to throw in a couple of one-liners. If he isn't at his office when you call, ask his secretary if he left any messages for you.

In view of the urgency to get the message into the hands of the people, I was curious about why McLuhan and his collaborators hadn't thought of the telephone extension media themselves. "Does this mean McLuhan has changed his mind about his seminal thought that books are obsolescent?" I asked the co-ordinator. "This book makes all other books on art and philosophy obsolete," Agel explained. "The message all the other reviewers are missing Is that what we have here is a breakthrough book. It's the first book designed for the TV age."

In those terms, this is one of the most carelessly edited shows (or books) in mixed media history. For example, some of the scenes (or paragraphs) are printed upside down, like this one.

Still other scenes can only be read by holding the TV screen (or page) up to a mirror, as in this case. Once you have gone to the trouble, you're liable to remember the words of the great American critic, Tallulah Bankhead, who said, "There is less here than meets the eye."

(Regarding your call to Toronto: to show that you really understand the working of media, try calling collect.)

And throughout the TV show (or book), we run into typographical errors, even in the title slide reading "The Medium is the Massage." I'm just probing, but shouldn't that have read "The Tedium is the Message"? An alert continuity acceptance department (the editor at Bantam) never should have allowed the misquotation from Shakespeare: "All the world's a sage," The correct is "stage."

Many viewer-readers will also be puzzled by the art work, which is as hard to understand as anything McLuhan has written in the past. For example, what is the meaning of the picture on page 17? Quentin Fiore is a distinguished, award-winning graphics designer and artist, and everyone assumes the art work was his responsibility. Could it be that the secret of why the text can be understood by any bright child is that McLuhan and Fiore reversed roles in the production of this major work?

(Don't let the Toronto operator tell you the number I gave you is not a working number.)

Having criticized the medium, I would also like to add a few words about a minor point, McLuhan's basic theories on what is happening to us in the Electric Age. The one flaw in his ideas may be the part about watching television. In the old days, before I got the McLuhan message, I used to punish my children by not letting them watch TV. Today I require them to watch what McLuhan calls "the charge of the light brigade" so they will grow up to be Happening Adults. "What are you doing reading that book?" I found myself yelling at my son last week. "If you don't sit down and turn on the TV set, you're going to be sent to bed without supper!"

"But I hate TV," he said.

I caught him reading a book under the covers in his bedroom last night.

A factor that McLuhan may have accidentally left out of his formula for an electric world is youth's traditional rebellion against parents who know what is best for their children. I'm just probing again, but I can't help wondering if the invention of McLuhan's ideas isn't his subtle way of trying to destroy the television industry?

(Still no answer in Toronto? Why not call a medium and ask her for a message.) [7]

1. What is the pervading tone of Mr. Kitman's review of *The Medium Is The Massage?* Whether or not you are familiar with the book, how does the attitude conveyed by Mr. Kitman affect you as you read his review?

2. If you are not already familiar with it, obtain a copy of *The Medium Is The Massage,* and compare your own reaction to Mr. Kitman's upon your first reading of the book.

MARSHALL McLUHAN AND THE TECHNOLOGICAL EMBRACE

Michael J. Arlen

Marshall McLuhan, who, as just about everybody ought to know by now, is the Canadian agricultural expert and author of "The Romance of Wheat"—No. I am mistaken. Marshall McLuhan, who, as just about everybody ought to know by now, is the Canadian communications whizbang and author of a number of books about media, was on TV the other Sunday afternoon, on one of the new "N.B.C. Experiment in Television" programs, and although McLuhan didn't say anything he hasn't said before (actually, he almost never says anything he hasn't said before, although sometimes he says it differently, and very reassuring is this note of constancy in a world gone mad), it was a mighty hippy, moderny, zim-zam-zap performance all the same, complete with the full Pop ritual of flashy, splashy lighting, electronic sound, fancy cutting, zooms, lots of stop action—in fact, the whole art-director's kit of exciting-visual-effects: go-go girls zazzing away but as if the film ran side-

MICHAEL J. ARLEN'S radio-television column, "The Air," is a regular feature of *The New Yorker* magazine. This appeared in *The New Yorker*, April 1, 1967, pp. 135–138.

wise (why do they never show go-go girls dancing straight up, the way their mothers would want them to?), and, toward the end, a cute little bit of I-can-be-as-cool-as-you-are-buddy contemporary graphics showing an H-bomb exploding in the shape of an exclamation point as the narrator intoned, "The hydrogen bomb is history's exclamation point." (Once, I remember, McLuhan was pleased to describe a hydrogen-bomb explosion as "information," which goes to show you the sort of pressure the dictionary-revision people have to work under.) It was a snappy show, really. Interesting. But, for all its snap and flash, it was awfully reverential in tone—reverential toward McLuhan and reverential, more especially, toward the whole idea of modernism and technology. I don't know that it was supposed to work out that way. I don't know that McLuhanism is supposed to work out that way. Now and then, McLuhan will waft out to us a sentence ("There is absolutely no inevitability as long as there is a willingness to contemplate what is happening") that gives the impression, or maybe gives *him* the impression, that he is making some sort of evaluative confrontation of the onrush of technology. But a sentence like that doesn't ever appear to be connected to anything else, to any other thought—to any other sentence, even—and when you get right down to cases, it seems to me, the confrontation turns out to be largely illusory, turns out to be instead an almost bland embrace. The N.B.C. program provided a fairly broad embrace, as these things go. "The electric age is having a profound effect on us," intoned the narrator, paraphrasing McLuhan. "We are in a period of fantastic change . . . that is coming about at fantastic speed. Your life is changing dramatically! You are numb to it!" And "The walls of your rooms are coming down. It is becoming a simple matter to wire and pick out of your homes your private, once solely personal life and record it. Bugging is the new means for gathering information." And "The family circle has widened, Mom and Dad! The world-pool of information constantly pouring in on your closely knit family is influencing them a lot more than you think." Well, O.K. But it all sounds rather too much like the revival preacher, who doesn't really tell you anything about hellfire you didn't know before but who tells it to you more forcefully, with all the right, meliorative vogue words ("fantastic change . . . fantastic speed . . . dramatically . . . numb"), and so makes you feel appropriately important and guilty in the process. In this instance, McLuhan tells us, the fire next time will be technological and lit by an electric circuit, but, having told us that, the preacher seems content to take up the collection and walk out of the church, leaving us with happy, flagellated expressions and a vague sense of having been in touch with an important truth—if we could only remember what it was.

For myself, I'm not so sure about McLuhan's truths. He has the Big Idea, which he pushes, about the effects on Western man of the alphabet, movable type, print—how this visual-mental dependence on little letters all in a row, lines of type, lines, one word right after another, has created in man a linear response to the world, has created specialization, compartmentaliza-[135–136]tion, civilization even, mass production, and sundry other evils. It's an interesting idea, all right, and there's a lot of substance to it, but, in the first place, it seems plain foolish to try to rest the full breadth and weight of man's linear sense of order on a single factor even as large as the alphabet and print. Art, after all, imitates life, and life is surely, among other things, intrinsically geometric. Nature is geometric. Trees, tides, plants, planets don't move psychedelically, they move geometrically, and as long as nature exists in any recognizable form the paths of force and tension and, consequently, the order that man intuitively responds to will in the main be linear, too. In the second place, it seems worse than plain foolish to be so modernistically airy about man's sense of logic. McLuhan seems to have the idea that man's dependence on print has been constricting and unnatural and has resulted in an imbalance of the senses, and that, with the disappearance of print and the concomitant rise of electronic information-feeding technology, man will once again come into a fuller life of the senses. "Television . . . reintegrates the human senses, thereby making books obsolete" is one of the ways he put it that afternoon. Oh, boy, some life of the senses is my thought for the week, with Brother and Sis upstairs in the kids' communication room watching "Uncle Don's Visit to the Fulton Fish Market," which they can't smell, and Mom and Dad curled up on acrilan grass in Dad's windowless information center holding hands and watching a twenty-four-hour weather program. In any case, just because an electronic circuit looks circular, or sounds circular, and just because the hippy teen-agers that McLuhan admires so much (by gosh, fellows, I admire them, too) go floating about absorbing sense impressions and otherwise having a fine old time doesn't seem to me much of a reason for supposing that we're going to start wanting to do without logic—intuitive, deductive, analytical, linear, call it what you will. After all, logic, brains, intellect, sustained formal thought are how we splendid, wonderful people got to be so splendid and wonderful in the first place, and when a philosopher-king like McLuhan starts saying things like "The way you react to them [television and computers] is what is important, not what is in them or on them," it's hard to forget that the first thing that boring old Gutenberg printed was the Bible and the first thing television gave us was Uncle Miltie—and, on present evidence, [136–137] there doesn't seem to be any very pressing basis for tossing out the first because of the second. McLuhan is so cheery and accommodating to the hard bewilderments of technology. I don't know, maybe he worries like hell about them, but he comes on cheery and accommodating. ("There is nothing sterile about television, except in the eye of the beholder.") I guess if you live here and now, you might as well enjoy it. Still, there's an appalling inevitability to this onrush of technology, and since much of it is likely to bring secondary effects that will just as inevitably diminish the possibilities of natural human life, I don't really see that you're doing much of anything when you toss up a line like "The new electronic interdependence recreates the world in the image of a global village," or "We have begun again to structure the primordial feeling," or "Our new environment compels commitment and participation," and leave it hanging. I don't really see that you're doing much of anything except, possibly, trying to ride with the winners.

It seems a pity, because McLuhan is an original man. A lot of people,

I know, are down on him these days, because he's been so much in the public eye (all those cover stories; even *Family Circle* had something on him this month, in which it referred to McLuhan as "the most sought-after dinner guest of our time in New York") and because, they say, he's inconsistent, which he is, and often wrong, which he is, and unfunny, which he certainly is, and even (they say) unoriginal. The thing is, about fifteen years ago, when Mc-Luhan—then, as now, a teacher of undergraduate English courses—began writing about print and communications and media, he didn't claim to be entirely original. Most of these notions about print and type and Western man had been written about for a number of years by a number of people (even though the editors of *Life* may not have been reading them then). What McLuhan did that *was* original was to put them together in a new way and add a sort of twist of his own that gave them relevance—and expansiveness. One got a feeling, in reading those earlier books, of rooms being opened up. But that was a while ago. These days, I get the feeling, especially watching McLuhan on something like the N.B.C. show, which was content to present his views pretty much at face value (as, indeed, most of the mass magazines have been), that, for all his talk about how he's mainly an investigator, a prober, how he's in-[137–138]terested in getting people to think about their environment, the principal result of what he writes and speaks—partly because of what he says, partly because of how he says it—has been to diminish discussion. When he touches something ("The technology of the railway created the myth of a green-pasture world of innocence." "Pop Art simply tells you the only art form left for you today is your own natural environment"), he seems to do it in such a way that although there's often substance or interest in his thought, the effect is somehow to close the subject off, to leave it in the end (despite the aphoristic crackle) more dead than alive. At least, it's odd that for all the talk of controversy surrounding his work, most people trying to come to grips with it, in conversation or in print, rarely ever seem to do much more than helplessly paraphrase what he's already said. On the N.B.C. program that afternoon, he appeared sometimes in darkness, sometimes in light, sometimes with a red light flickering on his face. He appeared, disappeared. Sentences hung in the air. Print. Electronics. Technology. The alphabet. Western man. Life. Death. Pop Art. The motorcar. The Beatles. Gutenberg. Civilization. Quite some time ago, Archimedes said, "Give me a lever long enough, and a place to stand, and I will move the world." McLuhan seems to be intent on moving the world, all right, and thinks he has found the lever—"the clash between print and electric technologies." But the lever keeps bending, and it's hard to find a place to stand. At least, he hasn't found one yet, which is perhaps why he keeps skittering all over the place. Maybe, one day, he'll settle for something less.   [138]

Note that Michael Arlen approves of McLuhan as an "original man" (p. *137*) but that he generally deplores that facet of McLuhanism

which the N.B.C. television program represents. On just what basis
does Arlen attribute originality to McLuhan, and, specifically, what
does Arlen object to in the McLuhan image projected by the television program?

GRAPHICS CONVEY
MESSAGE IN
MEDIUM IS
THE MASSAGE

Publisher's Weekly—Unsigned Feature

The power and message of Quentin Fiore's graphics in "The Medium Is the Massage" not only amplify the text by Marshall McLuhan and Quentin Fiore; they help make "McLuhanism" intelligible to many people for the first time. The generally straightforward text, occupying less than half the book's pages, is an exploration of some of the main points in Professor McLuhan's philosophy about the effect of the new technology. The book employs highly imaginative visual displays to get the points across. It was published in paperback by Bantam, March 1, and in hard covers by Random House, March 17.

"Marshall and I planned this book together," Quentin Fiore told *PW* in his New York office recently. The basic element of design idea was the use of motion picture techniques to express the ideas.

Some images are spread over several successive pages to emphasize certain statements. For example, the text says (also note in this passage an explanation of the book's title): "All media work us over completely. They are so pervasive in their personal, political, economic, aesthetic, psychological, moral, ethical, and social consequences that they leave no part of us un-

From *Publisher's Weekly*, April 3, 1967, pp. 62–64. Reprinted by permission.

touched, unaffected, unaltered. The medium is the massage. Any understanding of social and cultural changes is impossible without a knowledge of the way media work as environments." Also: "All media are extensions of some human faculty—psychic or physical. The wheel is an extension of the foot."

Facing this statement is a full-page bleed photo of a toe. The next spread shows the middle toes, and the next focuses on the big toe, looking very round, with the words "the wheel" appearing in the upper right. The last spread of the sequence has an action photo of an auto wheel, and the rest of the sentence, "is an extension of the foot," appears in the upper left.

A different photographic approach is used to convey the essence of a book to the reader: a spread with a bleed halftone that is blank except for life-size thumbs at each outside page edge.

These are samples of the unexpected, the visual verbal puns and games that appear throughout the book. They are there to jar the reader out of his line-by-line reading habit and his step-by-step inspection of illustrations, causing him—or so the designer intends,—to become actively involved with the material. There are mirror images. Type is upside-down, slanted, and jumps in size or from regular to boldface. The graphics are humorous, sometimes tongue-in-cheek, often subtle. The form of "The Medium Is the Massage" bespeaks the content. When content is highly abstract, as in this book, a totally new design approach must be developed to convey the feeling and spirit rather than merely to illustrate the text.

The profound influence that the technology of the alphabet, and of movable type, has had on the thinking processes of Western man is basic to McLuhan's philosophy. This technology fostered the step-by-step reasoning process, the habit of "logical" sequence, according to Mr. Fiore, and the notion of categories. The new technology has changed all this. The text says:

"Western history was shaped for some three thousand years by the introduction of the phonetic alphabet, [sic] a medium that depends solely on the eye for comprehension. The alphabet is a construct of fragmented bits and parts which have no semantic meaning in themselves, and which must be strung together in a line, bead-like, and in a prescribed order. Its use fostered and encouraged the habit of perceiving all environment in visual and spatial terms—particularly in terms of a space and of a time that are uniform,

c,o,n,t,i,n,u,o,u,s
and
c-o-n-n-e-c-t-e-d."

Humor was an important criterion in both text and graphics. McLuhan feels that seriousness should not measure quality. Fiore, a friend and sometime interpreter of McLuhan, feels people are conditioned to favor something "profoundly" dull over the "superficially" brilliant. Fiore recalled that when James Joyce was accused of being trivial, he retorted he would be more pleased if he was considered "quatrivial." Mr. Fiore says this book is light but not trivial, and can be understood on more than one level, depending on the reader.

Three times as many picture ideas were collected by Mr. Fiore as were used. He and McLuhan selected the ones nearest to the book's main points.

The first page before the title page has a photo of a raw egg on a plate, with an advertising message on the [62–63] yolk. The photo is captioned "Good morning." Thanks to the new electric technology, information pours upon us all the time—it forms part of us—we are "information man"—we even eat information, Mr. Fiore said. He used this photo to express the idea "that all is changing in ways we've not even begun to understand. We thought we began our day with the breakfast egg, we now really begin with information."

The reader can begin at any point in the book after the introductory sequence. This sequence explains the effects of electronic technology on You, Your Family, Your Neighborhood, Your Education, Your Job, Your Government, The Others (Minorities). Each topic is introduced with a bleed illustration on the right-hand page. The following left-hand page carries a small reproduction of the same picture and brief text. Each picture is an inventive symbol of the topic and all are varied in style and content. There are line cuts, halftones, an old photo, a photographic montage, and photos of objects new and old—for example, an antique hatrack, and a computer circuit. The combined effect makes for an invigorating if not jolting experience in turning the pages.

Mr. Fiore stressed that books are not obsolete, they are merely obsolescent in their present form—a point which he said is frequently misinterpreted in McLuhan's message. Books will change, he explained, because the nature and amount of information is changing but will remain important at all levels of education. Layout of books evolved from scrolls which were read aloud to a group. With the advent of the book, reading became a solitary act. At about the same time, rooms and walled-off areas became more common in architectural designs. Today the concept of the individual is being dissolved by technology. Walls and distance have been overcome by television, airplanes, and computers. Facts about individuals are being recorded on tape, and the actions of the individual have become the interest of the group.

The eye will become progressively less important as a sense organ, Quentin Fiore continued. Records are selling in ever larger numbers on campuses. The younger people have adjusted to the audio media. To them the intensity of sound is stronger than the printed word.

McLuhan's comments on television and the education process will probably be influential in the future planning of multi-media teaching aids. Below are some quotations from the book:

"Today's television child is attuned to up-to-the-minute 'adult' news —inflation, rioting, war, taxes, crime, bathing beauties—and is bewildered when he enters the nineteenth-century environment that still characterizes the educational establishment where information is scarce but ordered and structured by fragmented, classified patterns, subjects and schedules . . . The child was an invention of the seventeenth century; he did not exist in, say, Shakespeare's day. He had, up until that time, been merged in the adult world, and there was nothing that could be called childhood in our sense.

"The student finds no means of involvement for himself and cannot discover how the educational scheme relates to his mystic world of electronically processed data and experience that his clear direct responses report. . . . Education must shift from instruction, from imposing of stencils, to discovery— to probing and exploration and to the recognition of the language of forms.

"The young today reject goals. They want roles—R-O-L-E-S. That is, total involvement. They do not want fragmented, specialized goals or jobs. . . . We now experience simultaneously the dropout and the teach-in . . . They belong together. . . .

"The dropout represents a rejection of nineteenth-century technology as manifested in our educational establishments. The teach-in represents a creative effort, switching the educational process from package to discovery. As the audience becomes a participant in the total electric drama, the classroom can become a scene in which the audience performs an enormous amount of work."   [63–64]

On television:

"It was the funeral of President Kennedy that proved the power of television . . . (to involve) an entire population in a ritual process. . . . In television images are projected around you. You are the screen. . . .

"Most often the few seconds sandwiched between the hours of viewing—the 'commercials'—reflect a truer understanding of the medium. There simply is no time for the narrative form, borrowed from earlier print technology. The story line must be abandoned. . . ." The motion pictures "such as 'The Knack,' 'A Hard Day's Night,' 'What's New Pussycat?'—would prove unacceptable as mass audience films if the audience had not been preconditioned by television commercials to abrupt zooms, elliptical editions, no story lines, flash cuts."

Quentin Fiore studied drawing with George Grosz and book binding with Gerhard Gerlach. He was a highly successful type designer and lettering artist for 18 years, until, he says, he "saw the future of type was film and switched to design of general printed matter." Mr. Fiore does free-lance design for university presses, leading publishers, corporations and foundations; he recently completed a five-year contract with the Ford Foundation, and is currently a consultant to the University of Michigan Press. Mr. Fiore showed us a book he made himself that he used as a portfolio, with two-piece binding, accomplished calligraphy, line drawings, and handset type.

In contrast to the format of "The Medium Is the Massage" is the rich aesthetic treatment he gave the recently completed first volume of a projected 8-volume set about Byzantine art, dealing with archeological findings at the Monastery of St. Catherine on Mount Sinai, for the University of Michigan Press.

Marshall McLuhan, professor of English and Director of the Center for Culture and Technology at the University of Toronto, has written "The Mechanical Bride," "The Gutenberg Galaxy," and "Understanding Media," and he has several more books in the planning stage. He was recently appointed Albert Schweitzer Fellow in the Humanities at Fordham University.

DUOTONE IN BOTH BOOKS

"The Medium Is the Massage" was coordinated by Jerome Agel. Quentin Fiore supervised the production very closely on the paperback and hardbound versions. Bantam reported that it received a number of calls from the printer, Regensteiner Corp., checking on whether some of the unusual effects weren't errors.

In order to get rich blacks and fine details in the halftones, Bantam printed the book by duotone sheetfed offset, a first for their mass market paperback line. The decision to use duotone and other special production techniques that the design demanded raised production costs two to three times above those of their average paperback. However, according to Ray Little, Bantam production director, the results were so favorable that he hopes to use more duotone in the future. Paper was a 60# free sheet. The cover is Chromekote, finished with an extra glossy coating. The first printing was 100,000 copies, followed by two more of 35,000 each. The book is priced at $1.45.

Both books were produced from the same original art, but the text was reset for the Random House edition, and some of the negatives retouched, after being photographically enlarged. An innovation in the hardbound book was the use of "one-plate" duotone offset printing, which was handled by the Kingsport Press. The two negatives were exposed together to make one plate. According to Steven Baron, who supervised the Random House operation, Random House's production department was especially impressed with this book and the work of Quentin Fiore. The hardcover edition, about one and one-third times larger than the paperback, is priced at $10.95.   [64]

Compare this description of the machinery that comprises *The Medium Is The Massage* with the *New York Times* review (March 26, 1967) by Marvin Kitman. Analyze the reasons, as you interpret them, for the distinct difference in attitude between these two sources. Study a copy of *The Medium Is The Massage* for yourself and report on which of these two contrasting opinions of the book contains the fairest and most useful critique.

NOT-SO-COOL MEDIUM

Robert Lewis Shayon

Had Marshall McLuhan, the eminent grammarian of the media, been faithful to his elliptical insights recently when he appeared in a one-hour documentary, *The Medium Is the Massage,* on NBC's Experiment in Television, the program would have been a valuable extension of his electronic gospel to popular audiences. The Toronto guru violated his own rules, however, and the program, which was based on and took its name from a new Random House hardcover and Bantam paperback that he has co-authored with Quentin Fiore, to this viewer's sensory balance was "hot" McLuhan.

One of McLuhan's basic propositions is that we are crossing a technological frontier dividing the age of the collectivist from that of the individualist: We are being retribalized. The all-at-onceness of the "field approach" to problems is rapidly replacing the fixed, visual approach of applied or "resolute" knowledge. This explains the tension between "an overall awareness and a merely private point of view." The simultaneity of events "imploding" upon us via the newer media drum out of consciousness 500 years of the fixed perspective of print.

In his book *The Gutenberg Galaxy* McLuhan describes "the origin of lineal, fragmented analysis with its remorseless power of homogenization. . . ." It was homogenization that tripped up *The Medium is the Massage.* The show was meant to explain McLuhan. Bantam Books had granted the television

ROBERT LEWIS SHAYON writes TV-radio reviews that appear as a regular feature of *Saturday Review.*

From *Saturday Review,* April 15, 1967, p. 46. Reprinted by permission.

rights to a producer; he had made a package deal with NBC, and after he had prepared a script, the author of *Understanding Media* agreed to appear. Two elements were involved: first, illustrations of McLuhan's themes shown in live footage, stills, trick photography, plus fragments of on-camera faces and voices of the Canadian's critics and admirers; and, second, the communications theorist himself presented in close-ups, explaining, "probing," prophesying, alerting all of us to the whirlpool dangers of a time of media turbulence.

The first element, the illustrations without McLuhan's corporeal presence, was at least well fitted to the field approach. It was in tune with his notion of a cool, mosaic presentation on television wherein the viewer is given merely an icon, an incomplete symbol as it were, made up of quick-scanned electronic dots on the tube. The viewer is required to complete the icon by himself, to fill in the gaps. This fluid process, in McLuhan's system, provides the magical participation or involvement of television. I can't recall a single shot of the illustrations; they added up to a cipher as they passed my literate-minded eye. But this, also, is genuine McLuhan—content is secondary, and the medium, per se, provides the thrill.

The live, in-person master, however, did not fit well in the cool montage: He was "hot," too highly defined, too complete, literal. He was in a frame. He tried to play it cool, of course—casual, elusive, understated, non-sequential; this is par for the role. This was indeed a steel trap, a fixed event in time and space; it dominated the entire hour and weighted the intended horizonless, boundless, tactile, oral mosaic with far too heavy a visual perspective.

A pity. McLuhan could have had his cool cake and conscience, too. Had he insisted on playing the game strictly according to his own roles, he could have easily saved the show by playing not Hamlet but the Ghost. Instead of the full head shot, filling the camera frame, or the shoulder shot, profile strongly sculptured against a flowing, changing tide of color, there could just as easily, and more imaginatively, have been McLuhan fragments— the lobe of an ear, the tilt of a chin, an eyelid aflicker. There could have been the edge of a shadow, hovering over our descent into the electric maelstrom, or a special television-effect negative, spectral image, or a superimposition of one camera's icon upon another. Such multidimensionality, imploding upon our involved sense ratios, would have cooled the heat of the private, personal individual on our vacuum tubes and saved the night for electric circuitry: the unified, the fused.

One suspects that McLuhan shared Hamlet's conflict of "conscience" (corporate responsibility and awareness) and "resolution" (the private peep-hole point of view), which he described in *The Gutenberg Galaxy*. One can also sympathize with the highly literate and individualistic mind resisting the pressure to become collectively oriented. The author is not yet a loosed happening. He is still, like all of us, somewhat prisoner of a dissolving world of print. He still feels print's "alternating flicker . . . the very mode of subjective doubt and peripheral groping." More power, then, to his probing.   [46]

1. What assumptions does Mr. Shayon seem to make about Mc-
   Luhan's media theories in this review of a TV broadcast? Is he
   generally favorable toward or critical of McLuhan's basic propositions?

2. In the light of comments McLuhan has made about himself in
   other places, how do you think he might respond to Mr. Shayon's
   criticism of his performance on the TV program?

UNDERSTANDING MARSHALL McLUHAN:

or Will TV Put A Zombie In Your Future?

Senior Scholastic—Editorial Staff

Anyone who talks about mass communications these days *has* to talk about Marshall McLuhan. Whether one agrees with the controversial Canadian or not, it's hard to ignore him. His influence is too widespread.

McLuhan has shot into prominence in just the past few years. Before that he was a rather obscure English literature professor at St. Michael's College in Toronto. Now he's the toast of "pop" society and a consultant to business firms as varied as Time Inc., and the Container Corporation of America. McLuhan's current academic title is director of the University of Toronto's Centre for Culture and Technology. In the fall of 1967 he will begin a year's leave to take the prestigious Albert Schweitzer Chair at Fordham University in New York, teaching and doing research.

But McLuhan's fame comes mainly from his books—works like *Understanding Media* (1964) and *The Medium Is the Massage* (1967). McLuhan's books shake people up. Some readers praise him as a brilliant thinker; others denounce him as a publicity-seeking fraud.

Many say they can't make sense out of McLuhan's books. Indeed, the term "McLuhanism" has come to be used by some writers to refer to foggy

From *Senior Scholastic,* April 28, 1967, pp. 13–16. Reprinted by permission of Scholastic Magazines, Inc. From *Senior Scholastic.* © Copyright 1967 by Scholastic Magazine, Inc.

prose in general—as when one national columnist accused a U.S. governor of sounding too much like McLuhan in a recent speech.

McLuhan himself adds to the confusion with comments like: "I don't pretend to understand it. After all, my stuff is very difficult." Another time he observed mysteriously: "I don't agree or disagree with anything I say myself." And still more confusingly: "Most clear writing is a sign that there is no exploration going on. Clear prose indicates the absence of thought."

McLuhan's writing jumps disconcertingly from deadly serious thoughts to lighter matters (such as *Mad* comics and jazz). He speaks glowingly of Edgar Allan Poe ("he made his readers work; made them do-it-themselves"). He draws on the techniques of the poet by using language to *suggest,* rather than to *specify* ("People don't actually read newspapers; they get into them every morning like a hot bath"). He is criticized by some as unscientific, and praised by others as a prophet. Few deny that he has challenged the communications media like few men of our century.

Out of the maze of sometimes contradictory statements that make up McLuhan's writings, many people believe they can discern some very important—and fairly simple—ideas that have major significance for our age. The main thing, they say, citing one of McLuhan's pet notions, is to see *the Big Picture*—to grasp the way the bits and pieces fit into an over-all pattern, even if some of the bits or pieces may be missing or misplaced.

One of McLuhan's central ideas is that changes are going on all about us of which we are not fully aware. Take the case of TV. The rise of TV has very subtly altered the way people *think,* McLuhan says. He hastens to add that this has nothing to do with the quality of TV programs. Those who denounce TV as a "boob tube" or as a "wasteland" really are missing the whole point, McLuhan contends. Even if TV programs consisted entirely of dramatizations of literary classics and first-rate news documentaries, TV would still make us think *differently.*

This may be a bit clearer if we step back for a look at [13–14] history. Like many other writers, McLuhan has searched for a general principle to explain the way history works. Historian Arthur M. Schlesinger, Jr., compares the sweeping nature of McLuhan's theories to the theories of the German Socialist Karl Marx. Says Schlesinger: "Where Marx located the motive force of history in changes in the means of production, McLuhan locates it in changes in *the means of communication.*"

According to McLuhan, the present "electric revolution" is the third major historical change that has had a profound impact on the way man thinks. The two previous important changes, he believes, were the invention of the alphabet and the invention of printing. The influence of each of these innovations occurred in two steps.

ALPHABET

Before the alphabet was invented, man led a much more "natural" life—in close harmony with the world of nature. Information about the outside world was picked up in many ways, using the five major senses (sight, hearing, taste, touch, smell) in roughly equal proportion. But the invention of the alphabet between 2000 and 1500 B.C. upset the natural harmony of the senses. Man began to get more and more of his information from the written word alone—through the one sense of sight. Thus began what McLuhan terms the *visual orientation* of modern man. The sense of sight became more important than the other senses.

This development illustrates one of McLuhan's major points about the effect of new inventions: that they inevitably alter the existing ratio between the five senses. And this new ratio, in turn, influences how men think— the second step.

For example, before the invention of the alphabet man thought of "reality" as a jumble of events, McLuhan believes. The way man understood this "reality" was a result of intuition or feeling rather than of logical reasoning. Man was aware, for example, that rain and being wet went together—but he didn't necessarily think of rain as the cause and wetness as the effect.

The idea of cause-and-effect was a result of the alphabet. When man began to write down the jumble of his thoughts, he wrote a string of words. Those words took their meaning from the way they were strung together, one after another. Gradually man began to think the way he wrote—in terms of propositions that followed one another in logical order. This, says McLuhan, is the special logic that developed as a result of the alphabet and the written word.

PRINTING

The second major innovation was the 15th-century invention of printing by movable type. The resulting mass production of books again changed the way men thought, says McLuhan—by a process quite similar to that just described for the alphabet. "The portable book was like a hydrogen bomb," declares McLuhan. "For the first time, [14–15] man could read and think in isolation. Individualism was born."

Two other effects were noteworthy: (1) Emphasis on the sense of sight was stepped up even more. (2) Men got to thinking in terms of assembly-line production (for instance, the task of making a printed book was broken down into several distinct jobs that could be divided among several people and performed in series).

These developments made possible the stupendous growth of industry and mass production over the past few centuries, McLuhan says. But they also froze man's thinking into certain "linear" patterns—that is, in the coldly logical, step-by-step matter of the assembly line. Man learned the art of detachment. He was able to stand off and look at what he was doing and to judge it according to abstract standards. But, contends McLuhan, he lost many of the qualities of intuition and deep emotional involvement that characterized primitive man before the invention of either the alphabet or printing.

ELECTRICITY

This was man's state of mind when he suddenly found himself plunged into the "electric revolution" in the 20th century. One after another came radio, television, computers. Slowly, almost imperceptibly, man began to *think* differently.

Radio, says McLuhan, was a "tribal drum" that stepped up man's sense of hearing and added a person-to-person dimension to world affairs. Man no longer just *read* about important speeches and events—he *listened* to them. Like illiterate men in primitive tribes, modern man could get the feeling of direct contact with all of his fellow "tribesmen" in "a global village." McLuhan says that radio also introduced the *all-at-once atmosphere* of modern man—seen in the popular student practice of studying with the radio or phonograph on.

Television added sight to sound and brought the world even closer. ("Any highway eatery with its TV set, newspaper, and magazine," McLuhan says, "is as cosmopolitan as New York and Paris.") But TV did something else too—it tore man away from his detached, noninvolved attitude. Where print looked at experience from a distance, TV *involved* man. In McLuhan's view, a TV screen reveals just a pulsing sequence of light and dark dots that must be pieced together in a man's mind before taking on meaning. Thus the glassy-eyed man lounging in front of his TV set is no passive blob merely absorbing sight and sound, argues McLuhan. Instead, that man is *actively involved* in creating for himself a visual image to go with the sound that reaches his ears.

TV also involves man in a second way, McLuhan believes. Direct TV coverage of events such as civil rights marches, the Viet Nam war, or the Kennedy funeral brings the world into the home in an intimate manner. The TV viewer finds it hard not to become emotionally involved in what he is watching. For this reason, McLuhan asserts, TV has [15–16] "doomed" the Viet Nam war. "The young oppose the war not out of pacifism," he says, "but out of their pain of involvement."

This "urge toward involvement" is one reason the TV generation is so restless, McLuhan contends. But he finds another reason also: TV brings a change of perspective, so that young people growing up under the influence of TV have a different idea of life from their parents.

McLuhan explains this assertion as follows: With TV, Telstar, and other high-speed communications annihilating space and time, man is not the "fragmented, visual" man of recent centuries. He no longer depends solely on his visual sense or solely on his sense of hearing. Instead, he brings into play *all* of his senses in much the same way as pre-alphabet man. And in so doing, he begins to lose the sense of perspective of "visual" man—the idea of life as a series of separate events that stretch out behind and before us in uninterrupted sequence.

"All the remote visualized goals of usual culture seem not only unreal but irrelevant," McLuhan declares. "It is the total involvement in all-inclusive *nowness* that occurs in young lives via TV's mosaic image."

McLuhan says this is a major reason why so many of today's young people reject the job-goals philosophy of their parents (that's "linear" thinking) and the impersonal materialism of the so-called "consumer life." Instead, he says, these youth want *roles* that will give them personal involvement—*now*.

Most people, says McLuhan, simply do not realize that all this is happening. But TV, along with other modern devices, *is* changing their way of thinking—even if much of the press goes on as if the "age of print" will continue forever. People go through life looking through a rear-view mirror, he says, aware of the environment only after they have left it. They accept as "natural" a way of thinking (visual, assembly-line, chain-of-events) that, far from being natural, is a result merely of one stage (already past) in our rapidly changing technology.

"We are witnessing a clash of cataclysmic proportions between two great technologies," McLuhan asserts. The print culture is fighting a rear-guard action, vainly striving to absorb the electronic culture, "to force the new media to do the work of the old." But the press itself is in for far-reaching changes—in a "new social environment in which print will interact" differently than ever before with a great variety of communications media.

We can't stop TV from changing people, he argues. But by understanding those changes, we can prepare ourselves for them. One way: education. It can serve as civil defense against "media fallout." The ivory tower, he says, must become the control tower.

McLuhan, of course, doesn't stop with the framework we've sketched out here. The scatter-shot sweep of this theory encompasses a phenomenal range of material. And his vocabulary abounds with catch-words to which he has attached his own special meanings.

Perhaps his most famous catch-words are "hot" and "cool." For instance, the printed page is a "hot" medium because it projects plenty of information (which makes it "high-definition") yet involves mainly *one* sense—sight. In contrast, TV is "cool" because it is "low in definition" (that is, the dotted image provides a minimum of information) and because it involves all the senses at once. In short, a "cool" medium is one that requires the individual to supply his own "heat," while a "hot" medium supplies it for him. Observes McLuhan: "Any hot medium allows for less participation than a cool one, as a lecture makes for less participation than a seminar, and a book for less than a dialogue." He catalogs radio and movies as "hot" media, the telephone as a "cool" one.

Another of McLuhan's key concepts is the idea that a medium is really an extension of one or several senses. The caveman's ax, for instance, is an extension of his hand. The book is an extension of the eye. TV is an extension of the entire central nervous system.

"As extensions, the new media offer both possibility and threat," warns U. S. literary critic Richard Kostelanetz in a review of McLuhan's books, "for while they lengthen man's reach into his existence, they can also extend society's reach into him, for both exploitation and control."

If McLuhan is even partly right, what is happening today in the communications media may well be the single most important event of our time. For those media affect politics, economics, sociology, psychology, everything—"reshaping patterns of social interdependence and every aspect of our personal life," as McLuhan puts it.   [16]

1. How does this discussion, written for high school students, differ in style and emphasis from articles which have appeared in the news magazines, professional journals, and book review sections of popular periodicals? Is this as thorough and useful a summary of McLuhanism as the "standard" periodicals have published? Does it represent any biased point of view that tries to urge a strongly pro or con response from its readers? Does it neglect, through oversimplification, anything critically important about McLuhan's message?

2. Do you recognize any of this information in this article as having appeared in articles published earlier?

3. In view of the probable audience for this article, comment on why it includes McLuhan's belief that "Most clear writing is a sign there is no exploration going on. Clear prose indicates an absence of thought."

PROJECTS:

A McLUHAN
DO–IT–YOURSELF KIT

Convinced as he is that there can be no learning without involvement, Professor McLuhan probably would approve of projects.

The following projects provide an opportunity for students to demonstrate their comprehension of the ideas of Marshall McLuhan and to test whether his ideas have application of value. In addition, the projects provide an opportunity for students to sharpen their research techniques and to develop mastery of standard bibliography and manuscript techniques.

As indicated, some of the projects would be more meaningful if students have read all of *Understanding Media,* in which case pagination refers to the Signet edition (Q3039, 95 cents). However, even in these projects, the critical articles in this casebook provide the information necessary for students to understand and profit from them.

Obviously, before you can appreciate and evaluate a man's writing, you must understand it. The questions in this section can be used either as study guides, discussion stimulants, or theme topics.

1. Define the following expressions as McLuhan uses them: *media, technology, message, cool, hot, linear, sequential, history, fragmentation, definition, involvement, tactile, reversal, numbing, tribal, tribal culture, Narcissism, translate, implosion, auto-amputation, the electric age, the mechanical age, Western man, anti-environment, extension of the senses.*

2. Try to reduce to one paragraph what you construe to be McLuhan's message in *Understanding Media.*

3. The next questions are based on "Introduction to the Second Edition."

    a. Do you and Professor McLuhan agree on the meaning of "cool"? (vii)

    b. What is meant by "Environments are not passive wrappings but active processes?" (viii)

    c. Contrast the "oral and written cultures of the Greeks." (viii)

    d. Explain: "The poets provided specific operational wisdom for all the contingencies of life." Do you know of other such sources of instant wisdom? (viii)

    e. Explain: "Education by classified data has been the Western program ever since." Why does he limit this statement to "Western" areas? (viii)

    f. Explain: "data classification yields to pattern recognition." Illustrate. (viii)

    g. What is the "totally new environment" which has been created by "the electronic age"?

    h. How does each succeeding era in history make the preceding era an "art form"? (ix)

    i. Explain: "Art is anti-environmental." (ix)

    j. What was the "Hawthorne experiment"? Do you agree with Professor McLuhan's conclusion about its significance? (x)

    k. Explain: "TV has provided a new environment of low visual orientation and high involvement that makes accommodation to our older educational establishment quite difficult." Do you agree? Illustrate. (x)

    l. According to Professor McLuhan, "The power of the arts to anticipate future social and technological change by a generation or more has long been recognized." (xi) Have you "recognized" this power of art? Explain and illustrate.

4. The next questions are based on the "Introduction."

    a. What is the point to the James Reston quotation? (19)

    b. Explain: "Slow movement insured that the reactions were delayed for considerable periods of time. Today the action and the reactions occur almost at the same time." (20)

    c. Explain: "In the electric age, when our central nervous system is technologically extended to involve us in the whole of mankind and to incorporate the whole of mankind in us, we necessarily participate, in depth, in the consequences of our every action. It is no longer possible to adopt the aloof and dissociated role of the literate Westerner." Do you agree? Why is Professor McLuhan speaking only of Western man?

    d. In what sense can "the Negro, the teen-ager, and some other groups" no longer be "contained"? (20) Do *you* want to be "involved?" Defend your answer.

e. What are "the extensions of man"? (21) What do you think this book is going to be about? How does its subject concern you?

5. The following questions and suggestions require definitions and an understanding of *Understanding Media*'s first three chapters, published in this casebook. Try to discuss them in McLuhan's own terms and concepts.

a. Explain: "The restructuring of human work and association was shaped by the technique of fragmentation that is the essence of machine technology." (23)

b. What does McLuhan mean by "the message of any medium or technology"? (24) What single word might you use instead of "message"?

c. In what sense does the railroad have a "message" as McLuhan sees it? How would the railroad seem to be one of the "extensions of man"? (24)

d. Professor McLuhan writes that the "medium shapes and controls the scale and form of human association and action." (24) How does it square with McLuhan's idea that the "medium is the message"? Do the two statements contradict?

e. It is easy enough to understand that "electric light and power are separate in their uses yet they eliminate time and space factors in human association exactly as do radio, telegraphy, and telephone," (25) but how do they create "involvement in depth"? (27)

f. Explain: "So the greatest of all reversals occurred with electricity, that ended sequence by making things instant." (27)

g. What has this sentence to do with McLuhan's thesis: "And many have held that the American Presidency has become very much more personal and anarchical than any European monarch ever could be." (29) In your discussion of this question, be sure to introduce McLuhan's concepts of *implosion, involvement, fragmentation, sequence,* and *configuration.*

h. Explain: "Money has reorganized the sense life of peoples just because it is an extension of our sense lives." (33)

i. What does Professor McLuhan mean by "our human senses, of which all media are extensions, are also fixed charges on our personal energies, . . . and they also configure the awareness and experience of each one of us"? (35)

6. The preceding questions are designed, obviously, to promote close reading of *Understanding Media;* you may wish to devise similar questions for the remainder of the book. The next group of questions and suggestions invite you to discuss Professor McLuhan's ideas from a wider point of view. In addition to providing a basis for individual speculation and class discussion, they may suggest topics for writing projects. You will enhance your comprehension of McLuhan and McLuhanism if you give them the benefit of the doubt and try to consider the questions according to his frame of reference. Your opportunity to praise or condemn him—and to reject or utilize his ideas—will come later. As you discuss, or write, you should refer constantly to specific passages in the book, making their location evident by oral reference or written footnote.

a. Is it a paradox that McLuhan uses the printed word to describe the downfall of the printed word? Do you find this, or other parts of his argument, to be a basic contradiction? Is his case weakened by inconsistency?

b. Do McLuhan's special definitions for "message" and "medium" (or "hot" or "cool" or any other of the key words in his important pronouncements) demand a great readjustment of our conventional understanding of these words' meanings? Would it have been better if he had chosen different words, or coined some new words, to express his revolutionary new concepts?

c. McLuhan is quite persistently optimistic in his forecasts for man's future. Analyze the reasons why he seems to feel so encouraged about the world's next development. Do you share his cheerful outlook? Are there any flaws or gaps, as you see them, in his predictions of a better life for our descendants?

d. How does McLuhan feel about formal, systematic logic? In what ways does he justify his position? Do you agree with his attitude toward formalized, disciplined thinking?

e. What generalized impression does McLuhan convey of today's younger generation (20 years of age and younger)? Are the features in his portrait of adolescents accurate as you know them? In what ways has he been especially true to life in his description —or, in what ways has he distorted the image of 20th century youth?

f. McLuhan makes an important distinction between "doing a job" and "playing a role" as ways in which human beings adjust to their society. Can you provide explanations and examples which will make this distinction sharply clear?

g. McLuhan explains a vast range of modern phenomena as products of the new "electric media"; humor, sex, clothing, fashions, music and painting, architecture, education, athletics, etc. Can you identify some contemporary developments that he has *not* discussed (furniture design, perhaps? or trends in children's playthings?) and measure how well his inclusive formula explains (or fails to explain) their emergence?

h. The term "tribalize"—with its derivatives "detribalize" and "retribalize"—occurs very often and very conspicuously in McLuhan's scheme of historical analysis. Just what does he mean by a "tribalized" culture, and in what ways does he regard the world as becoming "retribalized" through modern technology?

i. Is there any *program of action* that is recommended, either implicitly or explicitly, by McLuhan's philosophy? Does he indicate certain steps that people should take or should not take in order to bring about the fulfillment of desirable goals? If there are such exhortations to action, what are they?

j. If you feel that McLuhan is *not* advocating any positive program of action, can you explain why he is so controversial a figure? Why should a person who is merely describing and analyzing what he observes (and not recommending any particular reforms or disturbance of the status quo) be at the center of so much heated debate?

k. It is notable how different scholars have attempted to submit final answers that sum up the total human condition: for example, Freud regards the whole spectrum of man's behavior as a function of the sex drive; Marx sees all history as an economic class struggle. Is Marshall McLuhan another in the list of important thinkers who have a formula that explains the whole of human experience? Do his ideas have more validity, or less, in your view, than some of the others? Is McLuhan contradicting people like Marx, Freud, Darwin—or is he amplifying and expanding on their views?

l. McLuhan, along with a host of other critics, is quite evidently impatient with today's educational institutions. Study some of the comments he makes about schools and see if you can discover and describe, in some detail, just what kinds of instruction he thinks would better serve youth in this electric age.

m. The importance of the artist as a creator of "anti-environments" is a concept that McLuhan has often emphasized. Can you explain, using examples from contemporary painters, playwrights, novelists, how the "anti-environment" operates in McLuhan's scheme?

n. Cultural historians have agreed for a long time that the invention of printing in the fifteenth century was a crucially important factor in the development of Western Civilization as we know it today. McLuhan echoes very strongly the traditional idea of printing's importance, but he sees its impact as something entirely different from what previous observers noted. Discuss.

o. A glance at the table of contents reveals that works about Marshall McLuhan appear in the most widespread variety of publications: scholarly journals, household-hint magazines, "highbrow" periodicals, best-selling paperback books. . . . Does a survey of his writings disclose any good reasons that explain to you why his ideas are so universally interesting at so many different intellectual and cultural levels?

p. How much do you have to suspend hostility or disbelief as you read McLuhan? What contradictions do you find? What distortions of fact or outright error? What gaps in logic do you find?

What misuse of evidence? In an article in *Vogue* (July 1966, p. 60) a student was reported to have charged McLuhan with having made twenty-eight contradictions in one lecture. "You're still thinking lineally," Professor McLuhan responded blandly. Do you see how McLuhan might think that the contradictions you've cited might be called the product of lineal thinking?

"You see, Dad, Professor McLuhan says the environment that man creates becomes his medium for defining his role in it. The invention of type created linear, or sequential, thought, separating thought from action. Now, with TV and folk singing, thought and action are closer and social involvement is greater. We again live in a village. Get it?"

Drawing by Alan Dunn, © 1966 The New Yorker Magazine, Inc.

7. In this *New Yorker* cartoon, the McLuhan message is being explained creditably. In addition, the artist, Alan Dunn, uses his own medium to convey McLuhan's theme. What do the books and lamp behind the man, the nearly undistinguishable sex of the youngster, his rhetorical question ("Get it?") and his guitar, symbolize in McLuhan's terms?

8. You can sharpen your understanding of McLuhan and begin to evaluate his ideas by seeing how they fit into your daily life. Either in an oral report or a written composition, use your own experiences or observations to illustrate one or several of the following McLuhan ideas:

    a. A medium or a technology is part of our bodies, an extension of our physical and nervous systems to increase power and speed.

    b. A new medium or technology changes the scale, pace or pattern of human affairs or human relationships.

    c. An electric medium eliminates time and space factors in human affairs, thus creating in us an involvement in depth in the lives of everybody in the world.

    d. By continuously embracing a technology or medium, we relate ourselves to it as a servomechanism (an automatic device for controlling large amounts of power by means of very small amounts of power and automatically correcting performance of a mechanism).

    e. The artist (any man of integral awareness) anticipates the effect of a new technology or medium and sidesteps its bully blow.

    f. We are numb in our new electric world, as numb as pre-literate people are when confronted by literacy and mechanical technology.

    g. Today's teenager, like the barbarian of old in contact with a more civilized society, is driven to furious restlessness by contact with, through TV, the life of a complex urban center that cannot accept him as an adult, cannot allow him to participate, to be totally involved.

    h. Electric media confer the mythic dimension, the dimension of instant vision of a long, complex process; therefore modern man, who sees so much so totally and so quickly, tends to study traditional myths respectfully rather than debunk them as did the highly literate, analytical, fragmenting and specializing pre-electronic print-oriented man.

9. Defenders of McLuhan maintain stoutly that "there is no area of human experience which he cannot explain according to his theories. For instance, when Peter Yarrow (of Peter, Paul, and Mary) was asked why he disliked television, he resorted to McLuhan's terms. According to the *Boston Globe* (August 30, 1967, p. 59) he responded, "The medium takes the human quality out of the message and substitutes a dehumanized massage." He then stressed the need for a "new, internal, and personal kind of commitment" to counteract a "technologically overweight age." Write a theme in which you explain in his terms any one of the following topics. Your instructor may indicate how long your papers should be. Whenever possible, make specific references to McLuhan's ideas, either from *Understanding Media,* or from the critical articles in this casebook. Use appropriate manuscript and footnote techniques.

    a. The Vietnam war.
    b. Student protest movements or activity.
    c. American acceptance and rejection of foreign cars.
    d. American acceptance/rejection of foreign movies. (You may wish to see how American audiences reacted to J. Arthur Rank movies in the early 1950's; contrast to present phenomenon of foreign-movie theaters.
    e. Mod fashions.
    f. Johnson's war. (Newspapers report that he sits up till three in the morning to see how the pilots did on each strike.)
    g. Return of the Negro to African "natural" names, clothes, and hair styles.
    h. Megalopolis.
    i. Air pollution.
    j. Athletics. (How is baseball combatting the popularity of football, basketball, and soccer? Is spectator sport really spectator sport?)
    k. Modern folk music.
    l. Teeny-boppers.
    m. Operation Bootstrap and OEO in contrast to the pre-1930 dole.
    n. The search for "respectable poverty".
    o. Black power.
    p. Ecumenism.
    q. Cubist art.
    r. Existentialism.
    s. Materialism.
    t. The death of God.
    u. The "do-it-yourself" fad.
    v. A "flow chart" illustrating responsibility in a military or industrial organization.

10. The following suggestions are related to the previous topics, but they are worded to give you more direction. Your instructor may ask you to write 250-1,000 word themes based on these topics. Illustrate profusely and cite references carefully.

    a. Project the future shape of one of today's major cultural institutions (education? religion? matrimony?) as it will emerge from increased exposure to the "electric media".
    b. Assuming that those who have something to "sell" (i.e., politicians, commercial advertisers) are perennially most sensitive to popular moods and trends, examine some newspaper magazine advertising and editorial techniques from the 19th century (the "pre-electric" age) and compare their appeals with the characteristic approaches of today's admen and vote-seekers. Does Marshall McLuhan's description of the impact of instant-media help explain the shift in tone and emphasis from the 1800's to today's advertising strategies?

c. On a "cool-to-hot" continuum, line up a dozen or so well-known figures drawn from the same walk of life (politicians, actors, musicians, athletes). Explain your reasoning for assessing each one to his relative niche on your scale of "coolness".

d. Observe the Federal Homestead Laws of the 1800's and the Poverty Program of today's administration as contrasting examples of "social legislation," each intended to promote national prosperity by answering some important needs of their respective epochs. What relationship do the 20th Century modes of media (as described by McLuhan) have to the changing shapes and purposes of today's welfare program?

e. With the wisdom of 500 years' hindsight, plus some guidance from McLuhan's analyses, write a tract addressed to Europeans of the late 15th century. Explain to *them* (as McLuhan is explaining to *us*) what measures they ought to take in order to accommodate themselves to the dominance of the newly-risen medium of printing.

f. McLuhan is able to interpret the famous slogan "Men seldom make passes at girls who wear glasses" in terms of his analysis of the "hot-cool" dichotomy. Discuss a few other popular expressions or aphorisms that might be analyzed in terms of the "media" they occupy.

g. During the past decade a notable resurgence of popular interest in arts and crafts or "do-it-yourself" projects has occurred. In considerable detail, using many specific examples, report on the extent to which the appeal of such homegrown enterprises can be interpreted as a function of the new media environment.

h. Analyze the lyrics of some of the popular songs that were in-inspired by America's entrance into World War I (or the earlier Spanish-American War). Compare these songs with the lyrics of today's rock 'n roll or folk favorites on the subject of America's involvement in Vietnam (à la Bob Dylan et al.) Can you account for these new songsters' attitudes in terms of the electric media?

11. Write a theme based on your synopticon notes up to this point in your study of McLuhan and his critics. Suggested topics:

a. The McLuhan lexicon.
b. History, as McLuhan sees it.
c. The effects of Mass Media on the individual (or society).
d. Modern education and Marshall McLuhan.
e. McLuhan's style.
f. McLuhan's thinking processes.
g. McLuhan's ideas in action.
h. An evaluation of McLuhan.
i. McLuhan responds to the critics.

12. Write a biography of Marshall McLuhan, the length to be prescribed by your instructor. First, assemble all the biographical information you have gleaned during your synopticon reading and notetaking. You should have two classes of information: (1) Vital statistics, i.e., birth date and place, parents, education, wife and children, teaching and experience. (2) Intellectual biographical information. Remember that each person's biography is shaped by his accomplishments. A soldier's biography will include his battles; a politician's, his campaigns, and a lawyer's, his cases. Marshall McLuhan is a purveyor of ideas, and you must give the biography of his ideas. Where did they come from? Who were his influences? From his early and from his later work, you can observe how his ideas developed; in your biography, you should trace these ideas. You may want to show how his ideas have influenced other people.

A really excellent biography develops a point of view. After you read and re-read your biographical notes, you may see that they seem to be making a particular comment about McLuhan—and you may wish to weave your major points and your details into a pattern which develops a central thesis. You may have noted that most of the articles in this anthology build up to a major point, usually an evaluation of McLuhan's ideas. You may wish to organize your biography into one of these:

    a. McLuhan's life as an explanation of his ideas.
    b. The transition from an English teacher to a communications expert.
    c. The influence of Catholicism on Marshall McLuhan.
    d. Parallels between Marshall McLuhan's life and recent Canadian history.
    e. The source of McLuhan's ideas.
    f. Marshall McLuhan's intellectual biography.

Be sure in all cases to footnote copiously to indicate your sources. When you find contradictions among your sources, indicate why you accepted one authority and rejected another. Be sure to include a bibliography indicating which articles of the casebook you have used.

13. Two Library Exercises. (a) Prepare a complete bibliography of the works of Marshall McLuhan. Suggested starting places: *Reader's Guide to Periodical Literature, Book Review Digest, Educational Index,* and *Books In Print.* (b) Prepare a complete bibliography of published information about Marshall Mc-Luhan. See the above suggested reference works.

14. The following topics, as they require the use of the library, provide opportunities to develop your research and manuscript techniques.

    a. The source of McLuhan's ideas. You may limit yourself to clues from the critics and from *Understanding Media,* or you may check the sources suggested in McLuhan's earlier works, particularly

The Gutenberg Galaxy (pp. 1–7) and *Explorations In Communications*, which he co-edited.

b. The authors of the articles in this casebook are very much aware that McLuhan does not think traditionally. Compton writes (p. 67) that McLuhan "regards the idea of cause and effect as an illusive linear abstraction," and many others point out that McLuhan avoids Aristotelian thought. From the articles in the casebook, *Understanding Media,* and the critics' comments, write a theme in which you describe, analyze, and evaluate McLuhan's mode of thought. If possible, contrast his mode to that of the scientific method, or to Bacon or Aristotle. What does McLuhan use as evidence? How does he organize an argument? What contradiction do you or the critics find? Which of the critics find his method sound and which find him unsound? In particular, consider Neil Compton's analysis of McLuhan's thinking.

15. McLuhan's free-wheeling, free-dealing writing style is almost as controversial as his ideas. Write a full analysis of McLuhan's prose style and the critics' reaction to it. Using copious illustrations, convey to your audience as exact a perception of his style as you can. You should touch on the following issues: Does he follow the conventions usually taught in English classes? Does he use a technical vocabulary? Where does he get his expressions? Does he make up his own terms, or does he stretch old terms to fit new concepts? What literary, scientific and mythic allusions does he make? How does he organize his material? What is the relationship and the proportion of general to specific statements? Are his sentences or paragraphs similar to those of any other writer you know? How are they different from other writers'? Is his writing like communication in any other, non-written, media? What do the critics think of his writing? What is meant by repeated references to his "mosaic" style?

On note cards accumulate a collection of comments made by the critics about McLuhan's writing style. Notice how vastly they differ, as from the Kostelanetz complaint that his writing is "horrendously difficult to read, clumsily written, frequently contradictory, oddly organized, and overlaid with their author's singular jargon," to Paul West's praise for McLuhan's "enchanting and rare" prose. Schickel (page 87) comments that McLuhan "blithely ignores all the conventions of critical historical exposition." In order to be sure that you raise all the questions pertinent to a study of style, check a good rhetoric or composition text. Unless you do, you might miss some of the important considerations (like the use of analogy or metaphor) or miss some of the relevant terminology, like *hyperbole* (exaggeration) or *litotes* (expressing an affirmative by a negative or suggesting an idea by means of its opposite, *not bad at all*). You must not ignore the concepts of *galaxy, configuration,* and *mosaic,* which McLuhan uses when he discusses all communication; certainly they are appropriate for a consideration of his own style.

16. McLuhan's humor and its response. Perhaps because of McLuhan's own outrageous sense of humor and his breezy whimsy, almost every commentator on McLuhan is compelled to get cute. McLuhan's puns ("collide-o-scope," "the medium is the massage") generate in kind; even the editors of this casebook were attracted into the act as we contrasted the prosaic versus the mosaic style (PROSE-aic, get it?). In *The Nation* he was called the "media guru from Toronto." A student titled a theme about McLuhan, "One Man's Media." Make a study of his humor and try to analyze its effect. You may wish to use McLuhan's system of analysis: his humor is not his message; it's part of his medium of communication. Does his humor fit his message? Does his message come through better because of his humor? What jokes has it generated? Does it distract from the seriousness of his message, if the message is serious?

17. McLuhan's theory of history. The professor's historiography is one of the simplest, neatest and all-encompassing theories ever expressed. Write an analysis of his theory of history. You may wish to show whence he derived the kernel of his structure—and here the first seven pages of *The Gutenberg Galaxy* will help you. You may wish to contrast his theory with others. Your library's card catalogue will list several books which explain history theories, for instance, *The Development of Historiography* edited by M. A. Fitzsimons and others (1954). You may wish to compare McLuhan's history with that of the originator of history, Herodotus, since both are concerned with the cause of man's actions. You may contrast McLuhan to Thucydides, who was concerned with exact dates and events, to Xenophon, who delighted in narrative, or to Hegel, who envisioned history as the result (synthesis) of the conflict between one course of action (thesis) and a contrary force (antithesis). You may wish to study him in context with other modern historians who had theories about what moves man: Karl Marx, James Harvey Robinson, Charles A. Beard and Vernon L. Parrington had varying ideas of how economics shapes history; Frederick Jackson Turner believed that American history, at least, was produced by waves of frontier living; Benedetto Croce believed that history is moved by a manifestation of spirit; Oswald Spengler argued that every culture has a life cycle of rise and decline, the cycle having its own irresistible dynamism; and Arnold J. Toynbee views history primarily as the way broad cultures respond to human and environmental challenges. To get some seminal ideas, you may wish to check the *Enclyclopedia Britannica,* the *Columbia Encyclopedia,* or another good encyclopedia under the entries of "history" or "historiography."

18. McLuhan and education. Directly and indirectly, Professor McLuhan has much to say about education's faults and future. How is it ill-adapted for today's students and problems? Is it related to the lineal-sequential form of communication or to the mosaic, impressionistic form? Where does education really take place? In what countries can we most likely expect sweeping reform and change in educational methods? How does "the frustration of the student need for participation in the learning process" increase the "drop-out situation"? (Do you agree?) Discuss these issues and others in a paper based on McLuhan's ideas and the reactions of his critics.

19. The soundness of McLuhan's critics. If we accept Professor McLuhan's terminology, the articles in this casebook have a message, but we cannot profitably examine them only as communication. An examination of the critics themselves may say something important about modern communication. Write a thoroughly documented paper based on these suggestions. Classify all the articles according to a series of criteria which you find meaningful, for instance, whether the judgments are relatively favorable, unfavorable, mixed, or neutral; the professional or religious backgrounds of their authors; the quality of the writing—accuracy, completeness, soundness of each article. By checking *The Writer's Market,* which is likely to be available in your college library, you can classify all the articles according to the periodicals in which they appear: business, religious, general editorial, literary, etc. After you have classified these articles, you may be able to write a documented theme in which you make some judgments about the writers or the periodicals in which their writing appears. Sample questions which you may be able to answer:

   a. Do the so-called "quality" magazines really do a better job than the popular magazines in keeping the public informed about intellectual developments?
   b. What religious or professional biases may influence an opinion of McLuhan?
   c. What classes of magazines have best covered McLuhan and his ideas?
   d. Which newsmagazine has best covered McLuhan? You will want to base your judgments on what you have read of McLuhan in *Understanding Media* and in the articles in this casebook, and you will want to check your judgments against what other critics have said. Of course, you will need to provide a great amount of footnoted evidence in this paper.
   e. Is there any difference in the level of difficulty or intellectuality from magazine to magazine, or from writer to writer? Which use the most learned vocabulary? Which demand the most technical and informed background? In this, as in all the judgments you make, we assume that you will qualify your conclusions carefully. You are not commenting on all quality magazines, or even on all the writing of any one of the authors, but you are making some limited, preliminary judgments which you may use later to add to other information you acquire; thus you may make wider, more definite judgments later about what periodicals you will customarily rely upon, and which authors you respect.

20. One writer in this casebook says he heard that a national magazine offered some well-known writer a thousand dollars to produce an article "against

McLuhan." Which article do you assume to be the one which resulted? Assuming you are right, what judgments can you make about the soundness and fullness of the article? Document your conclusions with footnoted evidence.

21. Marshall McLuhan has escaped being pigeonholed; he is variously called a literary critic, a historian, a pop philosopher, and a sociologist—to cite only a few labels—but he has perhaps made the biggest splash as an authority on the general field of communication. You can get a feel for this comparatively new area of intellectual inquiry by reading the entry under "Communication" in the *Encyclopaedia Britannica*. Note its ramifications into philosophy, rhetoric, drama, literature, linguistics, semantics, learning theory, Gestalt psychology, psychoanalysis, sociology, political science, journalism, advertising, mathematics, computers, radio and television. Make a comparison between McLuhan's ideas and those advanced by Franklin Fearing, 1954, (Chapter 8, "Social Impact of the Mass Media of Communication," *53 Yearbook, Part II*, of *The National Society for the Study of Education*).

    Your study of communication may suggest other subjects for a thoroughly-documented, fully-researched paper. You may prefer to select an aspect of the subject which is related to your own academic major or to some of your own intellectual interests.

22. McLuhan and Expo 67. Parallels between McLuhanism and Expo 67 are almost inescapable: both Canadian, both revolutionary, both concerned with changes in environment, both interested in communication by electronics, symbols and mosaics. Pierre DuPuy, Commissioner General of Expo 67, listed its aim: "to provide an explanation of the world we live in"; certainly McLuhan would approve. You can heighten your awareness of the parallels by noting some articles about Expo 67 and re-thinking your synopticon notes from McLuhan and the critics. (Use *Reader's Guide* and *Educational Index* for Expo 67 bibliography.) The *Expo 67 Official Guide* (copyright, 1967, MacLean-Hunter Publishing Company, Limited, Montreal, Quebec) may give you some ideas about the world's fair. Can it be that McLuhan and Expo 67 are the twin beacons lighting up a whole new stage of intellectual history? Do not treat this topic lightly; both McLuhan and Expo 67 may assume large places in history.

23. An evaluation of McLuhan. There comes a time when a student of the modern scene has to decide just what he thinks of McLuhan. Write a fully-documented, carefully researched evaluation of McLuhan and his ideas. You may wish to consider these questions:

    a. What is your general opinion of his value to you individually?
    b. What is your opinion of his value to society?
    c. Does he clear up any questions which have long puzzled you?
    d. Do you understand modern society, mankind, education, history, the Western world, the President of the United States, or anything

else, any better after having read McLuhan? What? Why? How do you explain it in McLuhan's terms?

e. What are the most significant ideas you have gleaned from McLuhan?

f. With what writers do you agree about McLuhan, and with which ones do you disagree? Why?

g. What claims or suggestions by McLuhan might be the basis for important reform or progress?

GLOSSARY of
McLUHANISMS

Page numbers refer to the first three chapters of McLuhan's *Understanding Media* as printed in this book. Other key terms, like *auto-amputation,* which do not occur in these chapters but which are important to a total comprehension of McLuhan, are listed under "Projects" and are defined in the critical articles.

Configuration (16, 18, 24, 27) McLuhan contrasts communication by the phonetic alphabet in lineal-sequential writing or print to communication by "configuration", figures and patterns which more closely resemble the concept they symbolize, for instance, the roadside sign "Children" in contrast to a silhouette of a child. The telegraph and the book communicate via lineal-sequential, non-representational symbols whereas television communicates at least in part by configuration, i.e., pictures of people and things. Often the configuration is "total field" (the whole picture). A conglomeration of configurations, called a "mosaic", communicates an impression but not an orderly sequential thought.

Cool medium (24, 25, 27, 30) A medium for which "low definition", (relatively little information), need be transmitted because the transmitter expects "high participation", that is, "much is to be filled in by the listener". A conversation is cooler (less definition required; more participation from listener) than a lecture in which the speaker has to provide all the information he wishes his audience to assimilate. He can take no chance with, say, technical vocabulary, because his audience cannot ask a question for clarity. A dialogue is much cooler than a book.

Cross-fertilization (36) The joining of two or more media, usually to correct the deficiencies or "overheat" of a preceding medium. Motion pictures were at first a single-sense medium (sight); then they became double-sense (with sound). They are tactile extensions (as when man's presence or "involvement") could be extended in space and time to life with the Bengal Lancers). Tele-

232

vision has even greater extension; man can do all this in his living room. Motion pictures retaliated with an attempt to extend smell, ("Smellorama") and to widen sight (CinemaScope, Wide-screen) and to improve proximity ("tactility") by 4D and Cinerama.

The Electric Age   (20, 26, 33–34)   After the Gutenberg age, also referred to as the age of literacy, which was most influenced by lineal-sequential communication and thought, characterized by the line of printed material, the electric age brought a speed-up which made civilization resemble the tribal age. Communication and decisions were hastened to face-to-face speed by the telegraph and the radio; involvement was increased by two-way radio and telephone; impressions came not by lineal-sequential, non-ideographic, printed symbols, but by mosaic, total-field configurations—as in television.

De-tribalization   (20, 26)   The breakdown of face-to-face, sound-and-sight communication into communication in which one sense dominates, as when the printing-press (sight) became the dominant medium.

Explosion   (See Implosion.)

Hot medium   (24–25, 27–31)   "One that extends a single sense in 'high definition'. High definition is the state of being well filled with data." "Hot" is a relative term; a medium may be hot in comparison to one medium, but cool in comparison to another. The radio is hot; a telephone is cool. The radio announcer knows that he can expect little involvement from his audience; he must supply all information; that is "high definition". A speaker on a telephone does not have to transmit so much information because he knows his listener can become involved: the listener may ask questions or add to the dialogue. Hot media are low in participation on the part of the audience.

Implosion   (33, 35)   Aware that there is much talk currently of the "explosion", (of population, of knowledge, etc.,) McLuhan points out there is also an "implosion". The print culture was characterized by a fragmentation (explosion) in which people took specialized responsibilities: a farmer, helped by the wheel and the high-speed train (new media) could raise artichokes and let someone else raise beans. A Detroit mechanic, helped by printed directions and assured of farm vegetables from California, (caused by the train and refrigerated cars, another medium because they extended man's ability to touch summer foods in winter, California vegetables in Michigan) could accept a job so fragmented that he spent his day putting one nut on a special bolt. In the electric age, with man returned to his home because of spectator sports (television) and the shorter working day, he became interested again in do-it-yourself gardening and handicrafts, which are neo-tribal. This is a reverse explosion, thus, an implosion. In addition, by means of another extension, television and on-the-spot newscasts, man could see Pakistanis fighting Indians at the Rann of Kutch, and the Viet Cong being captured, making possible a new emotional involvement with distant people whose faces (configurations) he had seen. Thus, McLuhan notes that civilizations remote geographically are blown together again, implosion.

Medium (14) Usually any method of mass communication, such as radio, television, and newspapers. McLuhan, however, extends the term to mean anything that extends man's capacities or man's senses; thus, an electric light bulb is a medium because it extends man's sight into the darkness, and a wheel extends man's physical being, and thus his senses, into remote distances.

Message (14) Usually the verbal thought content of any medium. McLuhan extends the term to mean "the change of scale or pace or pattern that it introduces into human affairs." The message of the railroad—another medium, according to McLuhan—is the enlargement of "previous human functions" that the railroad made possible and inevitable, including "new kinds of cities and new kinds of work and leisure."

Narcissism (26) McLuhan, believing that all media are extensions of the self, points out that developments of media are narcissistic, that is, they are examples of self-admiration and ego-building. A man might buy a flashy foreign sports car. In the sense that it extends his tactile ability to be in another place quickly it is a pure medium; in the sense that it also extends his personality, in an image-building way, it is an example of narcissism.

Numbing (21, 22, 27, 31) Too often, according to McLuhan, man cannot appreciate the message of media; he is bored by or oblivious ("numb") to them. He may appreciate their "content" (verbal message) but he will not perceive the message (i.e., the changes in his life) that is the real message of the media. If the "numbing" is deliberate, as when we shut out advertising on a street car, or when we ignore a crime on the street, McLuhan, in chapters 4-7, calls it "auto-amputation."

Participation (15, 25, 28, 30) During a large-auditorium lecture, the listener sits passively, supposedly absorbing information. In contrast, during a conversation, a listener is animated, quick to retort and to contribute. This response McLuhan calls "involvement" or "participation." He extends the definition to include any contribution by the audience. The receptor can make no contribution to the message of a telegram but to the verbal message of television he can add much because his eyes take in the configuration of the picture. At the lowest level of participation he can separate the good guys from the bad guys by seeing which wears the white hat. McLuhan's perceptions of education are based on his appreciation of the need for the student to get involved, to contribute creatively during the learning process.

Overheated media (25, 26, 28, 34) As a medium extends the sense of man, it can go so far as to cause tensions or "heat". Communication via print made extension of nationalism possible, and nationalities came into conflict. Fragmentation made occupational specialization so prevalent that life on the assembly line became a tension-producing bore. Forces come into existence against these overheated media; usually they are in the form of joined media; (cross-fertilization, p. 36); for instance, canned music was a temporary respite for the worker. Summers on the lake with the worker putting on a captain's hat and piloting a power boat (extensions) are another current solution. The heat of the old medium takes a form that actually resembles heated emotionalism, as perfervid patriotism. Older people may remember the heated voices of H. V. Kaltenborn, Walter Winchell, talking excitedly to "all the ships at sea", and "Thundering Ed" Thorgerson when radio was in its last days of dominance. Television newscasters are "cool". "Big-beat" hot music is popular on the "Top 40" of radio, but a fizzle on Ed Sullivan's television program. Overheat of media is usually followed by a reversal, numbing, auto-amputation, or cross-fertilization.

Re-tribalization (26)   When a civilization reverts from the lineal-sequential dominance in media to a configuration dominance, as when television replaces the book and the newspaper. The electric age resembles the tribal age because, by the extension of the new media (Telstar, Early Bird, television, short-wave two-way radio), men may communicate as though they were face-to-face.

Reversal (33–36)   A revolution is often in the form of a reversal, that is, a change in direction, from explosion to implosion, from extension to withdrawal, from lineal-sequential communication to configurational. For instance, warfare—after the development of the printing press—became fragmented, with the general directing the distant battles via the telegraphed field order; with the development of Telstar, Early Bird and television, the Pentagon and the President direct the war in Vietnam almost as though they were tribal leaders, with the President sitting up till three o'clock in the morning to find out if the "boys" all returned from their mission.

Tribal civilization (15–21, 26)   In the pre-literate stage of history men lived close together. They communicated orally or by gestures. They tended to make instant decisions, and they had no writing for remote communication. Both sight and sound were used to communicate; instead of predominantly sight as in the literate stage. Note that McLuhan thinks we are returning to a neo-tribal culture since the electric age has returned civilization to tribal characteristics.